Parachuting
From Student to Skydiver

Parachuting
From Student to Skydiver

Jim Bates

TAB BOOKS
Blue Ridge Summit, PA

FIRST EDITION
FIRST PRINTING

Copyright © 1990 by **TAB BOOKS**
Printed in the United States of America

Library of Congress Cataloging in Publication Data

Bates, Jim, 1926–
      Parachuting : from student to skydiver / by Jim Bates.
          p.   cm.
      Includes bibliographical references
      ISBN 0-8306-3406-1 :
      1. Parachuting.   2. Skydiving.   I. Title.
   GV770.B38 1990
   797.5'6—dc20   89-78100
                                                                   CIP

TAB BOOKS offers software for sale. For information and a catalog, please contact TAB
Software Department, Blue Ridge Summit, PA 17294-0850.

Questions regarding the content of this book
should be addressed to:

      Reader Inquiry Branch
      TAB BOOKS
      Blue Ridge Summit, PA 17294-0214

Acquisitions Editor: Jeff Worsinger
Book Editor: Tracey May
Production: Katherine Brown

Contents

3 From Student to Skydiver   51

4 How Parachutes Work   85

Acknowledgments

All the skydivers who have ever made a parachute jump have contributed in some way to the contents of this work—but there are those who deserve special mention.

Numero Uno!—Marge Bates, my wife, whose steady encouragement and continuous selflessness were major factors in getting this book started and completed. Not merely an indulgent spouse who sits about while her husband is gone and busy with parachuting matters, she has been involved with sport parachuting in many ways for many years. She has logged six hundred skydives, has been a competition judge for a long while, and currently holds a United States Parachute Association (USPA) rating as a Conference Judge.

Dave Drake used sharp eyes during attentive reading of parts of the manuscript. His perceptive comments helped improve various sections.

Jan Arnault looked over the manuscript from the viewpoint of a 50-jump skydiver and asked pointed questions, some of which brought about clarifications and changes. She has joined the ranks of competition aficionados by winning her first meet trophy as a novice accuracy champion.

Jim Mowrey provided much documentation about the broad educational, training, and safety programs of the United States Parachute Association (USPA) and answered question after question.

Bob Hunt—graphic designer/exparatrooper/veteran skydiver—was consulted on front cover suggestions. The front cover "stars," on both sides of a camera, are Nick Riciardelli, in a classic "frog" freefall position, "geeking" photographer Wayne Armbrust.

Last, but certainly not least—and in a special category—David E. Smith, who had a hand in hiring me for a job at one time, and who saw to it for many years that I learned the craft of writing according to the "Sullivan Doctrine."

Author's Note

This book is intended to provide accurate and authoritative information about the risk-taking activity of sport parachuting, also known as skydiving. It is meant to complement other material also available and not to provide all that is known about parachutes and parachuting.

Great effort has been made to have this book be as complete and accurate as possible; however, it should be used only as a guide. It is not the only source of information about sport parachuting/skydiving, parachute rigging, equipment, teaching methods, or any of the various other facets of recreational parachuting. Also, this book has information available as of its printing date.

Due to the risks inherent in the sport of parachuting, the author and the publisher shall not have liability or responsibility to any person or entity with respect to loss or damage caused or claimed to be caused by information in this publication.

Foreword

As sport parachuting in this country matured from pioneer beginnings since the early 1950s as an organized recreational activity, the "how-to" word began to appear in print. A sketchy history was usually included, to at least give some sort of perspective on parachutes, parachuting, and parachutists. The public knew little about this field of aviation, and people generally looked sideways at someone discovered to be involved in parachute jumping.

Earlier, during World War II, when airborne soldiers became the elite of military forces on both sides of the global conflict, parachutists had taken on a substantial degree of "legitimacy." Nonetheless, parachutists were still considered by most of the public to be reckless daredevils, fools who needlessly volunteered to do something perilous. Parachuting as a military duty, even in peacetime, was one thing, something that needed to be done to protect the country; but people who wanted to make parachute jumps as a "recreational activity," for "fun," had a hard row to hoe.

People who were writers as well as parachutists filled the need for information wanted by adventurers of all kinds: those thinking about getting involved with parachuting—at least to make one jump, to see what it's like; others who had become students with a few jumps in a log book, wanting to know as much as possible about their new and incredible sport activity, this thing so unlike anything else they had ever done; and experienced jumpers who were always on the lookout for tips and detailed accounts of how skydiving could be simplified, varied, and enhanced.

Many handbooks, manuals, and guidebooks appeared throughout the years, some broadly covering sport parachuting/skydiving, others closely examining and defining specific facets, such as freefall relative work and canopy relative work. The communicators helped make learning easier.

The author of this handbook started sport parachuting in 1961 and went on to become involved in a number of areas in the sport. He was also employed as a writer in the nonparachuting field for most of the time. With this work he has combined knowledge and experience to produce a book primarily for two types of people—those wondering about making a skydive (at least *one*, anyway), and particularly for those novice parachutists who have become enthralled and want to know what they can do in the sport of skydiving beyond simply jumping from an aircraft.

A particularly useful section of this work is its Glossary. It simplifies quickly learning about something specific that piques a reader's curiosity. Instead of sifting through a table of contents or flipping pages hoping one's eye will catch sight of one word out of many, the Glossary can provide a speedy answer.

Parachuting: From Student to Skydiver can be a boon to anyone who is a nonjumper but thinking about making at least one jump, just to see what it's like. It can also be very helpful to every novice sport parachutist wanting to go onward to become a *real skydiver.*

William H. Ottley, Executive Director
United States Parachute Association
Alexandria, Virginia
January 1990.

1
The Skydiver's Realm

Man small.
Why fall?
Skies call.
That's all.
    Skies Call

[A photographic essay]
—Andy Keech

The attraction of the vast expanse of sky that envelopes planet Earth—
and the apparently endless space beyond—must certainly go back to the
first humans. After wandering and searching, dealing with existence
and survival, then getting settled into various environments round the
globe, men, women, and children had to have wondered about all that
surrounding blueness that could not be felt. They must have wondered about all those pleasant-looking, white, puffy things in that blue:
things that clung together; things that towered to mighty heights; things
that sometimes were only wisps painted across long stretches;
things that often obscured the blue that ranged from a mere tint to a
deepness that was stunningly beautiful; things that sometimes turned
gray, sometimes dark, even black and frightening-looking.

They must have been puzzled about the bright yellowness that was
often noticeably warm, that very often burned tender flesh, that blinded
those who stared at it too long. They had to have been curious about
what it was that fell from above that was exactly like the strange, odd-
feeling stuff that flowed along the ground in narrow, convoluted shapes,
that slithered and trickled and dripped, that lay in every size of depression in the ground on which the people moved and lived, a substance
that gathered in enormous bodies, some of them endless to the eye.
Surely they were awestruck by the deep rumblings and sharp claps that
pummeled their ears, sometimes frightening them mightily; wondered
with fright about flashes of jagged light splitting gloom or blackness.
Humans were inundated with heavenly mysteries as they carried on
their lives.

Then, suddenly, a living creature was seen moving in that great over-head openness, sometimes wildly flapping things protruding from its body, other times only moving those appendages gently, sometimes keeping the broad surfaces extended fully, the creature gracefully soar-ing and wheeling, sometimes darting and tumbling, growing smaller to the eye as it rose higher and higher, sometimes disappearing. Where did it go? How was it possible for the creature to move about with such ease? There must have been an inquisitive human who tried flapping his or her own arms in unsuccessful attempts to emulate those mysterious soaring creatures.

When the first person—perhaps a hillside cave dweller of the earliest times, or someone scrambling up a tree for food or desiring some prize—was mildly or seriously injured, maybe killed, by falling from some height, it was quickly realized that there was peril in leaving the ground. Rising above it was regarded with caution. Most people chose to keep their feet on the ground. Why care about getting off it? Why care about soaring like birds? However, despite the perceived danger, fascination with the flyers continued.

Millennia passed, and fascination with the heavens continued, but humans remained earthbound. However, inquisitive minds kept won-dering about and probing the mysteries of how living creatures could rise above the earth, stay there, and safely return to solid ground.

It seems likely that there were those among the curious who tried to create devices that looked like birds' appendages, fastened them to themselves, then tried to imitate the flight of a bird. The closest version of such a happening is recorded in ancient Greek mythology. Aviation and parachuting lore both contain the regularly repeated legend of Daedalus and Icarus, a father-and-son team of intrepid individuals from the Athens of more than 3,300 years ago (circa 1400 BC), with the talented parent being a well-known engineer, inventor, craftsman, and architect of his time. Daedalus also had the reputation for doing offbeat things. There is no parachute involved in the misadventure of father and son, but the legend—one of the best tellings is by the poet Ovid—does have to do with achieving conquest of the sky.

The myth goes: Daedalus was sent by Greece into exile to the island of Crete, accompanied by his son, Icarus. The industrious Daedalus was directed by Crete's King Minos to construct the strongest of prisons to confine the dreaded Minotaur, a fearsome monster imprisoned for devouring helpless maidens.

In time, Daedalus's work on the formidable, labyrinthine structure—one of the engineering marvels of the ancient world—was completed, and he asked King Minos's permission to leave Crete. The king refused him. Angered, Daedalus, approaching this setback with typical ingenu-ity, told his son: "Minos possesses the earth and the seas, but he does not control the air, and that is the way we shall go if Jupiter pardons the enterprise."

It didn't take long for the clever Daedalus to work up an unusual scheme—making wings—so he and his son could surreptitiously depart the exile site. Michael Horan, one parachuting researcher, adds this information that supplements Ovid's poetic account:

Daedalus, father of Icarus, spoke to his son, "Is it possible? Can we do this?"

Icarus replied, "Birds have them, therefore they have been made."

"But is it really possible, can man fly?" Daedalus questioned.

Icarus goaded his father, "You have made many things in your life that you have never seen before. And anything you have seen, you can duplicate."

Daedalus was convinced of his son's reasoning. "I will start immediately," he replied.

A gull was captured, and then very carefully its wings were copied. Daedalus was a master craftsman and he studied the shape of the wings, the hollow bone struts, and the delicate feathers with their wind-catching overlaps and hollow stems.

Ovid's poetic tale continues: Daedalus constructed two sets of birdlike wings using feathers, linen securing devices, and wax, with which he and his son would fly from the heights of Crete to soar across the Mediterranean to Italy and freedom. Sensibly, as a precaution, Daedalus ordered that the wings first be tested. After a furtive, brief, successful, flight by each would-be "bird man," Daedalus had only one reservation about the desperate plan. The wings, as legend has it, were attached to the arms and shoulders of each hopeful avian emulator. Because of this insecure means of holding the wings onto themselves, Daedalus warned his son not to fly close to the sun.

The launch, unsuspected and undetected by the king's guards, was successful, and the escapees were miraculously airborne! The pair flew cautiously, eagerly soaring past landmarks marking the direction to free lives. They first headed north across the broad Sea of Crete to the Aegean Sea between Greece and Turkey. Then they turned west, to pass over their homeland for the last time.

Alas, the son wouldn't listen to Dad well enough (not an unusual circumstance in any era of humans). Icarus, overjoyed by the sight of his native land and exhilarated by the wonder of flight, soared and wheeled and swung, ever higher, then higher still, despite his father's vigorously called warnings. The sun, shining brightly in a clear sky, did its unrelenting, awful work. Wax melted. Icarus, struggling to keep the wings in yielding grips, flew lower to escape the sun's damaging rays; but the time for mending the error of his ways was past. Unable to salvage the flying device and save himself, he plunged into the sea, leaving scattered feathers spread across the site of his death. One chronicler of sport parachuting, the late R.A. Gunby, macabrely commented that "Icarus's first and last act in achieving fame was to establish the world's first long freefall record with a smashing finality."

Daedalus, watching horrified and helpless, saw his flailing son plunge with increasing speed, then disappear beneath the water. The parent must have desperately wished his son had had some auxiliary device to shelter him from the fall after failure of the primary flying implement, something to protect the adventurer from harm.

Fig. 1-1. *A 1493 woodcut depicts the failure of the mythological aviator Icarus, after escaping confinement on the island of Crete. The flyer's horrified father watches his son fall to the sea after the sun melted the wax used in making the wings.*

Saddened greatly, but determined, the lone flier soared onward, reaching the safety and freedom of Naples, living into an embittered old age, according to the legend. Little else is known of Daedalus, and his first flight adventure appears to have been his last. As tribute to a myth, the water into which the reckless youth fell is known as the Icarian Sea.

Aerial myths continued, inspiring indomitable humans to keep pondering the mysteries of flight, to keep trying to figure how to easily rise into the awesome sky, remain aloft, then gently return.

Throughout centuries of experimentation, many ideas did not work well enough, and people were seriously hurt, terribly crippled, and sometimes killed because of poor designs that led to equipment failures and falls from heights of every altitude. Then, as an afterthought, planners put their minds to work for a device that could be used when all else fails, some means of letting an aeronaut return safely to earth.

Detailed recounting of the historical aspects of parachutes and parachuting will be reserved for the next chapter. However, to gain perspective, occasional historical references will be included elsewhere. Now jump ahead and learn about the realm that inspired "recreational" parachuting, which evolved into "sport" parachuting, which became "skydiving."

THE BEGINNING OF PARACHUTING AS A RECREATIONAL ACTIVITY

By most accounts, the Russians were the first to see the value of parachutes being used for widespread nonmilitary purposes. The post-World War Russians had enormous areas of country that were lived in yet were inaccessible by ordinary transportation. Severe weather often created perilous living conditions. For years the government had used parachutes to supply remote localities with food, medical supplies, equipment, and other essentials. In life-threatening emergencies, even doctors and nurses were parachuted into remote communities.

For 20 years following the Revolution scarcely anyone in the rest of the world knew what was happening inside Russian borders; but several years after the Civil War, military representatives of that country visiting the United States approvingly watched American soldiers carry out a successful test of landing a fully equipped eight-man machine gun squad by parachute during a military demonstration. Suitably impressed, the Russians returned home and went to work.

In 1927 the national hero Gromov made Russia's first recorded parachute jump. No time was wasted thereafter. In 1930, at the Sport Festival, and as a special military demonstration, the visiting world was treated to soldiers parachuting from planes to "occupy the headquarters of the enemy." Adoption of parachuting on a national scale quickly followed. In 1933, in order to make all of Russia and other countries in the Soviet Union air-minded, the government-sponsored organization Osoaviakhim was formed. Its stated purpose was to promote sports and other recreational activities among the young working people of the U.S.S.R. Parachuting was particularly promoted, the Russian military leaders wisely anticipating the value of the air in its country's future.

Promotion of parachuting was spectacularly successful. Branches of the Osoaviakhim were established over the vast expanse of the country. Every town's square, park, or carnival ground soon had its parachuting towers—a small one for children, a full-sized structure for adults.

To the Russians of the 1930s, parachuting became as common a form of diversion as skiing is to Americans today.

In the United States, in 1935, the first free-drop parachute tower was constructed in Hightstown, New Jersey, by the Safe Parachute Company of nearby Trenton. There was hope of having similar towers across the country as centerpieces for amusement parks, but the concept never flourished. However, a parachute tower was a highlight of the 1939-40 World's Fair in New York City. Its canopies descended along guide wires, and two passengers sat in seats. A canopy was gently braked at the end of the descent, and passengers simply got out of seats rather than experiencing a conventional tumbling, rolling parachute landing fall (PLF) that usually ends a parachute descent.

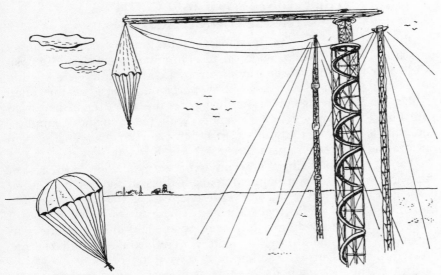

Fig. 1-2. A parachute tower used in Russia in the 1930s. There was also a smaller version for children. In 1935 Russia reported more than 800,000 jumps from such towers. Tower jumps were included in the tests for the first-class sports badge. In 1936 there were 559 such devices at 115 training centers in the U.S.S.R.

About this time airborne training services of the U.S. Army contracted for construction of several towers at its paratrooper training school at Fort Benning, Georgia. Many thousands of military personnel made tethered and untethered parachute descents from Ft. Benning's 250-foot-high training towers.

In this country, parachuting was getting recognition of sorts. It became a scheduled, albeit small-scale, event in huge annual National Air Races (the 1929 competition in Cleveland was a 10-day meet), and in 1932 Joe Crane formed the National Parachute Jumpers Association (NPJA).

By 1935 films of Russian Army maneuvers showed the great strides in military parachuting. A year later foreign nations were invited to see the missions performed, and at Kiev whole battalions of parachutists—many of them women—descended from a fleet of aircraft.

In 1936 there were 115 training centers and 559 parachute towers in the U.S.S.R., and by 1940 the Soviets had one million trained parachutists.

With such numbers it is little wonder the Russians held every one of numerous world parachuting records that were regularly being established.

(In World War Two Russian airborne assaults were minimal in number, in fact, nearly nil. The economic situation and manufacturing capabilities of the Russians precluded production of aircraft suitable primarily only for airborne missions. However, the rugged training of parachutists produced a great force of physically and mentally tough individuals who were then better able to serve as infantry soldiers.)

The German military establishment of World War Two—having witnessed effective Russian airborne training maneuvers—was the first to employ parachutists as a battle force. The Versailles Treaty, closing The Great War, forbade the Germans from having engine-powered aircraft. However, the wily, defeated nation, permitted to have unpowered soaring aircraft for recreation, used those silent devices to teach flying principles to its youth; then, in another step in forbidden military planning, allied themselves with the equally wily Russians, a recent former enemy. In short order, on Russian soil, Germans by the hundreds were using Russian aircraft and learning to be parachutists. Next, the first trainees became cadre for German military airborne training units, still in Russian territory, to train even more parachutists for Germany's future plans.

In May 1940 as part of "blitzkrieg" (lightning war) tactics, Belgium and Holland were struck and subdued by superb German airborne parachute and glider forces, and World War Two was begun. Germans later made the world's first completely airborne assault on an island and drove British forces from strategically important Crete in the eastern Mediterranean Sea (Operation Merkur/May 1941). However, Hitler was so depressed by the devastatingly high loss of paratroopers and aircraft that he forbade any further planning of such aerial attacks.

The Allies, impressed with the stunning success achieved with a large surprise assault by airborne units and understanding what went wrong for the Germans at Crete, doubled and tripled efforts to develop their own specialized tactical and strategic parachute forces. In the main, those Allied forces were used most successfully in a variety of circumstances throughout WW2, and parachutists as a military weapon continue as a standard in present times. As recently as December 1989, U.S. Army Airborne Rangers and the 82nd Airborne Division were used in "Operation JustCause" in Panama.

SPORT PARACHUTING IN THE U.S.

With the coming of peace, thousands of American paratroopers became exparachutists. Most of them felt that was a desirable status, since although jumping out of an airplane might have seemed a "glamorous" military role, it was also the scariest thing they had ever done. Now that there was no longer any demand on them to parachute, they decided to keep their feet planted firmly on the ground.

Nevertheless, here and there across the land, many of the erstwhile jumpers found that they sort of missed "that old feeling, " the once-familiar spirit of adventure. They set aside recollections of how scary it had been the first time, remembering only the elation that went with the open canopy, the glad feelings of a long, silent ride to firm ground. They vividly recalled the joys of jumps, somehow accepting and conveniently putting aside the less enjoyable aspects. They missed the anticipation that goes with getting ready for that next leap, missed the intrinsic excitement of the act of parachuting.

A small group of individuals in the country well knew and understood all those feelings. Many of them—jumping parachute riggers and parachutists only—were holdovers from barnstorming aviation decades of the twenties and thirties. At first, they had loosely banded together in a small group with the purpose of keeping in touch professionally and socially; to have kindred spirits with whom to associate; to communicate progress in their field of interest; to oppose, through strength in numbers, attempts to unduly restrict them, attempts to eliminate their activity. Eventually, exparachutists who had a yen to jump again, and who continued to experience the satisfaction of parachuting, learned of the organization, and many of the renewed parachutists became members. The fledgling group of a few riggers and parachutists of the Thirties grew until it eventually became a large, national, self-governing body for sport parachuting (going through three name changes along the way), affiliated with other national aviation groups and with international aviation and parachuting organizations.

Many of the scattered post-World War Two parachuting aficionados at first stepped out on their own. Some of them, having only limited knowledge and expertise, and not knowing where to turn but determined to at least try, paid severe penalties. With parachuting experience limited to making *static line* jumps at 750-1,200 feet of altitude (automatic parachute pack opening and canopy deployment by attachment to an aircraft), dauntless exparatroopers nonetheless decided to try *freefall* parachuting, usually without any guidance, usually with unexpected results, sometimes with comic occurrences, on occasion ending tragically.

Some careful aspirants, anticipating difficulties related to differences between controlled, military static line jumping and the unknown aspects of freefall parachuting, opted to jump from their planes at what they knew was a safe altitude—1,200 feet, just what they had become used to in their military days.

Unfortunately, many eager former military paratroopers were done in by things like wrong equipment, jumping without an auxiliary parachute and suffering a severe malfunction of one's only parachute, illegal rigging, improper self-packing practices, ignoring weather conditions, and lack of specialized skills. Those who survived harrowing circumstances benefited from errors, learned of others involved in parachuting, acquired new knowledge, sought more information, studied, paid attention, and experimented prudently.

In 1948 a young ex-82nd Airborne Division paratrooper, recently discharged from the Army at the end of his enlistment, acquired a freefall back-style parachute and arranged with a pilot to drop him over an out-of-the-way farm plot in mid-Florida. Letting go of the plane, he flobbled and flailed as he fell from about 1,000 feet, soon falling with his back to earth because of his bent-forward-at-the-waist-position. Today's standard, arched-back, face-to-earth freefall position was unknown to the now worried parachutist. Over his shoulder, the earth seemed awfully close, but at least it didn't appear to be rushing up at him yet. Memories flashed in his mind of what the ground had looked like when he jumped from military aircraft and approximately what it looked like under a slowly descending canopy. The jumper, nearing soundless panic, kicked his legs and twisted his body in one direction, then the other, but he stayed on his back. Now the grass looked terribly greener! He jerked the ripcord handle mightily—gripped tightly since his exit—from the harness pocket, pushed it away from his chest, and let out a sharp, satisfied yell as he saw the ripcord cable whipping about in front of him, a yell that lasted only about two seconds, until it became a whooshing "grunt" as the canopy abruptly stopped his hurtling fall a few hundred feet above the ground. Undaunted, the young man gathered up his gear, drove 60 miles to a federally licensed parachute rigger, and left the parachute to be packed for another jump the following week. His off-work time was filled with parachutes and parachuting. Thus, painstakingly, his civilian freefall parachuting experience increased.

Eventually, the young man decided it was time to make his first freefall night jump. He had made more than one military jump at night, so he knew what it was like to get down to earth in conditions ranging from gloom to pitch-black. With his then limited parachuting wisdom of 30-plus years ago, he chose 1,500 feet as his exit altitude, the extra height intended as a safety measure for his planned 10 seconds of freefall before pulling his ripcord. To uninitiated readers it might seem that the young man had planned well. However, the planning did not take into account that 10 seconds would mean falling about 1,000 feet and reaching an approximate speed of 100 miles an hour (or some 150 feet per second). If everything went perfectly, there would be no problem with pulling the ripcord at about 500 feet (with but three-plus seconds of freefall remaining). In a second and a half the parachute would be deployed in a flash and inflated smartly; but, if everything were *not* perfect, then—

Well, everything did go perfectly, and the young man was greatly surprised when he landed so quickly after the snappy opening of his parachute canopy. He made appropriate entries in his sport parachuting logbook, but that particular jump was not one he let students know about when he later became one of the country's foremost instructors.

The lucky pressed on—including the young, ex-82nd Airborne paratrooper—suffering whatever hardships and lumps needed to continue parachuting.

THE FRENCH CONNECTION

In 1951 a young pilot was logging flying hours on his commercial pilot license. Like so many other people—to satisfy a personal curiosity—Jacques-André Istel, who was a naturalized U.S. citizen, scion of a New York family with business holdings, a Princeton graduate, and a Marine Corps Reserve captain, made a parachute jump in an out-of-the-way place. That jump intrigued him so that he made several others. Parachuting became his way of life, and later he became an officer in the small national parachuting organization, since renamed National Parachute Jumpers-Riggers Association (NPJRA), and still headed by Joe Crane. In 1955 Istel attended an international parachuting conference in Europe as a U.S. representative. He learned much about advances being made in freefall parachuting techniques, particularly in France, his native land. Following the conference, he visited that country to see how parachuting was done there. He learned the mysteries of a stable, controllable, face-to-earth freefall body position; learned the technique of changing body position to add horizontal movement to ever-present vertical fall; learned how to do front and back loops; and learned how to vary falling speed in a "stable fall" position.

COMPETITION ENLIVENS THE SPORT

By 1951 several European countries had progressed to the point that an international accuracy competition was held at Bled, Yugoslovia. Six countries participated, with 15 men and 2 women competing. France took top awards. The U.S. was not represented.

The Second World Parachuting Championships were held at St. Yan, France, in 1954, and an American entered for the first time. The meet had grown to seven countries and 31 competitors. Army sergeant Fred Mason, stationed in Europe, the sole U.S. contestant, placed twenty-first in individual rankings. Russia won that championship and became next in line to host the succeeding competition, now settled on to be held biennially in even-numbered years, with locations to be decided by sponsor bidding.

The aggressive, determined Istel set about forming a U.S. Parachute Team to take part in various international competitions, with sights set on the Third World Championship to be held in Moscow in 1956. He recruited avid, experienced parachutists and added what he had learned to their store of knowledge and skills. What he had learned was also disseminated to parachutists everywhere in the country through the national organization, NPJRA.

In those mid-'50s days Istel talked parachutes to anyone who would listen. Among them were collegians in the east and northeast who swiftly took to making "sport" jumps, appropriately terming them "sky dives." Soon sport parachute ("skydiving") clubs were formed at Harvard, Yale, Princeton, Williams, Columbia, Middlebury, and other schools. In the Boston area the Cambridge Parachute Club, comprising about 20 Harvard undergraduates (including Edward T. "Ted" Strong, who would go on to become a force in sport parachuting) and one female student from Radcliffe, was one of the first in the country. On the West Coast, particularly in the wonderful weather of southern California, parachuting as a sport was taking hold also, with several clubs being formed there. Los Angeles Sky Divers was an early group.

Individual jumpers were scattered about the country. Eventually, through the national parachute group, enough were gathered to have a national parachuting "jump-to-the-line" accuracy contest during the 1955 National Air Races in Philadelphia, Pennsylvania, where a $300 first prize went to Bob Fair, a young Tennessean who said that luck had a great deal to do with his success since he had a mere 21 jumps. Two other contestants were Jacques Istel and a young exparatrooper named Lewis Barton Sanborn, the latter soon after recruited by Istel for the national parachute team he was forming.

Working closely with the renowned parachuting pioneer, Joe Crane, Istel did much to get parachuting into the public eye; then was instrumental in changing the national organization's name to Parachute Club of America (PCA).

The geographic realm of sport parachuting spread rapidly from east and west coasts into inner America. One thing followed another, and the once mysterious art of controlled freefall was ever wideningly mastered. Jumpers overcame slowness and awkwardness, learned how to make proper right and left turns in freefall, learned front loops and back loops, and learned to "track" for horizontal motion.

With credit going to Istel, a major comfort factor was introduced to the sport in the mid-'50s with the advent of the "sleeve," a deployment retardation device that slowed the deployment/inflation sequence of a parachute canopy to a reasonable, physically endurable "opening shock" level. (Development of the sleeve is said to have started in England, followed by additional modification attributed to the Germans, and possibly the Russians. A sleeve was finally put to widespread use in France, from where Istel introduced it to American sport parachuting.) With a sleeve encasing the folded canopy, canopy/suspension line deployment/inflation time was about doubled, to three seconds from a former rough, sometimes injurious, second and a half. (Deployment retardation devices will be explained further in Chapter 4.)

As training methods became increasingly sophisticated, jumpers became more accomplished. Military surplus parachuting equipment became available, then rapidly improved technologically by dint of engineering students and inventive minds putting their gray matter to work and making things different and better (often illegally) by means of pencil and paper, with scissors and sewing machines. Nylon parachute canopies were cut and taped and sewn and tested by willing, everyday, run-of-the-mill "fun jumpers" lacking any sophistication about what they were doing. Commercial sport (also termed *recreational*) equipment started being developed and produced by recognized parachute manufacturers.

It wasn't long before jumpers in groups everywhere started challenging one another about who the better parachutists were, accuracy being the early sole criterion of ability. A "beer on the target" became a regular wager between some jumpers betting on who could land closest to a target. Collegiate clubs soon started challenging other schools' parachute clubs to see which club produced the more skilled jumpers. Competition, the lifeblood of most human endeavors, also put "zing" into sport parachuting. (The many facets of today's contests are explained in the chapter titled *Competition*.)

In 1956 a financially struggling American team (led by Jacques Istel), in its first international meet, entered the Third World Parachuting Championships in Moscow, Russia, and took sixth place of 10 countries entered, beating four well financed European teams. This event had 73 competitors, of which 23 were women. The U.S. could field only a men's team.

By 1957 America's sport parachute activity appeared well on the way to steady growth. In 1955 there had only been some 10 proficient freefall parachutists in the entire country (though there were hundreds who tumbled and fumbled as they fell, but who exulted in their jumps nonetheless). Five years later there was an estimated 1,000. In 1956 there were four PCA-affiliated clubs; in 1957 the number had grown to 18. By mid-1960, PCA records showed 150 recognized clubs and just over 2,000 paid members.

In 1957 Istel was ready to take steps to establish sport parachuting in America. The concept of a commercial sport parachute center became a reality with the founding of Jacques Istel's Parachutes, Incorporated.

"I became a convert when my first parachute opened," he said in an interview. "The sheer beauty was a very deep emotional experience. But originally, I was not the least bit interested in making a living out of parachuting. However, the only way to make a skydiving school was by making a business of it."

Istel's idea was to follow the lead of Europeans and develop sky-diving centers, similar to ski resorts, places that would lead to sport parachuting being a popular weekend sport.

When Istel founded his company, France had 10 government-sponsored sport parachuting centers, with 1,000 students enrolled and 10,000 graduates. In that country an average of 40,000 civilian jumps were made annually. Russia's longstanding interest in sport parachuting had not waned in the least, with an estimated two million jumps being made each year.

Istel's first step was to establish a center in sun-drenched California at a small airport in Hemet. That state was already home to several small, loosely organized bands of parachutists who jumped as often as they could at a few widely scattered small airports. With the constraints of a limited supply of parachuting equipment, few qualified instructors, difficulty in finding willing pilots and suitable aircraft, most club activity was at a low level measured against today's customary day at an average drop zone (DZ). One account of that time described the Los Angeles Sky Divers as one of the most active of the group of clubs in the southern California region, yet with its 25 members (encouragingly, five of them were women) the club logged only 170 jumps in its first five months. However, things did get better in southern California. Istel's operation—highly structured, with its own small planes, and with specially designed and commercially made parachutes and related equipment—was off to a good start.

In 1958 the Fourth World Parachuting Championships were held at Bratislava, Czechoslovakia. The number of competitors had grown slightly, to 78, with 21 women entered. As in the previous world championship, America again took sixth place, but the number of countries entered had grown to 14.

By early 1959 the number of individual parachutists in the U.S. had grown significantly. Also, the number of clubs in the contiguous states was growing, two had been started in Alaska, and three were now in Canada. Istel's company, Parachutes Incorporated (PI), closed the Hemet operation and moved to the more densely populated east coast. There, in May 1959, he opened a commercial sport parachute center in Orange, Massachusetts, a small industrial town in the north-central part of the state.

In 1960 the picture changed in America's favor in international competition. The Fifth World Parachuting Championships were held in Sofia, Bulgaria; 137 competitors from 12 countries included 42 women. For the first time Americans were winners. Though the U.S. Team did not place among the winners, individual medalists were Jim Arender, World Style Champion, and Dick Fortenberry, Second Place Overall, Men.

The next world championships were held in 1962 at the Orange Sport Parachute Center (OSPC), just north of the vast, slender Quabbin Reservoir. Jacques Istel's three-year-old commercial venture had become a veritable Mecca for parachutists.

Twenty-five nations competed in the Sixth World Parachuting Championships, and the 133 contestants included 35 women. Americans did themselves proud in their "home park," taking seven medals, of which four were gold, one was silver, and two were bronze. Muriel Simbro and Jim Arender became Overall World Champions; American women won first place in team accuracy; and the men placed second in team accuracy.

In the early 1970s, with increasing sophistication of techniques and equipment, there were 500 sport parachute clubs and 20 commercial parachuting centers across America. Sport parachuting took hold in Canada. The already popular recreation in some European nations became even more so in those countries and also spread to others.

The fun of parachuting had been discoverd.

SKILL DEVELOPMENT AND
TECHNOLOGICAL BREAKTHROUGHS

The realm of the skydiver was indeed growing at the close of the fifties. The next three decades were to see that realm grow vastly. Sport parachuting, or as many preferred, skydiving, was to make great advances in every aspect:

- Worldwide participation.
- Increased membership in local and national organizations.
- Number and types of competitions.
- Highly developed relative work skills (RW—parachuting involving two or more skydivers):
  —Size and complexity of freefall formations.
  —Discoveries and development of both *sequential* freefall relative work and *canopy* relative work (CRW, pronounced "crew").
- Remarkable developments in equipment:
  —Ram air ("square" in skydiving jargon) canopies that fly 25 miles an hour in a no-wind condition, yet let a jumper wear jogging shoes, or even sandals, and make tip-toe landings on a five-centimeter target.
  —Complete main/reserve parachute assemblies that weigh in at as little as 19 pounds, down from 50 pounds of the early '60s.
  —High-performance "ram air" reserve parachute canopies.
  —Instrumentation (much of it miniaturized):
    • Altimeters.
    • Helmet-mounted, buzzer-type warning altitude warning devices.

- Automatic devices for opening reserve parachute containers in emergency situations.
- Military applications:
  —HALO (**H**igh **A**ltitude, **L**ow **O**pening).
  —HAHO (**H**igh **A**ltitude, **H**igh **O**pening).
  —LALO (**L**ow **A**ltitude, **L**ow **O**pening).
  —Covert personnel/equipment insertion by tandem parachute.
- Parachuting instruction:
  —Tandem parachuting—state-of-the-art training for both student sport parachutists and for teaching emergency parachuting techniques to aircraft pilots and crew members.

REAL PEOPLE—REAL PARACHUTISTS: A BAKER'S DOZEN

Most people still think that making a parachute jump is a mere matter of "get out of the plane and pull the ripcord!" True, it was that basic at one time, and it still can be that fundamental in some flying circumstances where things go wrong and the sole means available for getting on with life is to use a parachute; but there is also a whole other world of parachutes, and being part of that realm can bring you much enjoyment, excitement, and satisfaction.

Sport parachuting—skydiving!—offers you the same rewards that have come to thousands of people who have spent many years in the sport. Interestingly, each of those people would more than likely say that he or she really only wanted to make one jump—just to see what it was like—because it was something that person had always wanted to do:

- **Bruce Randolph Thompson**, a university forestry student, decided to make a jump after attending an extracurricular campus meeting where he listened to two other students who had experience with parachuting and were forming a collegiate parachute club. Randy has since passed the 6,300-jump mark and has been a National Accuracy Champion. He continues to be a regular winner or runner-up in numerous accuracy money or trophy competitions. Also, he became a seasoned USPA-rated Accelerated Free Fall (AFF) Instructor, a rated parachute Tandem Pilot, a highly skilled RW (relative work) skydiver, an F.A.A. Master Parachute Rigger, and a working partner of a firm manufacturing award-winning parachute canopies.

- **Harley J. Mowery**, not long after becoming an ex-Army 1st Lieutenant, wanted to try parachuting just once, after hearing about it from his sister's girlfriend. Since his first-jump course in 1970 Jim has made more than 2,900 sport jumps, including many under test conditions as a Marketing Representative for Pioneer Parachute Co. He has also served the club that taught him by being one of its officers or directors several times, and by being its president four times. He has been a United States Parachute Association (USPA) Conference Director for years, recently being reelected to that office for his fifth two-year term. He has also been on the USPA Board of Directors five times; served ten years on USPA's Safety and Training Committee, with the past eight years as Chairman; and helped implement the USPA Accelerated Freefall training program as a USPA-rated AFF Instructor. He is also a rated Tandem Pilot. He has assisted in updating USPA's *Basic Safety Requirements* and aided in publishing USPA's "Skydiver's Information Handbook."

- **Rayelene Wilson** is five-foot-one, weighs a hundred-something pounds, and earns her living as a highly skilled Registered Nurse with a long list of credentials. Her specialty is heart trauma, and she is a longtime coronary care unit head nurse. Her medical experience has earned her a U.S. Naval Reserve commission as a Lieutenant. Raye is close to making her sport parachute jump number 3,000, which will earn her USPA's Double Diamond Wings. She has been a USPA Jumpmaster, parachute club officer and director several times, and a member of two U.S. Parachute Teams.

- **Richard G. Barber** is a Charter/Life Member of one of the country's oldest and largest sport parachute clubs, organized in December 1961 and state-chartered in March 1962. Besides serving as a club officer and director for several years as he was fun jumping and competing, Dick also got an early start with judging parachute competitions. Over the years he officiated in many meets, steadily rising through the parachute judging hierarchy, becoming a USPA Conference Judge, then later a National Judge, rated for Accuracy, Style, Relative Work, and Canopy Relative Work competitions. At various National Championships he served as an Event Judge, a Chief Judge, and a Chief, Training Judge Program. Ultimately, Dick qualified as an FAI. (Fédération Aéronautiqué Intérnationalé) International Judge, officiating at several international contests, and has served as U.S. Team Judge at three world meets. Most recently he accompanied the U.S. Parachute Team to the world meet in Sweden.

- **Carol Christenson** is blonde, five-foot-six, slender, of Norwegian extraction, an exceptionally skilled parachutist of long standing, and has been a member of a U.S. Parachute Team more than once. Starting her sport parachuting in Colorado, Chris jumped regularly, paying attention to those who helped because they wanted to see her succeed, and one day felt skilled enough to enter competitions. With a few awards to her credit, she went up against the "major leaguers" of parachuting at a national championship. She ultimately did well enough in such competitions to be selected as a team member to represent America in international meets. As she parachuted and competed she also worked at qualifying for her FAA Senior Parachute Rigger certificate. She later went on to qualify as a Master Parachute Rigger. Presently she is president of a parachute manufacturing company, even as she continues to intensively practice accuracy parachuting with the goal of continuing to have a slot on the U.S. Parachute Team. Most recently she was a U.S. Team member at an eight-country international competition in Sapporo, Japan. Chris took third place, and the U.S. Team won the meet.

- **George McCulloch** was 55 years old when he made his first parachute jump in Orange, Massachusetts. On the day he turned 76 he was presented a set of USPA Gold Wings during his 1,000th freefall jump. After sea duty as a World War Two Merchant Mariner he was a newspaper reporter in Syracuse, New York. He also became a sport parachutist, "to ease the stresses of a hectic workplace and pressures of deadlines." He and his wife, Harriet, became familiar figures at DZs, and she quickly and happily became George's helpmate, repacking his rig after each jump ("because," she claimed, usually with a wink, "I'm a better packer than he is!"). George retired at the paper's mandatory age 62, but soon after took a job with the city of Stamford, Connecticut. Unfortunately, the city also had a mandatory retirement age, and when he turned 65 George and Harriet returned to Rochester, New York. George was a "doer," and he and Harriet quickly got busy as volunteers working on behalf of handicapped persons and working extensively with a Search and Rescue unit—and he kept jumping. George ultimately eased out of skydiving after he passed his 78th birthday, but only because his weakening vision no longer provided the depth perception needed for easy, safe landings. By then he had logged more than 1,100 sport parachute jumps.

- **Dennis Testoni** has a "learn-to-live-with-it" medical condition, but he and his doctor have let it affect his parachuting activity only minimally. After he was solidly on his way to USPA Gold Wings, he started training to become an FAA Senior Parachute Rigger and did receive that federal certification. He also became a USPA Jumpmaster as well as an AFF Instructor. Then Dennis added to his parachuting expertise by becoming a freefall photographer, using both still and video cameras. To help AFF students he often followed a student and instructors from a plane and videotaped the student's 40-second freefall performance, providing the student with the best possible critique of how well he or she had done.

- **Valerie Fenton** made her first parachute jump in 1987. Her initial curiosity satisfied and other things making demands on her time, she didn't jump for another two years. The first four of these later jumps were made with "conventional" student gear (a main and reserve parachute on a single harness with the main parachute automatically opened by a static line attached to the aircraft); but the wonder of parachuting still tugged at her mind. One day she went to a parachute club's DZ, watched, saw the major changes in student parachute training and equipment, and decided to jump again. She now has made a transition "tandem passenger" jump, completed seven levels of Accelerated Freefall (AFF) training, and obtained a USPA "Basic Parachutist License". She has logged nearly 50 jumps, including relative work (RW) formations with as many as eight other skydivers.

- **William Beaudreau**, a university senior, sat in a Student Union auditorium with more than a hundred other undergraduate students, all of them intently listening to a guest speaker tell of sport parachuting. When the speaker asked how many people in the room wanted to make *one* parachute jump, every hand in the auditorium went up; but when the speaker asked how many wanted to make a *thousand* jumps, not one arm was raised. The speaker had made his point and explained it to the audience: No one sees him- or herself as making a lot of jumps, especially a thousand, but most people readily see themselves as making at least one.

  Bill made his one jump, then another, and kept jumping. Along the way he participated in local and regional competitions; then in Collegiate National Parachute Championships, regularly winning honors and trophies at every competition level. He graduated the university, went to work, kept jumping, married a parachutist with many jumps herself, kept jumping and winning and placing in local and regional competitions. He also became a USPA Parachute Instructor, then an AFF Instructor. Later he was appointed his club's USPA Safety & Training Advisor. He continues to parachute as a "fun jumper," fitting it in with working and helping raise three young children.

- **William H. Ottley** ("WHO") made his first jump in 1959, and after 30 years of close association with sport parachuting has over 4,000 skydives. "WHO" is also the longtime Executive Director of the United States Parachute Association (USPA). With his innumerable and wide-ranging USPA associations, Bill has been at the cutting edge of equipment development, changes in philosophy, federal legislation, the conduct of competitions, revisions in student training methods, updating doctrine and regulations, and many other facets of skydiving. He is a perennial competitor at U.S. National Parachute Championships, has multiple pilot and parachuting ratings, has received many personal awards, and is on a variety of high-level national and international parachuting committees. The list goes on—notable achievements for someone wanting, way back, to make only one jump.

- **Howard L. Burling, II** was a U.S. Marine Corps parachute rigger trainee in 1954. A Navy Department requirement was that, as part of qualifying to be a rigger, each trainee had to make a freefall jump with a parachute he had packed. He made his jump, got his rating, and served the Corps as a parachute rigger. Thirty-three years later Howie was awarded USPA Gold Wings in recognition of making 1,000 freefall parachute jumps. In between there was a family; a job as a police officer, eventually becoming a captain of the department; a career change into personnel training for a major state bank; then, in time, a vice presidency of that bank. Throughout those years, the yen for sport parachuting never waned. Some skydiving "freaks" earned their Gold Wings in two to three years, but commitments kept Howie from reaching that goal as soon as he would have liked. However, he was persistent, and one day he reached his cherished goal. He hasn't stopped there; Howie goes on skydiving—jumping for fun, competing for fun.

- **Daniel F. Poynter** started skydiving in the early 1960s. As he became more involved with parachuting, he decided he wanted to be a parachute rigger as another step in being a "complete" parachutist. He discovered that there was little documentation from which to learn and that what was published was hard to find. The little he could gather revealed there was a large information gap for parachute riggers and rigger candidates. He kept on with his research, however, as he improved his skills and progressed through informal and formal hierarchies of the sport. In several years he had garnered, sifted, sorted, and collated a huge amount of technical data about parachutes. When information was lacking, he researched published history and lore. He wrote narratives, descriptions, and captions. It took Dan more than eight years to compile his work. Then he entered the publishing field, producing the first edition of *The Parachute Manual* in 1972. A single information source was finally at hand for everyone involved in parachuting.

More printing runs were needed to meet the demand. Meanwhile, evolution in parachuting was taking place rapidly. Dan steadily compiled more information to keep pace with changes and in 1975 published a second, revised edition of the manual. Parachuting evolution did not slow at all. Dan's research and information gathering continued. In several years it was time for another new, updated version. In 1984 the "Third Edition, Completely Revised" was published, an extraordinary store of information in 581 detailed $8\frac{1}{2} \times 11$ inch pages. Dan Poynter's technical treatise is today considered the standard in parachuting—and not just in skydiving. In fact, it is referred to as the "bible" by parachute riggers everywhere. All branches of U.S. military services use it for reference, as does the U.S. Forest Service. Many foreign governments have also ordered it.

At the start of the '60s a curious young man made a jump to see what it was like. At the close of the '80s he is a respected authority on parachutes and is widely involved in parachuting activities.

- **Norman Kent** was another who said, "I was going to do it only once." That "once" was on his 19th birthday. At the age of 31 he has 4,600 jumps in his logbooks and has the reputation of being one of the world's premier freefall photographers. He wanted to start his parachute photography while making his first jump but was not allowed to—he was reminded that there would be enough for a first-timer to do just to make a satisfactory jump. Norm took to parachuting readily and progressed quickly; well enough that he did shoot his first freefall picture on his 27th jump, using a Kodak Instamatic 126. "I bought a twenty-five dollar wind-up camera, and that's how I started." Today Norman Kent's still photographs, calendars, and entertainment and training videotapes are in demand throughout the world. His production company is kept humming, and Norm's star shines brightly.

With this "baker's dozen" of profiles of people just like you, you can see that there is much that can be done in the world of sport parachuting. These people, too, were uncertain about getting involved in something that many other folks about them viewed as madcap, to say the least. But in parachuting they each found excitement, pleasure, success, and an enduring interest. Skeptics unwilling to test themselves against something unknown missed out on what this baker's dozen discovered. Furthermore, many achievers like them also found something completely unanticipated. You can too!

2

Parachute Folktales, Lore, and History

Much of the early information about parachutes is from a body of folktales that had been passed along through the ages with little or no substantiation of historical worth. Eventually, written records started being kept, verifying documentation was gathered into archives, and a burgeoning lore accrued credibility.

You are about to learn more of the background of one word than you probably want to know, but it is a word that got your attention at some point, and holds it even now—*parachute!*

Parachute is said to have come about by combining a prefix *para* and a noun *chute*. Some examiners of word structure have decided that the whole word is a blending of two French terms; others say the prefix is of Italian derivation and was combined with the French noun for the modern word. Since both tongues are Romance languages and both prefixes date back to an ancient Greek prefix that includes a definition similar to the meaning of both later prefixes, it seems to make little difference who gets credit.

However, it is confusing; and because you will likely come across varying descriptions and wonder why the different explanations, the following is meant to clear the matter.

In the ancient Greek language there was a prefix *para* that had several usages, including "against." That prefix is the basis for the Italian *parare*, "to ward off," from Latin *parare*, a combining word form meaning "a thing that protects from."

The French prefix *para* means "protect against" or "shelter from" as used in *parasol* ("protect against"/"shelter from" and "sun"). The French noun *chute* is based on the Old French word *cheute*, meaning a fall, or a declivity (downward slope, or descent); but the term was meant to describe a means by which objects moved from a higher to a lower level, more in the sense of water conduits, or coal chutes to move fuel from a street level down into a building cellar. However, later users decided the *fall* was also in the sense of one falling from a height.

There was not a real need for parachute development until balloons began to proliferate in the 18th and 19th centuries. The need became urgent in the 20th century, when powered aircraft became a reality.

When Frenchmen started producing a great number of hot air balloons and made a great number of ascents, it was only a matter of time before there were in-flight failures, and finally there was a search to produce something that would protect against an injurious, or fatal, fall. We'll never know who actually coined the new word *parachute*, but it certainly seems that some man or woman of France is the likely choice.

Italy's renowned and wondrous Leonardo da Vinci (1452-1519)—engineer, mathematician, scientist, architect, inventor, painter (*La Gioconda* a.k.a., *Mona Lisa*), sculptor, musician, dabbler with countless interests—did not use such a term or anything like it when he cogitated briefly about a device that could be used by trapped people to escape fires in tall buildings. In his 1495 book *Codex Atlanticus* he refers simply to his idea as a "tent roof": "If a man have a tent roof of caulked [var., calked] linen 12 braccia broad and 12 braccia high, he will be able to let himself fall from any great height without danger to himself."

Another translation says, "If a man have a tent of closely woven linen without any apertures, twelve braccia across and twelve in depth, he can throw himself down from any great height without injury." (The year 1485 has also been given as a date for da Vinci's "parachute" design, by no less an authority than the Smithsonian Institution's National Air and Space Museum in Washington, D.C. Two illustrations captioned "Da Vinci Parachute Design 1485" are included in a variety of depictions of aviation devices on wallpaper sold through the museum's gift shop.)

It has been difficult to determine the actual size of da Vinci's design because of the unit of measure he detailed—a *braccio*. That term is from the Italian word meaning "arm." Thus, da Vinci's unit of measure was defined as "an arm's length." But whose arm?

Various people came up with differing figures for an arm's length, ranging from 15 to 39 inches. Some unnamed decision-maker stated it was exactly 18.4 inches (the basis for the decision is unknown). Calculating the canopy size using the variety of dimensions and their volumes gives a shape of anywhere from a square 15 feet on a side to one 39 feet on a side. So you can see that with such variance, da Vinci's canopy is more in the realm of lore than fact.

Fig. 2-1. *The renowned Leonardo da Vinci, painter of* La Gioconda (*the half-smiling* Mona Lisa), *sketched a design for a "parachute" and wrote minimal notes about his idea. It is said he was searching for some means of people being able to rescue themselves from burning buildings.*

FIGURE 2-1, said to have been reproduced from da Vinci's notebook, has also appeared in various other sketch forms, all of them similar in depiction.

Fig. 2-2. *Leonardo da Vinci's basic design has often been illustrated. But no records exist showing that a working model was ever built, nor has it been documented that a jump was actually made.*

The "parachute," a rigid shape pyramidal in configuration, has its air-gathering/air-holding shape held by long wooden poles. The whole affair seems unwieldy, but latter-day aeronautical engineers and parachute jumpers generally concede it could have worked. Its efficiency and ease of use, though, are doubtful.

Thus, based on his brief commentary and a sketch, Leonardo da Vinci was awarded yet another credit by admirers—"father of the parachute." However, no working model has ever been found, and there is no record of a descent ever being made with his drawing board design; not even an unsubstantiated rumor to that effect.

About a century later, another Italian, Fausto Veranzio, said to be an architect of Venice (but also said to be a Hungarian mathematician), published *Machinae Nova*, a book about new devices of his design. In the book was an engraving titled "Homo Volans" ("Flying Man"), and it seems to be the first printed depiction of a parachutelike device in use, showing a man descending from a tower, with four lines secured to the jumper's body to form a harness of sorts, with the upper part of the lines knotted to the framework corners of an oblong, horizontal "sail."

Veranzio's description read:

> Flying man. With a square canvas spread between four equal poles [though not shown as equal in the illustration], and having four cords attached to the four joints, a man could, without danger, throw himself from a tower or similar eminence. Even though there is no wind at the time, his weight will create the wind which inflates the canvas; he need have no fear of falling swiftly, for he will descend little by little. The man should proportion the spread of the canvas to his own weight.

Like his countryman's concept, Veranzio's seems to have remained an idea only. Though his idea was greatly publicized, no evidence has been found that there was ever a *homo volans* of his or any other time who tested and proved Veranzio's plan.

The Chinese have been credited for a variety of parachutelike activities, going back several centuries. Even then China had a highly cultured society in many respects and had people with the imagination, creativity, and technical understanding to have come up with what, as we now know, is basically a simple device. After all, China is the country that introduced paper money, spaghetti and many other forms of pasta, movable type for printing, gun powder and fireworks, the magnetic compass, ocean navigation, and contributed a great number of other useful or enjoyable innovations. Furthermore, a special characteristic of the Chinese people is their contemplative nature, their observation and understanding of the forces, beauty, and grace of nature. Surely many among them must have studied birds in flight, analyzed the gentleness and smoothness of their return to earth, and seen the shapes and actions

Fig. 2-3. *Fausto Veranzio's idea of a parachute resembled his countryman da Vinci's design. This illustration of a "Homo Volans" ("flying man") appeared in Veranzio's book,* Machinae Nova. *Publishing date varies from as early as 1595 to as late as 1618.*

of seed pods moving in winds and settling to earth. Surely some among them would have tried to duplicate nature.

There have been reports that the balloon was a Chinese invention to celebrate the coronation of Empress Fo-King in 1300 AD, but nothing tangible exists to support that claim.

The Chinese, very likely, also invented the kite, but even if they did not invent the aerial contraption, they certainly became masters of design, complex construction, and lifting capacity.

However, it is doubtful that the Chinese ever came up with anything at any time that could truly be considered a parachute. No documents or illustrations exist that even suggest anything purposefully constructed with the appearance or function of such a contrivance. It appears that China's main source of credit will be for storied innovation in adapting whatever was at hand to carry out parachutelike activities.

One bit of lore is that as far back as the 1100s Chinese amused themselves with contrivances that resembled umbrellas. Other lore says that it wasn't until 1306 that Chinese acrobats used hand-held devices in balancing acts billed as audience entertainment, devices whose shape seemed to have been a cross between an umbrella (or parasol) and a small, rigid parachute. Still other lore tells of actors leaping from theater heights with umbrellalike things to make spectacular surprise entrances onto a stage, to the "oohs" and "ahs" of delighted audiences. Another bit of lore, also dated 1306, relates that umbrellalike parachutes were used by Chinese to descend from the Great Wall of China, apparently as a personal diversion. One of the legends is that China's Emperor Shih Huang Ti was one of those who enjoyed leaping from the top of what is today nearly a 4,000-mile-long protective structure marking a major portion of China's northern border, his device described more as a parasol than a parachute, but serving the same purpose. It would seem that a fully open, rigid-canopy device had to have been required equipment for such diversion. Even so, any thrill would have to have been extremely brief; the Wall itself is only 25 feet high. Even the sentry towers spaced every 100 to 200 yards along the Wall's length are only 40 feet high.

One account stands out in Chinese story-telling. It is the tale of Emperor Shun, who lived during the approximate period of 2258–2208 BC (4,000-plus years ago!). According to an ancient Chinese publication, *Annals of the Bamboo Books*, when the emperor was a boy he was captured and held prisoner by his father's enemies. He was said to have later escaped by putting on "the work clothes of a bird," then flying over the prison's walls.

The *Annals* go on to tell that when he became a man, he recalled the excitement of the aerial part of his daring escape. To recapture some of "that old feeling," he took to jumping from the top of a tower, protected from harm by supporting himself with "two large reed hats." It is known that such reed hats, as large as three feet in diameter, existed at that time, but they would had to have been sturdily constructed, and even with the largest of reed hats, the Emperor would have had to be of light weight to make any kind of comfortable landings.

Perhaps the most amusing bit of Chinese "parachute" lore has to do with a young suitor who is said to have escaped an angry pursuing father by scrambling upward in his love's house, reaching the rooftop. High above ground, with no other means of evasion open to him, he improvised. Grasping the chin strap of a large, circular reed hat firmly in each fist (it's never been explained how he happened to have *two* hats), he desperately leaped from the roof, safely reached the ground, and scrambled joyously away from the threatening parent.

One tale remains to be told here, one that is closer to being history in a genuine sense. During the period 1687 to 1688 Simon de la Loubère was the envoy extraordinary from the King of France to the King of Siam (now Thailand). He later wrote a two-volume work about the relationship of the two countries. One of the chapters was titled, "Concerning the Shows and Other Diversions of the Siamese," and in that chapter he devoted a section to "A Tumbler Exceedingly honour'd by the King of Siam":

> There dyed one, some years since, who leap'd from the Hoop, supporting himself by two *Umbrellas*, the hands of which were fix'd to his Girdle: the wind carry'd him accidentally sometimes to the Ground, sometimes on Trees or Houses, and sometimes into the River. He so exceedingly diverted the King of Siam that his Prince had made him a great Lord: he had lodged him in the Palace and had given him a great Title; or, as they say, a great Name.

The "Hoop" must have been a very high place indeed, perhaps a spire or rampart of the king's castle, but in any case high enough that there would be enough time for a wind to occasionally carry him some distance. The risk might have been great, but the rewards proved to be worth the trouble. Many a skydiver today would give eyeteeth for a deal like the Tumbler's.

NOW—TO LINGERING QUASI-HISTORY

16th and 17th Centuries

In the 16th and 17th centuries, scientists diligently and persistently studied gravity and the mysteries of falling objects and terminal velocity. The discovery that a falling body accelerates at a specific rate until it reaches a terminal velocity was to produce calculations that would be useful to parachutists of the mid-20th century and later.

1783, France

The [de] Montgolfier brothers, Joseph Michel (1740–1810) and Jacques Étienne (1745–1799), were sons of a papermaker of Annonay, a town 45 miles from Lyons. The brothers had a deep-seated interest in designing, constructing, and flying hot air balloons.

It has been reported that Joseph had, as a 16-year-old boy in the mid-1700s, made a leap from the peak of the Montgolfier home using a crudely formed parachute, tightly gripping the lower ends of the canopy's several lines in his clasped hands. He is said to have become interested in the idea of jumping because of a desire to in some way fly through the wide sky about him. He had learned of da Vinci's "tent roof" and had also heard of bold men who had made leaps from buildings. One day, after long wanting to satisfy his curiosity, Joseph took action, to the amazement of neighbors and other townspeople.

The brothers grew to manhood, worked for a living at manufacturing paper, and started their sideline hot air balloon endeavor. Thinking far ahead, and recalling Joseph's teen-age exploit, the thought of a parachute came quickly to mind as an emergency device should a balloon fail during flight. The brothers made and tested a variety of parachute models, first using inert objects as weights, conducting their experiments from the tops of high towers and buildings. Ultimately, said to be about 1779, using a parasollike device, seven feet, four inches in diameter, they dropped a live sheep in a basket secured below the small "parachute" canopy. The animal landed without injury, though it was skittish for several minutes afterward. Test animals were the only living creatures to use the Montgolfiers' experimental lifesaving devices, but the brothers were satisfied with their rescue concept. However, they redirected their attentions and efforts almost completely to their first love—making a hot air balloon that could take a human passenger aloft and return safely to earth.

On June 4 (or 5), 1783 they partially succeeded with a balloon (without passenger) that rose to about a thousand feet, drifted for some 10 minutes in a gentle wind, then settled lightly into a vineyard a mile and a half away. Ballooning history had been made. Later that year, on November 21, a huge Montgolfier balloon 54 feet in diameter with a capacity of 55,000 cubic feet soared into the sky above Paris with two men aboard as passengers, traveled about five miles, and dramatically landed with both passengers safe. Each of the brothers was granted lifetime pensions by the King of France, in addition to being given a substantial royal grant for further experiments. Their spectacular successes gave impetus to widespread development of balloons in many countries and greatly encouraged development of parachutes as a lifesaving alternative in case of aerial emergencies.

1783, France

On December the 26th of the year of notable ballooning achivements by the Montgolfier brothers, it is said by one chronicler that Sébastian Lenormand, a French physician (also described by another as Professor of Technology at the Paris Conservatory of Arts and Handicrafts), created a great stir in the newspapers of Paris when he jumped from that city's Montpelier Observatory with a crudely made 14-foot, conical device, with the converging lower end of suspension lines lashed about his waist. He was said to have proclaimed that his purpose was to demonstrate a practical means of escaping from a burning building. It is not known whether the idea was his alone or if he had been inspired by Leonardo da Vinci's early similar purpose.

However, "history," as recorded by several other sources, is murky as to whether Lenormand ever actually made such a demonstration. One recorder said the parachute maker could not work up the nerve to make the leap; but it is generally conceded that the "professor"/"physician" did make test drops, using animals, with a parachute variously described as being made of silk, coarse cloth, or "oil-silk."

1783–1784, England

Thomas Martyn published *Hints on Aerostatic Globes* in 1783 (or 1784), dealing with construction of aerial craft. In this book he made mention of a lifesaving device for aircraft, support it with a detailed illustration, and said that his design theory included "an Umbrella to afford easy descent, should the Balloon burst." There doesn't appear to be any record that his advice was followed. When he was criticized in print by Jean Pierre Blanchard, he concluded his rebuttal by adding that "the air's natural resistance must have occurred to anybody who carried an umbrella in a strong wind." Blanchard apparently later reconsidered his opinion about Martyn's advice, as noted in the following section.

1777–1793, France

Jean Pierre Blanchard, a diminutive, feisty, professional showman, is said to have done quite a bit involving parachutes; but, here again, details are fragmentary and hazy. Not much was faithfully recorded about his activities, but accounts of him persistently appear in ballooning and parachuting information resources. One chronicler of 1930 told of Blanchard's association with ballooning as early as 1777. Various accounts tell of Blanchard's numerous balloon ascensions. One of those accounts had an illustration of his aerial craft equipped with a parachute resembling Martyn's *Hints on Aerostatic Globes*. Other illustrations of different balloons show similar riggings, though there is no evidence that Blanchard did actually use such equipment during flights. There is also a report of Blanchard's first experiment with a parachute on June 3, 1785, when he was said to have released a weighted 20-foot silk parachute in midair. There are accounts of him several times dropping a small dog in a basket secured to the canopy's lines.

Blanchard is also debatably credited with devising a collapsible canopy with a light framework of ribs that could be folded, the whole unit being reduced to a small bundle, thereby eliminating the need for an awkward, bulky, rigid contraption that at all times held a broad expanse of fabric fully extended. To Blanchard's credit, he and a copilot are recognized as having "sailed" a balloon across the English Channel in 1785, from Dover to somewhere near Calais—completing the first aerial voyage over open water.

The next report on Blanchard is about his time spent in America. A 20th century narrator said that in 1794 Blanchard, with George Washington as his patron, made both the first balloon ascension and the first parachute drop in the United States, and that he acquired the distinction of being called the "father of American aeronautics." Oddly, there are no details of these events, which should have been milestones in American history.

Among other activities attributed to Blanchard, it is reported that he often released parachute-equipped dogs in testing various parachutes he designed and made; also that he once released a dog, a cat, and a squirrel attached to a single parachute (presumably in separate containers) from an altitude of several thousand feet. The outcomes of the animal experiments are not known.

There are also persistent accounts that Blanchard actually made a parachute jump himself, but these accounts do not withstand scrutiny. Dates for his alleged jump include 1777, 1785, 1787, 1793, and 1801; but no evidence exists to verify either his claim or anyone else's report that he really did jump. What does appear in some accounts is that he broke a leg making a jump; but details are varied, unclear, and inadequate. The only thing that seems certain is that Blanchard once did have a broken leg, though its cause is not clear.

Nothing is known of Blanchard after 1794. Apparently he lost interest in balloons, in being a parachutist, in devising parachutes. The date of his death is uncertain. His widow later became a highly popular balloonist in Europe. There are two prevalent accounts of Mme. Madeleine-Sophie Blanchard's last balloon flight, one with a clear parachute relationship to it:

Account "A." Mme. Blanchard enjoyed night ballooning and, with a great sense of adventure, was one of the first to set off fireworks from a balloon. Her daring one night got her into terrible trouble: A fireworks spark accidentally ignited the highly inflammable hydrogen lifting gas of her balloon. Without a parachute on board, she fell to her death.

Account "B." After her husband's death, Mme. Blanchard supported herself by making balloon ascensions at fairs. To dramatize the ascents, fair promotors often set off dazzling fireworks displays.

On a fateful occasion, a rocket veered from its soaring climb and glanced off the bottom of the hydrogen-filled bag; but there was no explosion, only a brief fire. Most of the hydrogen rapidly escaped as the fabric was burned away, then flames expired. The upper fabric of the bag remained intact, embraced by the large net over the bag, a net designed to support the passenger basket. The fabric hemisphere thus served as a parachute to slow the descent. Mme. Blanchard, worried but hopeful, certain that she was out of trouble, happily waved small flags at spectators cheering what they thought was a new feature of her performance. Then Mme. Blanchard seemed to be out of danger. Suddenly the basket swung sharply against a roof, hung treacherously for a moment, then turned over and tumbled Mme. Blanchard to the pavement two floors down. Her back was broken, and the unlucky aeronaut died on the way to the hospital.

In either telling, for Mme. Blanchard it was the ultimate fireworks show.

1797, France (and an Ensuing Period of Improved Historical Accuracy)

André (curiously called "Andrew" by some parachuting chroniclers) Jacques Garnerin gets credit for being the first genuine parachutist. It has been noted above that occasional rumors had J.P. Blanchard being the first to make a jump, but repeated attempts to substantiate the claim produced nothing worthwhile. With the absence of proof and the presence of verifiable evidence of Garnerin's accomplishments, the latter's accreditation seems valid.

Garnerin, described as a "small, peppery man with a spade beard and waxed moustaches," has been credited with being the "pioneer exponent of free human parachute flight from aircraft."

The story goes that he had been captured during the battle of Marchiennes and imprisoned at Budapest, Hungary. Locked in oppressive solitary confinement, he is said to have conceived a parachute with which he desperately hoped to end his imprisonment once relieved from his small cell, but he was freed before ever getting a chance to test his idea. He returned to Paris, but the extraordinary concept would not leave his mind. He proceeded to build the device he so clearly pictured in his mind; then made public announcement of his scheme to rise into the sky, release from his aerostat, and descend to earth by parachute.

The parachute canopy was said to have been made of either canvas or silk, and the assembly allegedly included a long support pole extending downward from the canopy apex, with the passenger's basket suspended from that pole. One report on the size of the inflated canopy gave it as eight feet in diameter, but that is not a believable number: severe injury would have undoubtedly occurred if an average-weight male of that time had used a canopy that small. Most accounts said it was 23 feet in size. The latter is a credible figure, being much closer in size to some parachutes in use today. Garnerin's entire parachute assembly was reported to weigh more than one hundred pounds.

That first test was on October 22, 1797, at the Park of Monceau. Garnerin secured his parachute apparatus to a small basket in which he would ride during ascent and descent. Then he further secured the combination of parachute and basket to a special fitting on his expendable hot air balloon, everything rigged so that he would only have to pull a release line to break away from the balloon when he reached what he calculated to be a sufficiently high altitude. (Accounts of later ascensions—one of them in his words—have Garnerin using a knife to cut the connecting line between balloon and parachute.)

When the balloon was inflated and all else was ready, Garnerin hopped blithely into the parachute's basket and in a moment or so signaled he was ready. Above his head slack canopy fabric and suspension lines dangled. His assistants let go of restraining ropes and, to the cheers and applause of a large crowd, the balloon rose quickly over the roofs of Paris, drifting slowly to the west in a mild breeze. At an altitude that has been reported as between 2,000 feet and about one and a quarter miles, Garnerin firmly tugged the line that was to free the parachute and basket from the lifting device. Garnerin and his rig dropped quickly at first, the canopy fabric fluttering as suspension lines extended and the parachute gathered precious air. One report had the hot air balloon skyrocketing up when the load was released, then bursting into shreds. Other reports make no mention of what happened to that aerial craft.

The descending canopy was seen to be oscillating, with reports varying from "mildly" to "wildly." One account said that Garnerin was dazed when he landed and greeted wellwishers. It is not known whether it was because of pure joy and excitement or due to illness brought on by oscillations of the parachute.

Hundreds of spectators followed his short journey and greeted him when he safely landed in a surprised farmer's vineyard. While his helpers gathered his parachute and basket, Garnerin went by horseback to the site of the lift-off, returning to more cheers and adulation. He went on to be named a hero of the newly founded French Republic, and his fame spread throughout Europe.

To his benefit, Garnerin's feat had been duly witnessed and recorded. However (and curiously, considering his vision of the project's magnitude) there are no technical descriptions or illustrations by Garnerin of his first rig.

Enthused by the success of his first parachuting venture, Garnerin turned to full-time involvement with his new interest. He made three more exhibition parachute drops in France, receiving many plaudits and achieving much recognition. He kept wrestling with the problem of stable descent, trying conservative modifications with the hope of reducing canopy oscillation. Garnerin was to note later that he "usually experienced [painful vomiting] for several hours after a descent in a parachute." The solution ultimately was a simple one, but for quite a while it escaped Garnerin and others who occasionally tried to solve the puzzle.

In 1802 Garnerin was invited to England to make that country's first parachute descent, his fifth. It was said that his audience would include King George III and the Queen. This time attention was paid to Garnerin's parachute device, which is described in *Jump!/Tales of the Caterpillar Club*, by Don Glassman (1930), as being:

> . . . umbrella-shaped, 23 feet in diameter, and built up of 32 gores of white canvas or sailcloth. [Another report said the fabric was silk.] Distended, its area was 860 square feet, and it was thought capable of conveying 230 pounds to earth at an average speed of 10 feet per second. [That figure does not seem believable. Present-day canopies, a foot larger in diameter, have a rate of descent of about 20 feet per second, based on carrying a 170-pound passenger.] The landing impact . . . equivalent to a drop from 12 feet . . . the top of the parachute . . . held a truck or a round piece of wood 10 inches in diame-

ter, with a hole in its center, fastened to the canvas by 32 short pieces of tape. At about 4 1/2 feet from the top of the canvas, a wooden hoop 8 feet in diameter was affixed and secured by a string from each seam, so that when the balloon ascended the parachute hung like a curtain from the hoop, and appeared cylindrical. . . .

On September 21, 1802, a great crowd gathered at the Volunteers Ground, North Audley Street, Grosvenor Square, and waited expectantly. Garnerin later wrote, "I ascertained the height of the barometer, which was 29 1/2 inches. I now pressed the moment of my departure and the period of fulfilling my engagements with the British public.

"All the cords were cut; I arose amidst the most impressive silence . . . and discovered from on high the countless multitude that sent up sighs and prayers for my safety. . . .

"I . . . rose through light and thin vapors, where the cold air informed me that I was entering into the upper region. . . .

"I examined my barometer, which I found had fallen to 23 inches. The sky was clear, the moment favorable, . . . I made every necessary disposition, prepared my ballast and measured with my eye the vast space that separated me from the rest of the human race.

"I felt my courage confirmed by the certainty that my combinations were just. I then took out my knife, with a hand firm from a conscience devoid of reproach, . . . I cut the cord.

"My balloon rose and I felt myself precipitated with a velocity which was checked by the sudden unfolding of my parachute. I saw that all my calculations were just, and my mind remained calm and serene. [Skydivers, too, are still always happy that *their* "calculations" (read "parachute packing") are "just"; and their minds, too, are "calm and serene" with the sight of a properly inflated canopy overhead] . . . the oscillation which I experienced increased in proportion as I approached the breeze that blows in the middle region: nearly ten minutes had elapsed, . . .

"I came near the earth, and after one bound, I landed and quitted the parachute, without shock or accident. . . . A crowd soon surrounded me—laid hold of me, and carried me in triumph till an indisposition, the consequence and effect of the oscillation I had experienced, obliged me to stop.

"I was then seized with painful vomiting, . . . "

Throughout the descent, oscillations persisted. Garnerin, in his basket suspended from the confluence of the suspension lines, swung to and fro like a pendulum, in small arcs first, then in greater swings, until so much air spilled from within the hemispheric dome that the canopy would collapse slightly and drop some distance before reinflating fully and stabilizing briefly. Then the cycle of increasing oscillations would begin again. Some of the greatest arcs were said to be so wide that Garnerin's body was brought nearly level with the top of the parachute. The sequence kept repeating itself through Garnerin's landing.

Fig. 2-4. *André Jacques Garnerin made his fifth parachute descent—England's first—on September 21, 1902. The large crowd was greatly pleased. Garnerin's parachute oscillated wildly at times, enough to make him sick soon after he landed; but later descents improved when a vent hole was cut in the top of the canopy. Above him, the freed balloon drifts to a landing some distance away.*

The balloon from which he had separated landed without damage some 36 miles away, in Farnham, near Surrey. The parachute was reported as having been carefully preserved and later exhibited in the Pantheon in Paris, where thousands of proud French men, women, and children viewed it.

Later the parachutist would discreetly avoid talking of the one detracting feature of his display. Published illustrations emphasized the oscillations, however, and Garnerin was ultimately obliged to give explanations. He admitted that the swinging had finally caused brief unconsciousness, but only because the oscillations, for some unknown reason, were worse than on previous descents. Garnerin attempted to define what caused the oscillations and tried to explain how they could be eliminated. Antagonists disagreed, offering their own unproven theories. One young spectator, 24-year-old Robert Cocking, a water colorist by profession, was greatly impressed with Garnerin's successful descent but greatly alarmed by the terrible oscillations. Inspired by the parachutist's feat and motivated to improve parachute design, Cocking, among many others, set about to make a better parachute.

When Garnerin returned to France, he continued his balloon ascensions and parachute descents. The adulation of the French public continued without letup, and it has been reported that one of Garnerin's sisters took up her brother's activity, making some 40 parachute descents.

As Garnerin continued making parachute descents, he pressed on with trying to eliminate oscillations. Apparently the pleasure and excitement of the parachute descents were worth any discomfort felt as he returned to earth. Others also worked at coming up with an explanation and a solution.

One of Garnerin's contemporaries is generally credited with arriving at a solution. In 1804 Joseph Lalande, a scientist and notable astronomer, who was also a member of the Institut de France, suggested cutting a hole at the apex of the canopy. This would allow air trapped within the fabric to escape through that outlet, in additon to the air which indiscriminately escaped from all about the lower periphery of the parachute. His concept, decided on from scientific theories he thought were applicable, was that pressures inside the canopy would be eased through better control of airflow. His reasoning was that air trapped within the canopy escaped from beneath the skirt at some point, spilling that air and causing the canopy to tip in an opposite direction. The suspended jumper would, of course, serve as a pendulum weight and start moving in an arc direction opposite the spilling air. With canopy and suspended load off-center, the pendulum would next swing back, go past center, spill more air from the opposite side, swing back again, spill more air, and continue the uncontrollable swings until stopped by contact with the ground—or a tree or a building or some other structure. It is little wonder that people who continually subjected themselves to such hazard were looked at sideways.

Lalande's idea worked. It became a matter of determining the best size of the special vent, and only a few trials were needed to greatly improve what had been a nearly unbearable condition of parachute descents. Garnerin's descents became far more enjoyable to him, and Lalande's concept remained as a distinctive feature in the design of "round" parachute canopies, a feature that remains in use today. Though canopy oscillation was not eliminated with the simple solution, the minimal swings became a practically negligible factor in parachute design and use.

1808, Poland

Statistics, in the form of the "law of diminishing returns," finally came to the forefront. The old saying of "sooner or later" that haunted the minds of those battling to get up into the sky and stay there at leisure finally took on importance.

On July 14, 1808, the "fire balloon" of Polish balloonist Jordaki Kuparento rising over Warsaw suddenly ignited at a "considerable elevation." The flames from his portable heat source (said to be bundles of straw lighted as needed—a forerunner of modern propane fuel tanks) blazed up, reached the fabric, and burned rapidly. The balloon lost its form; Kuparento started his fall to earth. Fortunately, the balloonist had had foresight. Restraining panic, he quickly equipped himself with a parachute he had wisely brought along, then leaped from the useless aircraft. His lifesaving apparatus, which he carried aloft on all his flights, was said to be a foldable silk parachute that he had made himself, one with hand grips formed at the ends of suspension lines. Unexpectedly astounded by his sudden misfortune, he kept his wits about him and lost no time turning to his last resort. Firmly clutching the hand grips of his folded canopy, he launched himself and his parachute bundle from the basket. The canopy snapped open sharply, almost causing Kuparento to lose his tight grasps. But he hung on desperately and landed safely on the ground. Kuparento entered history as the first person to save his own life by using a parachute.

The era of the hot air balloon began to wane after the discovery of hydrogen by an English chemist, Henry Cavendish. The gas's lighter-than-air characteristic made it a far better and quicker way of raising balloons to great heights. A French physicist, J.A.C. Charles, constructed an unmanned model balloon and inflated it with hydrogen. It rose quickly to an estimated 3,000 feet and was carried by the wind for some 15 miles. On December 1, 1783, Charles and another man ascended in a hydrogen balloon designed for passengers and rode to a landing 27 miles away. Next, Charles went on a solo voyage that reached a 9,000-foot altitude.

Despite cost and the danger of inflammability, hydrogen-filled bags grew in popularity as a lifting method. However, since the gas was expensive, many balloonists continued using hot air as their choice for achieving flight.

Balloons were being widely used for entertainment at fairs all about the country, and parachute descents from lofty balloons continued to be made by daring men and women. Designs of both balloons and parachutes kept being toyed with, though progress with parachute concepts was at a much slower pace, the need for improvement seemingly not as important to most inventors.

Having become accepted as practicable as a means of viewing from on high, many balloons were used for military observations during the French Revolution of 1789-1799. Napoleon had a fleet of observation balloons built in time for a pending major battle, but they were destroyed beforehand by the enemy. Since balloons could be used at heights beyond the range of ground fire, there was little rush to equip observers with a parachute as a lifesaving device. That thinking was to change a century and a quarter later, with the onset of the Great War (subsequently termed *World War One*).

People by the score continued for years to experiment with parachute designs. An English scholar, Sir George Cayley, proposed a conical parachute, to be used with the tip down—in other words, an "upside down" canopy. Sir Cayley published an article titled *Aerial Navigation* in February 1810, holding that André Jacques Garnerin's parachute was "nearly the worst possible," saying that a canopy with an inverted surface would be better, that "the apex downward is the chief basis of stability in aerial navigation." Sir Cayley's opinions were readily accepted, due to his exclusive study of aeronautics, and he came to be acclaimed the "Father of British Aeronautics." But an avid parachute designer, Robert Cocking, was to pay a harsh penalty for his unshakeable belief in Sir Cayley's design criterion.

Sir Cayley's idea was said to have been actually developed, first in theory, then with models, then next put to successful "live" use by a German, Lorenze Hengler. One parachute researcher of our time noted that Hengler had made a few jumps from heights of 100 to 400 feet "without experiencing the least discomfort."

1838, England

Robert Cocking, the young Irish artist who saw Garnerin make his unnerving parachute descent in 1802 was puzzled by what had made the intrepid man's apparatus oscillate so drastically. From that point on, for the betterment of parachutes as an entertainment means, his life's major avocational interest was to develop a device that would function better than Garnerin's.

For three and a half decades Cocking worked diligently toward perfecting "a nonoscillating fall-breaker," principally taking signals from the writings of Sir George Cayley. Eventually, Cocking developed his own hypothesis. It is reported that early on his ideas were favorably enough received that in 1814 he spoke before the London Institution about his hobby. It is said also that at a later date he received a medal of honor for presenting a similar talk to the Society of Arts.

For many years he concentrated on refining his ideas on paper. Ultimately, he constructed models of an "inverted cone" parachute, then is said to have made successful test drops of models from the top of the Monument at London Bridge. Later, at Hampstead Heath, he used miniatures of his design in connection with a small hydrogen balloon, apparently employing a ground-release mechanism to free the parachute model from the lifting device. Jubilant, Cocking went ahead with plans for the full-scale parachute.

During this phase, he foresaw problems in building a large-scale version of his vision: His design called for a large intricate apparatus, and the weight of his device would exceed the lifting capability of extant balloon designs. Nothing was available that could get his rig to a satisfactory parachuting altitude.

In 1835 his first attempt to gain the financial support he needed to get his parachute built ended in disappointment; but in 1837, when he learned a gigantic balloon was being built by the owners of Vauxhall Gardens, Cocking again applied to have his parachute taken aloft and dropped. This time he was listened to, and he wangled a contract with Vauxhall: he would make the first descent for no fee in return for the management's financial support to help have the parachute constructed.

Cocking supervised every detail of the construction of his invention, which was to be put together on the grounds of Vauxhall Gardens. Thorough descriptions of Cocking's parachute have remained. The following description is paraphrased from *Jump!/Tales of the Caterpillar Club*:

> Three metal hoops (or tubes) were used to give the parachute a circular form. The upper hoop was made of block tin and measured 107 feet in circumference. Two other hoops, made of copper, measured about four feet in diameter. The resulting inverted cone measured ten feet in height, with the angle of slope at 30 degrees. The upper and lower metal hoops were connected and made rigid by braced wooden spars between the two tiers.
>
> A means of lifting the parachute assembly and its passenger was needed. A set of "crown lines" had one end fastened at many places about the large upper periphery of the inverted dome with the opposite ends joined together to form a confluence above the upper hoop; that juncture was then secured to a release fitting at the base of balloon basket. The 124-square-yard surface (1,116 square feet) was then covered by 22 gores of Irish linen.

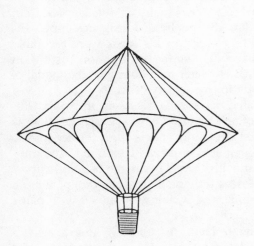

Fig. 2-5. Robert Cocking, on July 24, 1837, after nearly 35 years of imagining, designing, and dropping models, entered history with a parachute descent on which he was the passenger. Cocking's concept was radical, but aeronautic authorities of today concede that it was a workable design. His rig was so large and heavy that a specially constructed balloon was needed from which his parachute assembly could be slung for the ascension.

As a finishing touch, the scenic artist employed by Vauxhall Gardens decorated the inverted cone with brilliant colors.

The whole parachute apparatus weighed an astounding 233 pounds; to be added to that was Cocking's 170 pounds, for a total weight of 393 pounds. Despite the weight, Cocking calculated optomistically that the rig would descend at about 10 feet per second. To be on the safe side and to ensure as soft a landing as possible, the passenger basket was padded with inflated bladders.

On the perfect summer evening of July 24, 1837, the diligent Robert Cocking prepared to achieve his dream. All preparations had been completed. Charles Green was the balloon pilot, to be assisted by Edward Spencer. A "liberating iron" had been rigged so that Cocking would be the one to release the huge parachute assembly from the balloon (fearing the worst for the parachutist, the pilot did not want such added responsibility); and, as one more contingency, a "tackle" had been rigged by which the 61-year-old inventor could be drawn up into the balloon basket if he so desired, should he have a change of heart.

Nearing eight o'clock, the balloon pilots released 750 pounds of ballast, and the aerostat started its rise to 5,000 feet.

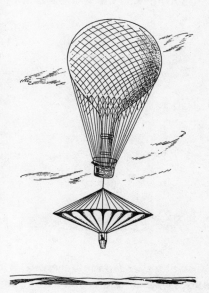

Fig. 2-6. *Robert Cocking's rig was attached to the balloon basket by means of a confluence loop made by gathering the loose ends of a group of "crown lines" secured about the circumference of the upper metal ring that formed the inverted cone of the radically new "upside down" parachute.*

As Cocking neared the moment of decision, Green shouted down to the parachutist asking, "if he felt comfortable." Cocking replied, "Yes, I never felt more comfortable or more delighted in my life." In a moment he added, "Well, now, I think I shall leave you." Green called out again," I wish you a very good night and safe descent, if you are determined to make it and not use the tackle."

Without hesitation, Cocking's voice sounded strongly in the summer stillness: "Good night, Mr. Spencer. Good night, Mr. Green."

With two tugs of the rope connected to the liberating iron, the balloon shot upward and the parachute dropped. The inverted cone started to descend as planned. Cocking must have smiled broadly, even grinned with delight, now quickly certain that after all the years of imagining, his idea was correct; but any pleasurable excitement was to be terribly short in duration.

Unexpectedly, the "upside down" parachute started to oscillate, slowly, then more quickly; a bit of fabric tore loose from the frame; vertical descent increased with each oscillation; rushing air tore at more fabric; air surged about inside the open framework, tearing at the construction; the large hoop buckled; suspension lines were jerked about violently, nearly snapping; the cone lost its shape; and falling speed increased even more, causing the collapsing cone to whip still more roughly. Suspension lines could no longer stand increasing strain and started breaking in two. At about 300 feet, the parachutist's basket finally separated from the rest of the structure, carrying Cocking to his death in a field at Lee Green, in Kent. The hopeful, unfortunate dreamer entered history as the world's first parachuting fatality.

Fig. 2-7. Robert Cocking's parachute only worked properly for a brief time after he separated himself from the balloon. It started oscillating slowly, then more rapidly; the descent rate increased. One thing affected another. Excessive forces caused the parachute structure to break apart. Cocking died of injuries, entering history as the world's first parachuting fatality.

Cocking's escapade received widespread attention in the press. Countless explanations were given about the failure. In the end a court rendered a verdict of "death as a consequence of serious injuries received in an accident."

In later experiments it was generally decided that Cocking's concept of an inverted-cone parachute was valid, though it would need to be more strongly built. However, such a device would not be practical today because of its inordinate size and weight. Far more sophisticated devices of infinitely better design have been made and are in regular use.

Despite Cocking's failure and demise, the search for a better parachute went on. In the year after Cocking's terrible misfortune, John Wise, an American, twice took a balloon to about 13,000 feet for the purpose of demonstrating his strong belief that a burst balloon could be converted into a parachutelike device, "relying upon the friction and resistance of the atmosphere for a safe decent." He shunned glorifying press accounts of his descents and later, similar descents by others as being "miraculous escapes." Wise did not view his experiments as being extraordinary. Feeling instead that results were as he had fully expected, he argued, "We might as well call the descent of the flying squirrel a miracle."

As the century ended, parachutes lingered in the province of show business, used as a sure attraction at balloon meets, fairs, carnivals, circuses, and expositions.

Little of notable accomplishment in the field of parachuting occurred for many years, but persistence remained the name of the game. As with so many other things to which humans set their minds, success was achieved, but there was undue slowness in accepting a parachute's full worth.

THE 20TH CENTURY!
The First 20 Years—and The Great War

Even after the first flights by the Wright brothers, not a lot of thought was given to equipping aviators of powered aircraft with parachutes. However, in time, progress was made.

In 1901, before the Wright flights, Charles Broadwick, an American from North Carolina, designed and made a rig variously described as a "coat pack "(because it was put on like a coat would be), a "pack on aviator," and "automatic attached pack-type parachute "—*automatic* because it was a static line system, whereby a line from the parachute pack was attached to an aircraft and a falling jumper's weight would break lacing on the pack and the canopy would be deployed. Broadwick achieved worldwide fame, and the essence of his design became the basis for military static line assemblies.

A. Leo Stevens was a well-known balloonist of the beginning 1900s, and he had a balloon loft in New York City. He also spent time devising both static line and manually operated parachutes, though there is no record of the latter actually having been used. His static line rigs were used by jumpers making leaps from the city's river bridges and the Statue of Liberty, as well as occasionally from airplanes; however, his designs proved not as suitable as others in use.

In Italy, in 1910, an inventor named Joseph Pino devised and patented a back parachute with a line extending from it to a small "pilot " parachute compressed into an aviator's close-fitting leather hat. Descriptions of its operation vary greatly, and Pino's unusual hat design never became anything more than a curosity in parachute history, but there was a holdover from his vision: the "pilot chute" concept proved to be sound and is used in virtually all systems designs today. (A "miniature" parachute is deployed first to aid in orderly deployment of the main canopy.)

Parachute historical accuracy continued to be plagued by haziness in all too many cases, even as parachute developments proliferated rapidly, and discrepancies exist as to who made the first parachute jump from a powered airplane. Credit is given variously to either "Grant "(real name, William H.) Morton in 1911 or Albert Berry in 1912. Examination of accounts favor Berry, however, and he is generally conceded to be the first to jump from an airplane.

One vague report said that in 1911 Grant Morton, 54 years old and a veteran balloon parachutist, leaped from a Wright Model B "pusher" plane over Venice, California, a gathering place for balloonists and spectators; but the date seems to be in doubt. Another unsubstantiated account of that jump had Morton bracing between the fragile-looking biplane's wings, positioning himself at the trailing edge of the lower surface, then doing the first "pull-off " parachute descent.

What was said to have made his historic feat additionally notable, whether he jumped from the plane or was yanked off the wing, was that he simply rolled and folded a silk canopy into a small bundle that he held in his arms, then hurled the bundle away from him, where it whipped and snapped about and finally filled with air. In either case, he reportedly had a safe landing. It was said that he was greatly disappointed that his accomplishment was primarily viewed as a stunt rather than as a demonstration of a parachute's usefulness in escaping an airplane.

Interestingly, in that pattern of Morton's reputed jump, and more than a half century later, a sport parachutist seeking an unusual way of commemorating his Gold Wing jump stowed an unsleeved ParaCommander canopy and suspension lines in a large paper shopping bag, with the risers to extending up from the bag in his arms to his harness. Atop the bundle in the paper container, protected by an arm across the mouth of the open container, was the rig's uncompressed pilot chute. On that 1,000th freefall jump he leaped head-high from his plane, falling feet first, then in the next second flung the pilot chute into the airstream, and happily watched the canopy and lines rapidly and safely stream from the bag.

The other contender for the distinction of making the first parachute jump from an airplane was Albert Berry. He was sometimes billed as "Captain " but most likely that high-sounding nonmilitary rank was self-proclaimed and a holdover from earlier showman days working with his father, John, who also was experienced with balloons and makeshift parachutes.

In a rather haphazard plan, Albert Berry was taken aloft on March 1, 1912, leaving Kinloch Park to be flown over Jefferson Barracks, a military installation in St. Louis, Missouri. The ostensible reason for Berry's jump, which was really only a publicity stunt for a local flying school at Kinloch, was to have him deliver a "communiqué" to the army post commandant, the communiqué warning "the enemy has routed the left flank of the Kinloch Army, wounding the commanding officer, and is rapidly closing in on the remaining forces."

Berry's unscientifically designed, crudely constructed 36-foot muslin parachute was stowed in a conical metal container fastened to a nose skid framework just ahead of the plane's landing gear, as shown in a photograph made before takeoff. Berry sat to the left of the pilot, both of them without the least protection from wind, cold, and light snow flurries. A trapeze bar was to be Berry's suspension device during his descent. The bar was stowed in a fitting on the wing and a line ran from it to the base of the stowed parachute in the container at Berry's feet. After a half-hour flight to cover the 17 miles to Jefferson Barracks, the small plane, moving at 55 miles an hour, was at the prescribed 1,500-foot altitude. The parachutist tugged the trapeze bar from its place on the wing, got as firm a grip as he could, then daringly fell into space. The parachute worked satisfactorily, though Berry slithered rapidly earthward with a streaming, noninflating canopy for some 500 feet before it quickly filled. After almost a full minute more, the cold, shivering jumper landed safely.

The military people were not impressed. They apparently saw little worth in a device like Berry's for airplanes, despite the fact that military personnel had already died in crashes. Perhaps they were also irritated by an itinerant showman's self-glorifying use of a respected military rank.

Berry made a second similar jump. The airplane's owner had already collected admissions for a jump to be made at Kinloch Field and didn't want to make refunds because he needed the money. Berry, too, wanted his share of the gate and made the second jump nine days later, under much the same difficult weather and physically demanding conditions as the first time. Asked whether he would attempt the stunt again, Berry shook his head emphatically, "No sir! Not unless there's a lot more money in it!"

To give Morton his due, his jump of April 28, 1912, was duly reported in newspapers and illustrated by photographs. At least he achieved a measure of fame as a pioneer airplane parachute jumper.

In Russia, inventor G.E. Kotelnikov designed several parachute models with the idea of having them used by his country's military pilots, but the high command of the fledgling Russian Air Corps discarded his proposals, concerned that pilots might be tempted to resort to a parachute rather than try to save an aircraft.

World War I provided the impetus for widespread adoption of parachutes by ballooning soldiers, followed by occasional adaptation to engine-powered aircraft. With the latter it was a long time coming, and many lives were needlessly lost in the meantime.

Balloonists of the late 19th and early 20th centuries had long since demonstrated that parachutes were practical devices, using them to provide spectator entertainment at traveling carnivals and "air shows" of the times. Parachutes had also saved the lives of a number of balloonists whose aerial crafts had failed for one reason or another, which further proved their usefulness.

When opposing military forces initially established balloon observation units to eye the ground movements of enemy units of even the smallest size, parachutes usually were not part of the equipment taken aloft; they didn't seem needed. Balloons could be raised high enough behind friendly lines to be secure from enemy ground fire yet still be superior observation sites.

Improved war technology soon made that safety untenable. Ground weapons quickly ranged farther and became more accurate. When balloons, easier targets for ground-fire and enemy fighter planes, were routinely being set afire, parachutes became standard equipment for balloonists. Typically, an observer wore a harness while aloft, with a folded canopy stowed in a container outside the basket. If needed, a fitting at the base of the parachute assembly could be attached quickly to a harness fitting, and over the side went the balloonist. Parachutes saved lives, and soldiers were able to continue opposing an enemy.

Unfortunately, airplane pilots and crew members were not so lucky at first—particularly Allied aviators. The Germans were first to realize they were losing many pilots and gunners because they could not rescue themselves from disabled aircraft. It was one matter to have "acceptable" losses, but Germany soon realized it was terrible and wasteful to not give airmen a chance to fight another time, and several means were tried to adapt parachutes to airplane use. Some ideas did not work well at all; others were better than nothing; then, finally parachute use proved reasonably satisfactory, functioning much like the static-line-operated sack-type parachute used by balloonists. A pilot wore a minimal harness, with a line fastened to a bulky canopy stowed in a conveniently located container in the cockpit or on the exterior of the plane.

The Germans lost air machines, but they were deemed more readily replaceable than people. What the country needed was seasoned aerial combatants. Parachutes made that possible.

Reluctant American and British commanders—like the prewar Russian generals—figured that inexperienced pilots would all too readily leave a damaged, but flyable, recoverable plane if a parachute was handy. Pilots and crew members complained, but military planners kept stalling action. There have been reports that, on occasion, fighter pilots, as personal last-ditch insurance, risked military court-martial by covertly buying unauthorized parachute equipment and secretly rigging their planes for an emergency jump.

With mounting pilot losses, due attention was finally paid by Allied authorities to German successes.

E.R. Calthorp of England developed the "Guardian Angel" parachute. Finally, an American go-ahead was given to developing an emergency parachute. In the summer of 1918 work on parachute development started at McCook Field, Dayton, Ohio. Floyd Smith, a leading parachute expert, was one of the design and test group. However, bureaucratic red tape, production problems, and transportation slowness meant that not until shortly before the war ended in November 1918 were parachutes reaching pilots and crew members in Europe. There have been no reports of lives of Allied pilots or crew members being saved by means of parachute. Nonetheless, the lifesaving quality of parachutes became more appreciated. Thus, America continued parachute research, development, and testing at McCook Field after the war.

As a closing note to the World War, Colonel (later General) William "Billy" Mitchell conceived the first "airborne assault" stratagem, his plan being to equip thousands of soldiers with parachutes and to use hundreds of aircraft to drop parachutists behind German lines as a means of demoralizing and destroying the enemy. He argued his plan in the ranks of generals and got mixed reviews. The scheme was ultimately approved by General Pershing, the Allied Expeditionary Force supreme commander, but before anything worthwhile could be done the war ended. Nevertheless, Mitchell had made a point, and it was later to be reconsidered and applied by military establishments of several countries.

Between the Wars

The French, who had seriously approached parachute design and use as early as 1911, and who had sensibly supplied their wartime pilots with parachutes, went ahead with their efforts in the postwar era, making significant progress. Great Britain also kept working toward developing better parachutes.

The McCook Field parachuate project gained momentum; the War Department had come to recognize the importance of parachutes. Major E.L. Hoffman was put in charge of the work, and there were several parachuting notables on his staff, including A. Leo Stevens, wartime hold-over Floyd Smith, and Leslie Irvin, among others.

In 1919 Floyd Smith came up with the "Smith Aerial Life Pack," the acknowledged first "free type" (manually operated) parachute. At about that time Leslie Irvin joined the McCook Field parachute group. He liked what he saw in Floyd Smith's design (though it had not yet been "live-tested") and developed his own concept of a manually operated parachute. He promptly started the complex process of preparing a patent application and filed it on April 28, 1919. On the same day he made a jump with his parachute to prove his point that, from his personal experience as a high diver and someone who had made 200 balloon-release parachute descents, a person could fall free for several seconds from an aircraft and not lose consciousness, that human faculties would remain useful.

A curious event in parachuting had occurred. Though it was acknowledged that Floyd Smith had developed the first freefall parachute, it was not his device that was used to advance parachuting. A credible account of what took place and why, and what followed, is offered in the book *Parachuting Folklore/The Evolution of Freefall*, by Michael Horan (1980).

On the morning of April 28, 1919, the grapevine around McCook Field buzzed with excitement. The gossip going around said the newly designed freefall parachute was going to get its first practical test. Major Hoffman had given Les Irvin permission to make the jump and a chance to make history. For some reason Floyd Smith, whose basic design concepts started this whole experiment, would not make the jump. Just why Irvin was chosen over Floyd, who also had some jumping experience, was a mystery. It's a good bet that the decision was based on politics or personalities. Smith, of course, was very disappointed. More aggravating to him was the fact that he had been chosen to pilot the plane that would carry Irvin to meet destiny. . . . With Floyd Smith manning the controls of the airplane, Irvin took off, and climbed to 1,500 feet above the field. Circling in on jump run Irvin smiled and exited the airplane. He fell for several seconds and, completely in control, gave a healthy yank on the ripcord and watched as the canopy blossomed open perfectly.

His parachute had worked as he knew it would . . . Not only had he proved to some skeptics that his parachute could do what he said it would, he also became the first person to officially make a premeditated parachute jump. All in all, it was quite a historic day.

The jump was a convincing one to some, but not to everybody. A discussion still centered on the idea about how far a man could fall before he would lose his senses. So, on the morning of May 14, 1919, Floyd Smith walked over to Jimmie Johnson, who at the time was the chief civilian test pilot at McCook Field, and asked if he would fly him to make a freefall jump. Johnson was dubious about this but finally agreed to take Smith up.

Smith leaped from the airplane, fell about 500 feet, and opened his parachute. The system worked perfectly, and he landed uneventfully. Within the next several days more freefall jumps were being logged. The age of freefall had truly arrived, and the rest is history.

Both Smith and Irvin went on separately with their work and were important persons in the parachute industry for many years.

In the decades of the Twenties and Thirties, great strides were made in parachute development and applications. Test after test was made regularly on personnel chutes of every description—with inert test loads of light to extraordinarily heavy weights, with torso dummies, and with human test jumpers. Reassurance was sought constantly. However, there was an element of proof missing. What would happen in an honest-to-goodness, real-life emergency situation, one that might happen under the worst possible conditions, at a time when panic might be the major factor?

A little more than three years after Irvin and Smith had made their historic contributions to the art and science of parachuting, the answer was provided.

On October 22, 1922, 27-year-old Army Lieutenant Harold R. Harris was assigned to McCook Field as Chief, Flight Test Section, Engineering Division. While testing a plane with experimental ailerons, Lt. Harris lost control of the craft at about 2,500 feet during intentional violent flight conditions at full throttle. The plane started to shudder, then he lost all control. The control stick vibrated wildly against his legs. The plane roared toward the ground at 150 miles an hour in a thirty-degree dive. Parts began to break off. Lt. Harris suddenly remembered his parachute, his one remaining option.

He unbuckled his seat belt and pushed up out of the cockpit. The rushing air literally tore him from the plane at a low altitude. He tugged desperately at the ripcord handle to open the parachute. But he realized he was pulling at something on the harness instead of the handle. His hand found the handle, and he yanked it mightily. Inside of two seconds he was suspended beneath a perfectly formed white silk canopy. Some observers estimated that his altitude was about 200 feet. Within seconds he landed unharmed in a grape arbor, gaining a place in history as the first person to save one's life with a manually operated parachute after escaping a disabled engine-powered aircraft. The freefall parachute was awarded deserved legitimacy.

Parachutes were soon manufactured by the thousands. Their use as emergency aviation equipment rapidly came to be understood and appreciated.

The Caterpillar Club

A month after Lt. Harris rescued himself, an informal organization was created to recognize those who had saved their lives with a parachute. At first it listed only those who had used a specific manufacturer's equipment, but it soon made awards to anyone who survived an aerial emergency with a parachute. The club's name acknowledged the caterpillar, that small insect that produced a substance that became silk threads, from which, for a long time, most personnel parachute canopies and suspension lines were made, until the advent of synthetic fibers.

Membership in aviation's most exclusive association grew quickly, affirming the beliefs of many people closely involved with parachutes for a long time:

1924-15	1927-78
1925-27	1928-120
1926-40	1930-210

Wartime years saw the roster grow dramatically. By 1955, following World War Two and the Korean Conflict, Caterpillar Club records showed more than 40,500 members. In ensuing years many more names were added to the elite roster.

Two of its most famous members were Charles A. Lindbergh (four jumps while he was a mail pilot) and Jimmy Doolittle (three bail-outs).

As noted previously, the Russians used parachutes for many purposes, among them recreation, humanitarian, military, and setting world parachuting records. In other countries, particularly America, parachutes were used mostly by barnstorming balloonists and airplane jumpers to make a few dollars amusing spectators at air shows; but stepped-up, technical development with serious purpose was also underway, directed at improving technology and finding varied uses of parachutes.

One of the latter was first only a gleam in someone's eye in the mid-1930s—using parachutists to save the country's natural resources by quickly getting to forest fires and getting them under control. Airplanes had long before shown their worth in locating remote fires. The next step was to use "smokejumpers." The idea worked, and for 50-plus years using parachutes and parachutists paid great dividends to America.

Impressive strides were made in parachute development in the between-the-wars period, but only a limited amount of literature was produced about a field of interest that remained esoteric.

War Works Wonders

War accelerates technological progress. As related to parachutes and parachuting, a wide range of needs and wants were met with what once had merely been a last-resort device to save a hapless pilot's or crew member's life. Benjamin Franklin remarked in 1784:

Where is the Prince who can afford so to cover his country with troops for its defense, as that ten thousand men descending from the clouds, might not, in many places, do an infinite amount of mischief before a force could be brought together to repel them?

The Germans first—in Holland and Belgium in May 1940, then later in other countries—followed by the Allies over later years of World War

Two, showed that Franklin's vision proved correct. Today, still, airborne units of every size are tactical and strategic military forces.

Besides dropping personnel, with ever-changing techniques in doing so, other cargo of every conceivable description has been delivered from sky to earth, in a variety of ways, in every climate, under virtually all weather conditions. Nothing yet has proved too large or too heavy to use a parachute.

Fig. 2-8. *A flight of Fairchild ''Flying Boxcars'' drops scores of military para-troopers in a training exercise.*

In addition, parachutes are standard equipment on many fighter and bomber aircraft to slow aircraft when landing. "Drag chutes" do much to save wear and tear on complex, critical, and expensive aircraft braking systems.

Parachutes and the Age of Space

The latest challenge for useful parachute application has been recovery of enormous, ultraheavy space components, and every challenge has been met. State-of-the-art parachute development is now working toward a recovery system that can be used in a flight emergency during Earth reentry of a shuttle vehicle returning from a mission in space. The preliminary concept of such a parachute has it being a "ram air" canopy (similar in appearance to the "square" parachutes used by skydivers) with a span of about 150 feet and a chord of an estimated 50 feet, and capable of supporting 76 *tons*; but the concept doesn't end there. The canopy would be steerable and have the capability of being directly maneuvered by the crew or being remotely guided by ground personnel.

The Space Age Sport

Over 4,000 years of folktales, lore, and history form the backdrop for modern parachutes and parachuting, starting with perilous leaps from small structures using haphazard contrivances.

Today jumps from 15,000 feet are considered routine, and equipment and techniques for controlled freefall are quite sophisticated.

From the time of the early 1950s, when America had only a dozen or so proficient freefall parachutists and only several loosely organized clubs of a few people, each who had minimal skills (but a lot of desire), the stature of the sport has grown to where an estimated more than 30,000 parachutists make over two million jumps a year. The level of activity in other countries is now extraordinarily high.

The sport has become safe, too. The USPA reports that like other *action* sports, parachuting has its routine minor injuries. However, USPA research reveals that the majority of injuries happen when deviations are made from accepted safe jumping practices.

Reading on, you will learn what it takes to become a skilled sport parachutist.

Welcome to skydiving, the ultimate in free flight!

3

From Student
to Skydiver

Sport parachutists have a term used to refer generally to nonjumpers—
whuffo (the "whuff" portion rhyming with "muff"). Those who have
never made a "fun" parachute jump often ask skydivers why they make
jumps. The story goes that the term *whuffo* derived from the question of
a curious spectator in some backwater drop zone: "Wha' fo' y'all jump
out of an airplane?"; the "wha' fo" being the asker's form of saying
"what for" instead of "why." The story only took several tellings for
"whuffo" to take its place in American skydiving jargon.

As sport parachuting grew and started being done at airports in
more populous areas, pilots had the same curiosity about skydivers, asking: "Why do you jump out of a perfectly good airplane?" Jumpers had a
quick response: "There ain't no such thing as a perfectly good airplane!"

A SMALL BASE OF KNOWLEDGE

When parachuting for recreation and sport began in this country students went through a process that was slow, uncertain, cumbersome,
and drawn out. There were few places outside of military services to
learn the complexities of making a parachute jump, and to further com-
pound matters, the few knowledgeable sport parachuting teachers in
existence were themselves still learning much about a new parachuting
technique, a technique with only a small base of knowledge.

Any new endeavor needs time to get established, needs a "shake-
out" period, needs time to become accepted. Also, there are periods of
development, of change. Time is needed for the endeavor to be subjected

to "Murphy's Law," and there are usually periods of "back to the drawing board."

Sport parachuting/skydiving was no different, but the ramifications of nearly everything that was done were more serious than, say developing a board game or card game for social gatherings or working out at even strenuous physical activities like football, basketball, or countless other sporting activities.

Recreational parachuting is a risk-taking activity, and its rewards are on a par with those experienced by downhill skiers, aviators, mountain climbers, and automobile and speedboat racers. For many the satisfaction is on an even higher plane because of the relative briefness of a given jump and because of the extraordinary intensity of many experiences associated with skydiving.

The so-called "pioneering" days of sport parachuting started in the early 1950s. True, in the beginning many years earlier, and for a long while, there were people doing various things with parachutes on an individual basis, and many of the things those folks did were used when sport parachuting/skydiving started to have an identity; but improvements from early trials and tribulations were more part of an evolutionary process that occurred as most individuals worked at bettering equipment and techniques to protect themselves rather than a conscious effort of doing something for the greater benefit of parachutes, parachuting, and parachutists.

During World War One, with scientific knowledge and technological skills applied to parachutes, albeit slowly and oftentimes reluctantly, equipment was made better and worked better—and lives were saved in aerial combats, lives that might have once been lost. Still, there was a lot of room for improvement, particularly in attitudes. With the surging growth of aviation between the World Wars followed by the widespread use of parachutes during World War Two and the Korean Conflict, parachutes came into their own, at least insofar as "practical" use.

The fifties were difficult times for getting started when someone got interested in recreational parachuting—at least interested in making one jump, just to see what it was like, just to see if they could really do it. It was not easy to find written material that told about parachutes and parachuting, written instructional material that offered even a tip here and there about how the "pros" did things.

For those who pursued their interest in parachuting, it was also a case of trying to find a parachute somewhere—a complete assembly, if possible; if not a whole outfit, then components that could eventually be put together to make a whole rig. A common procedure was to watch every publication for notices of military surplus gear for sale, then find someone who claimed to know "all about parachutes" who would make sure it was O.K. for making jumps—and hope that person was right. If a rigger couldn't be found, then eager jumpers resorted to doing work illegally on their own equipment simply to get up into the air, make a jump, land safely, fix anything that might need fixing, alter something so things would work better, repack, and jump again; this process being repeated again and again.

THE EARLY DAYS OF STUDENT TRAINING

In the fifties, in this country, there was a single method of training someone to be a sport parachutist—a recreational jumper—and that was to make jumpmaster-assisted static line jumps. The technique was a combination of standard military training and new methods that had evolved in Europe.

Many thousands of parachutists had been trained by military services during and following World War Two and the Korean Conflict. When some of those rigorously trained parachutists decided to continue with parachuting in civilian life, some of them also undertook being self-appointed instructors and taught what they knew to others. Since theirs was primarily military knowledge and only surplus military equipment was available early on, sport parachuting clubs at small airports had a definite aura of quasi-military activity. Jump suits were surplus gray or orange multizippered, multipocketed army and air force flight suits. Back parachute containers and harnesses were colored army olive drab and navy gray. "Main" canopies (those actually used for each sport jump) were military surplus of various services. Some were air force 28-foot, orange-and-white "candy stripe," while others were four-color (white, orange, sand, green, for worldwide camouflage used by downed aviators). Some were white, 28-foot army, air force, marine, and navy canopies while still others were green, 35-foot army T-10 used by paratroopers (heavyweight skydivers were especially happy to have a canopy designed to support a 300-pound suspended weight).

Reserve auxiliary parachute canopies also varied in source, size, and appearance. Some were army O.D. and camouflage green 24-foot, while others were air force orange-and-white "candy-stripe" 28-foot. Some were navy white 24- and 28-foot "flat" canopies and an occasional 26-foot "conical" canopy could be found. (As a general explanation, *sizes* of "round-type," "flat" canopies are usually given as the diameter of a canopy when it is spread out on a flat surface (thus *flat* canopy). However, there are technical variances used by parachute engineers when stating canopy sizes. As an example, a 26-foot *conical* canopy measures well under that diameter dimension when spread on a flat surface, due to the manufacturing technique of cutting shaped gores to form the inflated conical shape of the parachute; however, sizes of round canopies used throughout this book are those that have became commonly used and thus fixed in the jargon of sport parachuting. The term *conical* refers to the appearance of the *form* of the canopy when inflated during use.)

Speaking of *appearance*, the T-10 paratrooper canopy is said to be "parabolic" in shape, thus the inflated diameter a short distance above the bottom of the canopy is larger than the mouth of the canopy itself.

Confusing, isn't it? Fortunately, however, you don't really need to know any of this to become a skydiver, and considering the state-of-the-art of student training in this day and age, it is not too likely that you might encounter such equipment any longer.

The nonmilitary aspect of student training that needed to be incorporated had to do with the manner in which a trainee left an aircraft when making a parachute jump. What exmilitary paratroopers now trying to master skydiving had to "unlearn" was the body position used when jumping. All their past jumps had been with their bodies in a mandated, strictly adhered-to airborne exit position, which had been carefully developed to meet military parachuting conditions—feet first!; ankles tightly together!; legs straight!; elbows in!; hands clutching sides of the chest-mounted reserve parachute, right hand ready at the ripcord handle; head down, chin tucked on chest!; body bent sharply forward at the waist into a near-fetal position.

Now all that instruction, absorbed in a tough, demanding learning environment, was "out the window," and the new object was to leave a craft in a full *spread eagle* form, arms slightly above shoulders and pressed rearward, head up and back, with a backward arch at the waist, belly pushing outward, legs straight and spread widely, toes pointing.

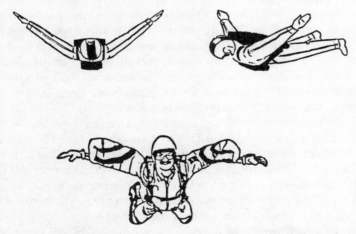

Fig. 3-1. *A "full-spread" body position taken as soon as a beginning student exits an aircraft. With a hard arch of the back and with arms and legs spread as shown, the jumper will quickly get into and then maintain a stable, face-to-earth freefall body position. With experience and confidence, this greatly tensioned body position will be relaxed substantially and a skydiver will use a comfortable "frog" position.*

The object was to achieve a configuration in which the center of gravity of one's body would cause a face-to-earth, "stable" body position while falling freely through space.

Even before you are in a first-jump course, there are easy ways for you to quickly learn "stable fall" principles and to gain confidence in methods that have been used by skydivers for more than a quarter of a century. Training aids can help you gain the understanding you need.

SIMPLE TRAINING AIDS

There are several training aids ground instructors at sport parachute centers use to easily demonstrate both stable body position and the importance of properly using center of gravity in freefall.

One is a shuttlecock used in the sport of badminton. You can do this on your own for a simple yet excellent demonstration of how weight distribution affects the position of a falling object. Because of the relationship of the weight of the object to other areas of the object, a low center of gravity is achieved with regard to areas of the object that offer resistance to relative airflow. No matter how you hit or throw a shuttlecock, it will always move through the air with the weighted area ahead of the feathered portion of the device. That movement is determined by the combined factors of mass and area of resistance.

Hand-toss a shuttlecock a few feet in the air and you will see it rise heavy end first until gravity takes effect and starts pulling it back down. Then the shuttlecock will turn on its own because of mass/area-of-resistance relationship, and fall downward. Toss it horizontally at an upward angle, letting the shuttlecock leave your hand in a backward position. It will quickly turn so its nose will be the leading point in travel, then fall to the ground, nose still ahead. Simply drop the shuttlecock from your hand in any haphazard fashion. Again, in an eyeblink, it will turn so the heavier portion of it will lead the way.

There is another good example of how a center of gravity can have a great effect, working for you or against you. It is an example you might already have experienced. It is much easier to fall out of a canoe from a standing position than if you are perched on a seat, and it is very difficult to fall out, in normal use, if you are seated on the bottom.

Using your center of gravity is just as useful if you are in freefall making an emergency parachute jump as it is to a canoeist in deep water or in a fast-moving stream or river.

Learning from a Paper Doll

Another visual aid a sport parachute instructor uses is nothing more than a paper doll figure that can be shaped to show right and wrong body position. After reading this section (perhaps even before going on further with reading), make your personal training aid to persuade yourself as soon as possible of what skydivers already know.

Cut your training aid from heavy or stiff paper, or from light cardboard. Shape it into an arched figure, with a curved spine to give it an arched back, with its stomach area below outstretched arms and legs.

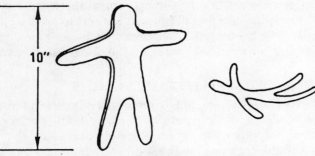

Fig. 3-2. *Cut a doll figure from lightly stiff paper and bend it into a slightly arched shape. Drop it from a height of six feet or so; it will fall curved side down, representing belly-down, face-to-earth, stable freefall.*

Drop the model from an arm's length above your head and watch it fall curved side (belly side) down, known to parachutists as a *stable* position. Though your body is not made of paper or cardboard, it will nonetheless react similarly to the same aerodynamic forces.

Next make a kink in the center of the paper or cardboard figure, to represent a bent-forward-at-the-waist body configuration, making it look like the model below.

Fig. 3-3. *Make a kink or bend in the center of the doll figure and drop it from a six-foot height. The figure's falling will be random and tumbling, perfectly illustrating what happens when a skydiver excessively bends forward at the waist in freefall.*

Again drop the model from overhead. Its fall will be erratic. "Unstable" freefall happens to a skydiver because of bending forward at the waist. Being unstable at ripcord pull or hand-deployment of a soft pilot chute could lead to "disorderly canopy deployment" and possible malfunction.

After you have tried this small demonstration a time or two to understand stable/unstable freefall, don't discard the model just yet. Keep it handy so every once in a while you can use it as a "persuader" to keep remembering one of the most important principles of skydiving. You will become a skilled student when your mind and body instinctively react to the lesson learned from the model each time you leap from a jump plane.

FIRST-JUMP COURSE TRAINING ("PARACHUTING 101")
WHERE IT STARTED FOR ALL SKYDIVERS!

Many people express a desire to make a parachute jump—"It's something I always wanted to do" is a refrain often heard when an instructor surveys a first-jump course class, whether one student or many. Think back to Chapter 1 and about the people characterized in the *Baker's Dozen*.

Thus, the purpose behind each student's first-jump course participation is to find out what it is like to jump from an airplane. Most people make their first jump to satisfy a curiosity. For some, once that curiosity is appeased, that's that! However, many others enjoy the experience so much that they continue learning and become skydivers.

All participants in skydiving—with one exception—are required to be an adult; the exception: a minor who is at least sixteen years of age and presents written and notarized parental or guardian consent can participate in static line or accelerated freefall (AFF) methods of parachuting instruction. Some parachuting operations require that the person providing consent for a minor observe all prejump instructions.

Whether jumping only once or continuing onward, a certain amount of knowledge and skill must be acquired to be a safe jumper.

A typical first-jump course will include comprehensive coverage on a variety of matters important to a student: personal equipment, aircraft procedures (including emergency situations), exiting an aircraft, parachute opening, parachute emergency procedures, canopy steering, and landing (including unexpected hazardous circumstances).

There are three customary methods by which someone can make a first sport parachute jump:

- Static line.
- A tandem jump.
- Accelerated freefall.

STATIC LINE PARACHUTING TRAINING

For years the traditional—also termed "conventional"—training manner for someone learning to become a sport parachutist was static line parachute training. *Static* refers to "acting by mere weight" and a *static line* is an item of parachuting equipment attached between an aircraft and a parachutist's back-mounted parachute container. A jumper's *weight* is used to separate the jumper from the *static line* attached to an aircraft, after the static line starts deployment of the canopy from the container.

A static line jump consists of a student making a solo exit from an aircraft and making a solo descent under a parachute canopy. The original sport parachuting training technique was a holdover from military-style parachuting, and the benefit of the method was that a student did not have to rely on his or her own initiative to actuate a parachute after leaping from an airplane. (Static line jumps actually date far back in parachute history.)

Student static line jumps are made from a minimum altitude of 2,800 feet above ground level (AGL). A static line is secured to a fixed point on a jump plane, and the opposite end of the static line is connected to the container (pack) and/or canopy of the main parachute worn on a student's back. The student, further equipped with a front-mounted (also termed "chest-mounted") reserve (auxiliary) parachute only has to exit the plane (notice how easily it is *said*?), and when the end of the static line is reached, the container is automatically opened and a "static line assist device" continues to assist deployment of the parachute canopy. In military use, static lines were 15 feet long, but, at the beginning of sport parachuting it was seen that those students who exited weakly and who tumbled and flailed while falling to the end of such a long line too easily got into "poor body position" situations where a canopy malfunction was highly probable. Experimenting, the static line kept being shortened until eight feet was settled on as an ideal length—long enough to let a student get clear of a plane before a container was opened, short enough to get a quick opening before a marginal-ability student got unstable. (Detailed information on deployment/inflation is given in Chapter 4.)

Once safely suspended beneath an inflated canopy, a student then steers the canopy toward a target area until landing. During the descent the student receives assistance from a ground instructor, usually by radio, less often by means of signal panels. Most drop zones equip students with radio receivers, using signal panels as a backup in case of garbled radio transmissions or failure of communication equipment. Less sophisticated drop zones (DZs) rely on signal panels only, an acceptable method, but such training sites are few and far between these days.

Static line first-jump course training requires a substantial amount of classroom and mock-up training, a typical course lasting about four hours. However, time needed for a first-jump course varies according to several factors, including number of students, how well they absorb information, and type of equipment being used. The goal of ground school training is to have students meet learning objectives, not merely spend a minimum amount of time in a classroom.

That training time, again going back to the early days of skydiving, was greatly reduced from holdover military practices. Military training included a lot of time-consuming physical conditioning so paratroopers would have strength and stamina for carrying on with a mission after using a parachute to get somewhere. Also, even though training to make nonmilitary sport/recreation jumps, members of military sport parachute clubs were still bound by many military regulations and often had to excessively train people for "fun jumping." As an example, in 1965, the Standard Operating Procedure (SOP) for individuals training with the XVIII Airborne Corps Sport Parachute Club at Fort Bragg, North Carolina ("The Home of the Airborne") required 22 1/2 hours of training in 19 segments that were mostly in half-hour and one-hour periods, but with one segment mandated at ten hours of "Drop Zone Observation." Fortunately for military club members, those requirements have been substantially reduced; but they still far exceed what goes on at civilian drop zones. (The training sequence for static line jumping is given later in this chapter.)

Fig. 3-4. 1961 first-jump-course students receive instruction from Jacques Istel in the fine points of doing a proper parachute landing fall (PLF); Orange Sport Parachute Center (OSPC), Orange, Massachusetts.

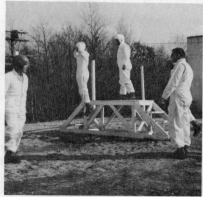

Fig. 3-5. Students quickly go through repetitive training from a proper parachute landing fall (PLF) platform with a height that aids in simulating the shock of a normal landing under a round sport main canopy of the type generally in use at the time.

Fig. 3-6. A student reaches the midway part of a prescribed five-points-of-contact roll (done much like a gymnastic tumbler), which takes a jumper through an acceptable, energy-dissipating proper parachute landing fall (PLF).

ACCELERATED FREEFALL (AFF) PARACHUTING TRAINING
(A FIRST JUMP FROM 10,000 FEET)

In 1968 talk show host/comedian Johnny Carson made a parachute jump, his only one. Sport parachuting received a great deal of favorable publicity as a result, and the jump was a forerunner of a training technique that is today one of the state-of-the-art parachuting instruction methods—accelerated freefall (AFF).

Johnny's 12,500-foot, 60-second freefall skydive more than two decades ago was referred to simply as a "buddy jump" made under the "direct supervision" of Bob Sinclair. The pair jumped simultaneously from a small plane, and the instructor held on to the entertainer's harness until Johnny pulled the ripcord. There was a lot of film coverage of every aspect of the event, and the videotape was shown on the Tonight Show. U.S. military services later adopted and refined the buddy jump technique for "High Altitude, Low Opening" (HALO) tactical missions.

Ken Coleman, Jr., a sport parachutist, refined the concept into a multilevel training system that is now in widespread use throughout the world. In the United States this training method is known as Accelerated Freefall (AFF). The AFF method is geared primarily toward a serious skydiving student who wants to become skilled in the basics in the quickest amount of time; however, it has also become an exceptional way of a one-time jumper truly experiencing skydiving.

The accelerated freefall method is based on three concepts:

1. Each student receives a private lesson and *direct* supervision by means of harness-holding techniques used by the instructor(s) *throughout freefall*.
2. Information is presented and student skills are developed in a logical and progressive manner.
3. Modern equipment and state-of-the-art skills are used so a student receives maximum benefits.

With AFF training a student receives the benefits of dual instruction. This training method requires completion of a ground school before making a jump. For Levels I through III, a jump is made in company with two highly skilled, specially trained instructors who provide direct assistance to a student during aircraft exit and throughout freefall. Once the parachute is deployed by the student, the instructors briefly continue their freefall, then deploy their own parachutes. (For Levels IV through VII, as student skills increase, only one jumpmaster accompanies the student.) The student makes a solo canopy descent, usually under the guidance of a ground instructor using a ground-to-air communication system.

AFF jumps are made usually from an altitude of at least 10,000 feet, allowing for freefall of about 45 seconds. A higher exit altitude would allow for longer freefall. On reaching an altitude of 4,000 feet, the student pulls a ripcord and deploys his or her parachute. As with the static line training method, an AFF student is required to carry out emergency procedures, if needed. Emergency procedures are detailed in a classroom part of ground school, followed by training and practice on mock-ups. (The training sequence for AFF skydiving is given later in this chapter.)

LIFE'S NOT PERFECT!—DEALING WITH EMERGENCIES

Sport parachuting has physical risk associated with it. Safety studies have been made over many years, and a consensus shows that emergencies resulting from parachute system malfunction are rare—but they do occur!

Thus, emergency procedures are an important part of every first-jump course, whether static line or accelerated freefall training is learned, and require the complete attention of every student as staff instructors explain and demonstrate corrective procedures. Students are put through repeated practice sessions until actions become reflexive. (On tandem jumps, the instructor—a.k.a., *tandem master, tandem pilot*—will be in complete control of performing emergency actions.)

Throughout student status, instructors and jumpmasters will have students explain or demonstrate (perhaps both) procedures for various emergency situations that might be encountered. The purpose is to be ready at any time under any circumstances. Some jumpers have needed the procedures on the very first jump. Other jumpers do not have a major malfunction for years and hundreds of jumps (e.g., 15 years and 964 jumps for one skydiver; five or six years and 1,780 or so jumps for another).

Smart jumpers never forget that a major malfunction, calling for extreme emergency measures, might—just might—occur on the very next jump; but the mere possibility does not make them paranoid about skydiving. The probability can be likened to the everyday activity of driving a car; it cannot be predicted when a threating moment will occur, so a driver learns what to do for a variety of perilous circumstances and remains alert and ready—but not paranoid.

STATIC LINE STUDENT PROGRESSION

Each lesson includes basic skills a student should perform in order to progress to the next phase of instruction; and theoretical knowledge should also be learned progressively. Each lesson is based on knowledge and skill learned in the previous lesson, so correct performance in each phase is needed for advancement. The skills include:

Equipment Preparation—Inspecting, packing, donning, and operating the parachute system and accessory equipment. Includes knowledge and skills a student should acquire before being cleared to jump without direct jumpmaster supervision.

Performance Preparation—Techniques students should learn to physically and mentally prepare for each jump. Needed to be learned so as to improve performance, add to enjoyment, and to maintain safety.

During Flight—Procedures to be followed during boarding, the climb to exit altitude, and the exit itself.

Freefall—Actions that occur after exit and until a canopy opens.

Canopy Control and Landing—Techniques of guiding a parachute to a safe landing to a designated target area. The cumulative effort of various steps improves a student's proficiency.

A static line program of training includes the following lessons:

Basic Orientation—Two *static line* jumps from 2,800 feet AGL:
—Aircraft procedures.
—Exit.
—Student's body position.
—Canopy check immediately after opening.
—Canopy control (steering).
—Landing.

Practice Ripcord Pulls—Three *static line* jumps from 2,800 feet AGL:
—Coordinated student movements.

First Freefall—One jump from 3,200 feet AGL (to be made on the same day as the last static line jump with a properly performed *practice ripcord pull*):
—Time awareness.
—Stability.

Ten-Second Delays—Two freefall jumps from 4,000 feet AGL:
—Introduction to spotting.
—Use of altimeter.
—Maintain a heading.

Fifteen-Second Delays—Two freefall jumps from 5,000 feet AGL; though some parachuting operations require three such jumps, breaking "controlled turn" requirements into two segments:
—Controlled turns; in a three-jump method, the second jump calls for holding a heading for five seconds followed by a simple 180-degree turn in a specified direction; the third jump will require maintaining a heading for five seconds, then doing controlled 180-degree and 360-degree turns in alternating directions. With a two-jump technique, the second jump is when the required 180-degree and 360-degree turns in alternating directions are made.
—Equipment checks (demonstrate ability to inspect, don, and adjust personal equipment without assistance).
—Briefing for "Supervised Training Progression"
  (NOTE: Some parachuting operations at this point permit students

"supervised" jumps on their own—that is, a student
nger be under the direct supervision of a Jumpmaster
ircraft. Nonetheless, the parachutist is still classed as a
l must perform other requirements to the satisfaction of
ment to be considered "off instruction." Very often
requirements match the qualifications for a USPA Class
achuting license. Those DZs might also require actual
of the license rather than being merely A license-quali-

Delays—Often only one or two "transition" jumps
from 5,500 feet AGL intended as a means of a student experiencing
making skydives without being under the direct supervision of a
Jumpmaster aboard the plane.

Thirty-Second Delays—Two freefall jumps from 7,500 feet AGL:
—Backloops.
—Delta body position (for achieving horizontal movement in addition to vertical fall).
—Introduction to relative work (RW); a "hookup" with a Jumpmaster/Instructor/*authorized* experienced jumper during freefall.
—"Wave off" technique—to assure proper clearance between jumpers during parachute deployment.

Forty-five-Second Delay—Two freefall jumps from 10,000 feet AGL:
—Frontloops.
—Barrel rolls.
—Relative work (RW) turns and "redocks" with an RW partner.

ACCELERATED FREEFALL (AFF) STUDENT PROGRESSION

Accelerated freefall (AFF) is a training method primarily for parachuting students making a first jump, though it is also used for students who have previously had some other form of experience, say a tandem jump or static line training, and who wish to learn skydiving in an efficient training program. All AFF jumps use harness-holding techniques with one to two USPA-rated AFF Jumpmasters (depending on a student's training level).

A key to the success of the accelerated freefall instruction method is teaching basic skydiving skills in a logical manner. The program is divided into seven levels (or steps). Each level is a convenient grouping of standard lessons; however, lessons can be tailored to fit circumstances or a specific student.

The accelerated freefall method stresses using up-to-date equipment so a student will have every advantage: a "piggyback" harness/container assembly that includes a spring-loaded pilot chute and where parachute activation is by means of a ripcord; a large, easy-handling, docile, ram air main canopy; a reserve (auxiliary) parachute equipped with an automatic activation device (AAD); and a visually accessible altimeter.

An accelerated freefall (AFF) training program encompasses a great number of lessons presented in the following sequence:

Level I—Basic Orientation (Free Arm)

Personnel required: Two Jumpmasters (JMs), one radio instructor.

- Thorough ground school training.
- Student and Jumpmasters practice entire skydive until smoothly done.
- Aircraft procedures.
- Exit; student in full two-handed grips by each JM.
- Exposure to continuous terminal velocity freefall.
- Body position.
- Heading awareness; focused awareness and attention; altitude awareness; JMs agree to release student's arms.
- Coordinated freefall body movements, including three practice ripcord pulls.
- Altimeter use.
- Time awareness.
- Actual student ripcord pull at 4,000 feet; Primary Jumpmaster and Secondary Jumpmaster maintain grips; Secondary JM assures pilot chute release and canopy deployment; both JMs open at 2,000 feet.
- Canopy check.
- Canopy control; radio instructor on ground guides student throughout descent until landing.
- Landing; JMs land near student, providing immediate counseling.
- Student debriefed, with student's self-concept first, JMs' critiques second.

Level II—Free Arm-Plus

Personnel required: Two Jumpmasters, one radio instructor

- Review previous skydive.
- Refresh previous training; give additional training; basic "spotting" guidance (determining ground reference point over which skydivers will exit an aircraft).
- Student exits in full two-handed grips by each JM.
- Stability assured by JMs.
- Heading awareness.
- JMs agree to release student's arms; with student displaying good body control JMs maintain harness grips with no tension.
- Coordinated movements; rehearsal of objectives, with emphasis on "trim" control (*arm and leg awareness,* body position changes by

means of arms in-out and legs in-out and returns to "neutral" position after each movement).

- Student does three practice ripcord pulls.
- Student pulls actual ripcord on own altitude awareness by 4,000 feet.
- Primary JM assures student's ripcord pull by 3,500 feet; Secondary JM assures pilot chute release and canopy deployment; both JMs deploy their parachutes by 2,000 feet.
- Canopy control; radio instructor on ground guides student as needed throughout descent until landing.
- Landing; JMs land near student, providing immediate counseling.
- Student debriefed, with student's self-concept first, JMs critiques second.

Level III (Release Dive)

Personnel required: Two Jumpmasters, one radio instructor.

- Review and discussion of previous jumps.
- Refresh previous training and present new training; alter in-air emergency procedures to accommodate intentional main canopy release ("breakaway," "cutaway") in event of a major malfunction.
- Complete equipment check before boarding aircraft.
- Additional spotting technique guidance in aircraft prior to exit.
- Heading maintenance; principles of turning.
- Optional practice ripcord pull (based on student's past performance and time elapsed since last jump).
- "Hover" control by JMs; by 6,000 feet JMs agree to release grips on student; Secondary JM releases first on signal from Primary JM and stays in position; Primary JM then releases grip and stays in position; both JMs are ready to regrip or correct a student's body position.
- Solo ripcord pull on own altitude awareness at 4,000 feet; JMs remain alert to assist in event of student delay, turn or spin movement, or loss of stability; JMs open parachutes by 2,000 feet.
- Canopy control; radio instructor on ground guides student as needed throughout descent until landing, minimizing control to allow student to achieve independence.
- Landing; JMs land near student, providing immediate counseling.
- Student debriefed, with student's self-concept first, JMs' critique second.

Level IV (Turns to Redock)

Personnel required: One Jumpmaster, one radio instructor

- Review and discussion of previous jumps.

- Refresh previous training and present new training.
- Student selects exit point and canopy opening point on a DZ aerial photo; assists JM in spotting process, actually dropping a wind drift indicator (WDI), if circumstances permit.
- Complete rehearsal of new exit procedures (movement into exit position is unassisted but controlled by supervising JM); student also explained use of head and arms to make a turn, plus use of arms and legs to achieve horizontal movement, and explained "docking" technique for performing basic RW with another skydiver, further explained "wave off" safety procedure to signal another jumper of intention to deploy a main parachute.
- Full equipment checks before boarding aircraft.
- Controlled turns and redocks—jump sequence:
  —When student demonstrates awareness (GAP—Ground, Altitude, Primary Jumpmaster), JM moves into a "hookup" position, facing student.
  —JM releases student and backs away five feet.
  —Student performs a 90-degree turn, then turns back to face JM again, then moves forward toward JM for redock (JM assists in redock, if needed); altimeter is rechecked.
  —Release is repeated for student 90-degree turn in opposite direction, return to heading, and redock; JM observes student's altitude awareness.
  —JM releases so student can pull.
  —Student waves off and pulls by 3,000 feet; JM pulls by 2,000 feet.
- Canopy control; radio instructor counsels student as needed throughout descent until landing, further minimizing control so student achieves independence.
- Landing; JM lands near student, providing immediate counseling.
- Student debriefed, with student's self-concept first, JM's critique second.

Level V (Turns to Redock-2)

Personnel required: One Jumpmaster, one radio instructor

- Review and discussion of previous jumps.
- Refresh previous training and present new training.
- Student and JM discuss *spotting*, effects of aircraft attitude in spotting, calling out corrections for direct instruction or relay to the pilot.
- Jump sequence:
  —Student gets into exit position unassisted, but gripped in a harness-hold by the JM.
  —After exit JM moves from side-by-side position to hookup position, facing student, maintaining grips on student's hands.
  —JM releases and backs away 10 to 20 feet.

—Student performs a 360-degree turn and moves forward to JM to redock. JM does not assist in closing the distance during redocking.
—Release is repeated, with student making a second 360-degree turn in the opposite direction, then redocking with JM, again with no assist by the JM.
—JM releases so student can pull.
—Student pulls by 3,500 feet; JM pulls by 2,000 feet.
- Canopy control; radio instructor still further minimizes control.
- Landing; JM lands near student, providing immediate counseling.
- Student debriefed, with student's self-concept first, JM's critique second.

Level VI (Solo Dive)

Personnel required: One Jumpmaster, one radio instructor

- Review and discussion of previous jumps.
- Refresh previous training and present new training; instructions given in performing a backloop, using a "delta" position to achieve "tracking" (horizontal movement in addition to ever-present vertical fall), "flaring" from a *track* position so as to reduce speed increased while *tracking*.
- Full equipment checks before boarding aircraft.
- Jump sequence:
  —Student gets into exit position unassisted to perform a no-contact, poised exit.
  —Student exits, recovers stability if necessary, then "lays base" for the JM.
  —The JM moves into position to face the student, makes eye contact (a hookup is optional), then demonstrates a backloop.
  —Student performs a backloop, recovers (regains stability, if necessary), and does a second backloop.
  —Student *tracks*, using the *delta* body position.
  —JM demonstrates *track* by passing the student.
  —Student *flares* at 4,000 feet, *waves off*, and pulls by 3,000 feet; JM opens by 2,000 feet.
- Canopy control; radio instructor still further minimizes control.
- Landing; JM lands near student, providing immediate counseling.
- Student debriefed, with student's self-concept first, JM's critique second.

Level VII (Half Series Plus)

Personnel required: One Jumpmaster, one radio instructor

- Review and discussion of previous jumps.
- Refresh previous training and present new training.

- Spotting is done by student without assistance (unless unsafe, then counseled by JM).
- Student does a diving ("unpoised") exit (a la "Superman/Superwoman"), followed closely by the JM.
- Student stabilizes and maintains a heading, then does a front loop.
- Student performs *half* of a "style set" sequence of maneuvers (a full *style set* consists of a 360-degree turn in one direction, a 360-degree turn in the opposite direction, a backloop, two more 360-degree turns, each in opposite directions and a second backloop); the half set should be performed as quickly as possible without loss of control; the purpose of the maneuvers is to develop a degree of precision in body control in all axes during freefall.
- Student *tracks* as necessary, *waves off*, and opens canopy by 3,000 feet; JM opens by 2,000 feet.
- Canopy control; radio instructor still further minimizes control.
- Landing; JM lands near student, for immediate counseling.
- Student debriefed, with student's self-concept first, JM's critique second.

NOTE: For official graduation, student's logbook must be signed by two Jumpmasters. A DZ's master logbook should also be so noted as to a specific student's "off instruction" status. An oral evaluation by a DZ's Chief Instructor is optional. Furthermore, a graduating student should be explained details of Level VIII skydives and other requirements that lead to a United States Parachute Association (USPA) Class A (Basic) parachuting license.

Level VIII (Graduate Student: Continuing Education)

Personnel required: One freefall (FF) coach (to be a USPA-rated AFF Jumpmaster or someone appointed by a DZ's Chief Instructor)

There are many other skydiving skills to be learned while a student continues to be supervised at Level VIII of accelerated freefall training until application for a USPA Class A license has been made. They include:

- Improving body control and awareness, performing a full style set.
- Launching two-person (and later, three-person) relative work (RW) formations from an aircraft.
- Improving relative work skills, including making a series of redocks while an FF Coach varies rate of fall; aggressive hookups; two-person sequential RW with completion of five maneuvers ("points") during one freefall period (with additional experience, the student progresses to doing three-person RW and completing five *points*); learning no-contact formation flying.

- Accumulating 15 minutes of freefall time (freefall time is a basic yardstick of measuring skydiving experience).
- Transition to personal equipment.
- Getting instruction and coaching in canopy control in order to make five landings within 20 meters of a target center; also learning to make a graceful stand-up landing.

A SKYDIVING STUDENT'S BIG DAY!

Hooray!—off instruction!—a student parachutist's big day!—all qualifications for a USPA *Class A Basic* parachutist license have been achieved. The only thing left is the paperwork and buying a set of silver USPA parachutist wings for proud display, as a tangible memento of a truly remarkable personal achievement, one that will be remembered always.

Fig. 3-7. *The silver wings of the United States Parachute Association (USPA) are coveted by student parachutists as a symbol of a significant personal achievement—becoming a skydiver!*

However, the "newly minted" basic parachutist must remember the operative word in the new skydiving ranking—*basic*; must remember that he or she is still learning, that attention must be paid continuously to what goes on at their DZ, what goes on in the sport, what goes on in a plane, what goes on in the air. There's an awful lot left to yet learn!

To learn what those things are, study the section later in this chapter titled *License Requirements*.

LEARNING FINESSE; WORKING WITH A MENTOR

The sophisticated accelerated freefall training program incorporates a "mentor" program of sorts in its Level VIII training schedule, through which a student gets one-on-one training for a period of time lasting until he or she acquires a USPA *Class A* (Basic) license. Generally speaking, most static line training programs do not include such one-on-one training as a requirement for "graduation" to full-fledged off-instruction status.

However, other DZs with a static line training program enlist the help of experienced jumpers approved by the DZ's Chief Instructor who agree to be available to assist student jumpers in analyzing and correcting particular freefall problems or help in developing specific skills for the student, such as relative work movements, freefall stability, performing *style* maneuvers, canopy handling, and so forth. Such mentor assistance is done on a per jump basis, with a student paying the cost of a mentor's jump. The practice amounts to a student paying for a private lesson, such as done in skiing and tennis. In return for a jump being paid for, a mentor agrees to critique everything about a student's jump and give an evaluation to the student (not merely go for a plane ride and get a jump paid for, all the while paying little attention to a student's efforts and contributing little or nothing to a student's progress). If a DZ offers a mentor program, it's a fine way for a student to improve progress.

TANDEM PARACHUTING—
STUDENT AND INSTRUCTOR ON THE SAME PARACHUTE

In 1961 there was a young woman who had made several static line sport parachute jumps, but whose husband decided against making any himself. He lacked confidence in his abilities when it came to the idea of parachuting. He said he was not sure he would do the right things as they needed to be done; but he added that he would probably give more thought to making a jump if there were some way two people—an instructor and a student—could be in one harness and under one canopy. Then, if he did not function, the instructor could make sure things were done correctly.

People smiled and voiced skepticism: It could not be done; there was not any way to make a harness for two people; there were not canopies large enough to support two people; and, besides, where would the thrill be of "doing it on your own"?

Static line jumps continued to be the order of the day for anyone getting into the sport of parachuting and remained the state-of-the-art instruction method for many years.

However, every now and then more thought was given to some way to providing better instruction to student parachutists. After all, every other air sport had historically used the concept of instructor/student dual training. First there was an introductory ride for a student, usually with the student briefly getting the feel of controls, followed by ground training and continuing aerial instruction until the student was ready for solo flight. However, until recent years in sport parachuting a student had to spend hours in a classroom environment and on mockups and in drilling from a jump plane still on the ground before actually flying to altitude to make a jump. Then, once letting go the aircraft at a jumpmaster's direction, the student was on his or her own—having to decide if the canopy had satisfactorily deployed; having to locate an airport and a target area; having to decide what the winds were doing; having to maneuver a canopy constantly until landing; and having to remember how to make a parachute landing fall (PLF). Sensory overload was most common for first-jump students and usually lasted well through a student's further training, but there was simply no other way to train students to become skydivers. Think of where the rest of aviation would be if there had been no dual flight training and students had to take up aircraft alone on a first flight.

Among experienced jumpers experimentation continued. Russian parachutists, when making exhibition jumps during breaks in world championships, often did two- and three-man trapeze acts using only one hugely oversized canopy. In military service certain U.S. paratroopers making static line jumps rigged special auxiliary harnesses that attached to their own and carried sentry dogs on jumps. In the mid-1970s two young jumpers decided they might have an answer, but they were wrong. Years afterward one of the participants in that adventurous attempt recalled: "I made my first tandem jump 10 years ago (two of us, both experienced jumpers, under an old 44-foot cargo chute). We were almost killed, and that put an end to my experiments for quite a while." A means of two persons using one harness remained unattainable for a while yet. In 1977 two parachutists made the first recognized tandem jump over DeLand, Florida.

Then two later developments ultimately made it possible to give serious attention to student/instructor dual flight. First there was the "piggy-back rig"—a single harness with both a main parachute and an auxiliary (reserve) parachute arranged so as to be worn on a skydiver's back. However, it was not developed with tandem parachuting in mind; piggyback gear was more an evolutionary step in providing better gear in response to other needs. Jumpmasters wanted to stop having reserve canopies in front-mounted reserves from being accidentally deployed while attending to static line students during their exits; accuracy competitors wanted a bulky reserve on the front of a harness out of the way in the final stages of an approach to a small target disc; and everyone wanted some way of achieving more orderly, more comfortable deployment of reserve canopies in malfunction situations.

The second development was the ram air canopy. In time it became possible to develop small-volume, high-weight-load canopies that would readily support the weight of two persons and their equipment. A ram air canopy (nicknamed "square" because of the appearance of early models) had a much lower rate of descent, a superior glide ratio—it could be flown about much like a glider—and its high forward speed could be fully "braked" so as to achieve a soft landing. What came to be known as "tandem parachuting" was now possible. Many years after the husband who lacked confidence in his ability to safely parachute on his own and expressed his "two-on-a-harness" imaginative idea, it became a viable concept that grew quickly into reality.

In the late 1970s limited research continued, and in the early 1980s intensive effort was given to coming up with equipment suitable for an instructor and a student to simultaneously make a parachute jump. Development and testing continued steadily by two American parachute manufacturers who, for a time, joined minds and efforts to produce an idea. Later, each manufacturer went a separate way, due to philosophical differences, resulting in two systems being developed, tested, produced, and ultimately put into widespread use, with each achieving a great deal of success. In mid-1984 each of the two manufacturers received an exemption from Federal Aviation Regulations (FARs), an exemption that legalized tandem parachute jumping. To date, the two manufacturers are the only ones in this country permitted by the Federal Aviation Administration (FAA) to commercially produce tandem parachute systems.

Each system resembles and performs much like the other, and each can employ a "drogue parachute" that is deployed at the beginning of freefall, thereby slowing a descent rate of about 180-190 miles an hour (depending on "pilot" and "passenger" weights) to 110-120 miles an hour, permitting softened, comfortable openings.

Each system gives a passenger a freefall experience of several seconds followed by a lengthy parachute ride, with hands-on opportunities for a passenger to manipulate steering lines, along with the pilot, to understand making canopy turns and to learn how to land properly, softly, and comfortably by assisting the instructor with "braking" the parachute's forward speed.

One system also, after completing a "standard" first-jump tandem training course, lets a passenger actually pull the ripcord on a second jump and successive ones thereafter.

As of now, thousands of jumps have been made with "tandem parachute systems," not only in this country but throughout the world.

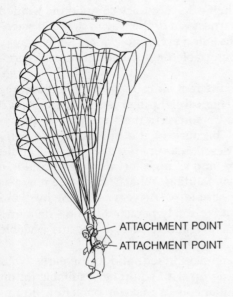

ATTACHMENT POINT
ATTACHMENT POINT

Fig. 3-8. An oversized tandem ram air canopy showing how a "passenger" (student in front) and a "pilot" (instructor in rear) are able to utilize a specially designed harness system for tandem parachuting. Only two U.S. manufacturers are allowed by the federal government to produce complete tandem parachute systems for use in this country.

An owner of a commercial parachute center in Washington state has said, "Due to the remarkable research done by those in the tandem field, skydiving has finally reached a level equivalent to that of dual flight instruction. Tandem allows for true one-on-one training and the implementation of an instantaneous instruction-performance-feedback-correction cycle. This cycle is critical in the learning process. I am amazed at the alertness of the first-jumpers as they talk, perform turns, read altitudes, and assimilate an incredible amount of information. The students have quickly learned canopy control, canopy characteristics, and how to flare for landing. I am continually awed by the system and the potential it offers its users."

Fig. 3-9. Instructor Bill Morrissey (dark jump suit) grips a student's wrists, pulling them rearward, and clasps the student's ankles together with his feet to demonstrate the "delta" body position for "tracking," used to gain horizontal movement in addition to ever-present vertical fall. (Such a maneuver is fully explained and demonstrated to a student during ground school training.) (Courtesy Strong Enterprises)

Fig. 3-10. A tandem student (in white) does body movements to initiate a left turn maneuver while in freefall. Instructor Bill Morrissey duplicates the student's movements so as to not counteract the turning movement by maintaining his stable fall, on-heading position. ("Shadowing" the student's movements also speeds making the turn, providing reinforcement to a student that such maneuvers actually do produce results.) (Courtesy Strong Enterprises)

The introduction of tandem parachuting brings sport parachuting both up to date and to the same level of professionalism as every other aviation activity.

TANDEM PARACHUTE MANUFACTURERS

Specific information regarding the tandem parachute systems of the manufacturers Strong Enterprises and Relative Workshop can be obtained directly from them:

Strong Enterprises
11236 Satellite Boulevard
Orlando, Florida 32821
305/859-9317

Relative Workshop
1725 Lexington Avenue
DeLand, Florida 32724
904/736-7589

General information about tandem parachuting and other training methods can be obtained from the United States Parachute Association (USPA), 1440 Duke Street, Alexandria, Virginia, 22314, 703/836-3495.

LICENSE REQUIREMENTS

At sport parachuting drop zones the terms *license* and *rating* are heard many times, all too often used synonymously. However, there is a distinction between a license and a rating, with the latter referring to instructional aspects of skydiving. This section will have to do with licenses; the complex system of ratings will be detailed in the following section, *Becoming A Parachute Instructor*.

About Licenses

Licenses issued by the USPA signifying sport parachuting skill-level accomplishments are coveted recognitions, so desirable that many US DZs require *A* license qualification before a student will be considered to be "off instruction" and permitted to jump without direct jumpmaster supervision.

USPA-licensing is sought also by jumpers of many other countries because, again, such a license is an indicator of having achieved specific skills. Most other countries have a licensing system, administered by a national sport parachuting organization, but American standards are often higher for comparable license designations.

"A" License (Basic). Persons holding a USPA *A* license are capable of parachuting without the direct supervision of a jumpmaster, know how to pack their own sport main parachute, know how to perform basic freefall relative work, and have been trained to make an unintentional water landing. Having an *A* license means that an individual has accomplished the following:

- Made 20 freefall parachute jumps including:
  - At least three controlled (stable) freefall jumps of 40 seconds or longer.

—Accumulated five minutes of controlled freefall time.
- Landed within 20 meters of a target center on five freefall jumps on which the candidate selected both exit point and opening point.
- Demonstrated ability to:
  —Hold heading during freefall.
  —Make 360-degree flat turns to both left and right.
- Demonstrated ability to safely be one's own jumpmaster, including selecting, without guidance,
  —Proper exit altitude.
  —Exit point.
  —Canopy opening point.
- Demonstrated ability to:
  —Properly pack a sport main parachute.
  —Conduct a prejump safety check on personal equipment and on equipment of other skydivers.
- Possesses documentation of training by a USPA Instructor for an unintentional water landing.
- Demonstrated ability to safely perform freefall relative work by:
  —Making satisfactory door exits.
  —Varying both rate of descent and horizontal movement.
  —Participating in at least three two-way (two-person) RW jumps.
  —Moving horizontally (tracking) away from other skydivers in freefall and checking surroundings so a parachute can be safely deployed without danger of collision with other jumpers, and when under an open canopy, accounting for location of other canopies to avoid collision.
- Passed a written examination administered by a USPA Instructor or Safety & Training Advisor (S&TA). (There is a USPA fee of $20.)

"B" License (Intermediate). The third highest of four skill-level licenses. Persons holding this license:

- Are capable of parachuting without the direct supervision of a jumpmaster.
- Know how to pack their own sport main parachute.
- Know how to perform basic freefall relative work (RW).
- Have been trained to make an unintentional water landing.
- Are permitted to make relative work, water, and night jumps.
- May participate in record attempts.

Possessing a *B* license means that a person has already accomplished the following:

- Either met all requirements for or has been issued a USPA *A* license.
- Made 50 freefall jumps including:
  —at least three controlled (stable) freefall jumps of 45 seconds or longer.

—Accumulated at least ten minutes of controlled freefall time.
- Landed within 10 meters of a target center on ten jumps.
- Demonstrated ability to perform a set of individual freefall maneuvers in 18 seconds or less (a figure-eight—defined as two flat turns—a back loop, a second figure-eight, and another back loop).
- Possesses documentation of water landing training with full equipment, such training to be in accordance with Section 9-2 of the current edition of USPA's publication *The Skydiver's Information Manual.* Section 9-2 comprehensively covers recommendations and procedures for:
  —First-jump course training for unintentional water landings.
  —"Wet" training for water landings, both unintentional and intentional.
  —Water jumps.
- Passed a written examination administered by a USPA Instructor or Safety & Training Advisor (S&TA). (There is a USPA fee of $20.)

"C" License (Advanced). The second highest of four skill-level licenses. Persons holding a C license:

- Are permitted to serve as a jumpmaster for other licensed skydivers.
- Know how to pack their own sport main parachute.
- Are qualified to make relative work, water, night, and demonstration (exhibition) jumps.
- May participate in record attempts and in certain USPA parachute competitions.
- Are eligible for the USPA Jumpmaster rating.

A C license defines what a person has already accomplished:

- Met all current requirements for or has been issued a USPA B license.
- Made 100 freefall parachute jumps, including:
  —At least 10 controlled (stable) freefall skydives of 45 seconds or longer.
  —Accumulated at least 20 minutes of controlled freefall time.
- Landed within five meters of a target center on 20 jumps.
- Completed at least four "points" on a four-way or larger randomly selected sequential RW skydive. (One scoring "point" is awarded for each completed formation of a series of predetermined freefall formations.)
- Passed a written examination administered by a USPA Instructor or Safety & Training Advisor (S&TA).
  (There is a USPA fee of $20.)

"D" License (Master). The highest of four skill-level licenses. Persons holding a D license:

- Are permitted to serve as a jumpmaster for other licensed skydivers.
- Know how to pack their own sport main parachute.
- Are qualified to make RW, water, night, and demonstration (exhibition) jumps.
- May participate in record attempts and in all USPA parachute competitions.
- Are eligible for all USPA ratings.
- Are eligible for appointment as a Safety & Training Advisor (S&TA).

A D license defines a person's exceptional sport parachuting accomplishments:

- Met all current requirements for or has been issued a USPA C license.
- Made 200 freefall parachute jumps, including:
  —At least ten controlled (stable) freefall skydives of 60 seconds or longer.
  —Accumulated at least one hour of controlled freefall time.
- Landed within two meters of a target center on 25 jumps.
- Demonstrated superior skills in performing freefall maneuvers, meeting the requirements in one of two ways:
  —Performed a set of individual freefall aerial maneuvers in sequence. Performing such maneuvers demonstrates that an individual has control of his or her body in all axes while in freefall. The maneuvers include: back loop, front loop, left turn, right barrel roll, and left barrel in a time of 18 seconds or less; or
  —Completed at least four points (four formations) of a randomly selected sequential series of formations on a relative work (RW) jump with at least eight participants.
- Passed a written examination administered by a USPA Instructor or Safety & Training Advisor (S&TA).
- Made two night jumps, with the guidance of a USPA Safety & Training Advisor (after initial night jump training by a USPA Instructor). Each jump included at least 20 seconds of freefall; one jump was a solo skydive; the other included relative work (RW). (There is a USPA fee of $20.)

Restricted License. The USPA recognizes that there are people who can experience many of the excitements and rewards of parachuting but who, because of physical limitations, cannot comply with all requirements for obtaining a USPA license. Thus, USPA, in specific, individually considered circumstances, might issue a *Restricted* license.

A person might be qualified for a *Restricted* A, B, C, or D license if he or she has:

- Met all license requirements except those detailed in a petition to USPA.
- Submitted a petition to USPA's Safety and Training Committee stating:
  —Type of license requested.
  —Specific license requirement(s) that cannot be met.
  —Circumstances that prevent compliance with license requirements.
  —A license application (USPA Form 104-1).

Each application will be considered separately and on its own merits, completely without precedent.

Exceptions to qualifications for each level of license will be listed on a *Restricted* license, thus: "*Restricted* licenseholder has not demonstrated the ability to (specific limitation listed)."

Restricted license numbers will be followed by the letter *R* (e.g., C-11276R).

BECOMING A PARACHUTE INSTRUCTOR

Becoming a parachute instructor is not an easy task! Every skydiving instructor started out with no jump experience, and it is a good bet that not one instructor, harking back to student days, was truly certain that another jump would ever be made after the first one.

To digress briefly—of course, as with practically everything in life, there is an exception to the positiveness of the latter statement in the above paragraph. This exception has to do with anyone who signed up for military airborne soldier training. In such a case, a paratrooper candidate, male or female, knows that a minimum of five static line jumps are required to be awarded coveted silver parachute wings, and every candidate, at the beginning of training, fully expects to achieve that personal goal. Actually completing the requirements is another matter, and the rigorous demands of military training can result in not qualifying for paratrooper wings. However, since this book deals primarily with skydiving as a recreational sport activity, the thesis continues as valid that there was practically no certainty that another jump would ever be made after the first one, that the first one was being made simply to see what it was like to make a parachute jump.

Most experienced skydivers didn't have the slightest inkling that they might go on participating in the sport after making that one jump to satisfy a curiosity, but many first-time jumpers liked what they experienced and stayed with sport parachuting. Of those, many who went on to become highly skilled skydivers also became jumpmasters and instructors, teaches willing to pass on what they learned earlier, all the time themselves still learning about skydiving, taking another step toward becoming a "compleat skydiver."

When an experienced parachutist sets his or her mind on becoming a parachute instructor, a vast area of knowledge and experience has to be acquired in order to accomplish that ultimate goal. Minimum skill levels—evidenced by qualifying for and acquiring USPA licenses—must be demonstrated. Then a variety of ratings, as additions to a license, must also be acquired.

About Ratings

After a parachutist acquires a USPA license, indicating personal skill levels, instructional ratings can then be added to a license, enabling a licensee to serve in an instructional capacity for student parachutists. There are a number of instructional ratings that can be earned:

- Static Line Jumpmaster; Accelerated FreeFall (AFF) Jumpmaster.
- Static Line Instructor, Accelerated FreeFall (AFF) Instructor.
- Static Line Instructor/Examiner; Accelerated FreeFall (AFF) Instructor.
- Instructor/Examiner. This rating is considered the "ultimate" instructional credential that can be acquired. (Though other ratings carry the label *Instructor/Examiner*—as shown above—the scope of achievement pertains to the particular form of parachuting to which the I/E complementary description is attached, e.g., *S/L I/E, AFF/IE.*)

USPA's complex rating program provides a realistic and practical system for issuing ratings for teaching static line and accelerated freefall sport parachuting. *Tandem parachuting* is still under the aegis of the FAA working in conjunction with two manufacturers in the closing stages of a formal approval program.

USPA instructional ratings are valid for one year. A renewal date coincides with a USPA membership renewal date.

A *Static Line Jumpmaster Rating* can be issued to a USPA *C* or *D* licenseholder who:

- Has demonstrated ability to provide practical instruction to and direct supervision of students in an aircraft and on static line and solo freefall jumps.
- Has presented documentation of completing all requirements on a USPA JM Proficiency Card.

- Has completed a USPA Jumpmaster Certification Course (JCC).
- Is at least eighteen years of age.
- Has made an intentional water jump (optional for a C license-holder, mandatory for a D licenseholder). (There is a USPA fee of $20.)

A *Static Line Instructor rating* can be issued to a USPA *D* licenseholder who:

- Meets static line Jumpmaster rating requirements by completing a static line *Jumpmaster Certification Course* (JCC).
- Has held a USPA *Jumpmaster* (JM) rating for at least twelve months.
- Has presented documentation of completing all requirements on the USPA *Static Line Instructor* proficiency card or the *Accelerated FreeFall Instructor* (AFF) proficiency card.
- Has completed a USPA *Instructor Certification Course*. (There is a USPA fee of $25.)

A *Static Line Instructor/Examiner rating* can be issued to a USPA *D* licenseholder who meets all the S/L Instructor standards and can additionally provide advanced instruction, training and guidance, and carry out duties covering a wider scope than expected of and permitted to a Jumpmaster. A Static Line Instructor/Examiner can serve a DZ and parachuting in general as a recognized skydiving expert.

An *Accelerated FreeFall (AFF) Jumpmaster Rating* can be issued to a USPA *D* licenseholder who:

- Has demonstrated abilities to instuct and jumpmaster at Levels I through VII of the USPA Accelerated FreeFall Program.
- Has documented at least four hours of freefall time.
- Has completed an AFF Certification Course.
- Has made an intentional water jump.
- Who is at least eighteen years old.

BECOMING A JUDGE

Being a judge can be as satisfying an accomplishment as many other achievements in skydiving. Being a judge means skydivers can be evaluated in whatever aspect of skydiving they choose to participate and have a chance to learn if they are as good as they perceive themselves to be. Objective evaluation by qualified judges can contribute greatly to an individual's skill improvement.

The USPA administers a comprehensive program of training, certifying, and recertifying judges at three levels of expertise—Conference, National, and International (Federation Aéronautiqué Internationalé (FAI).

A judge at any meet has the responsibility to see that each contestant receives an unbiased, equal opportunity to display competition skills.

This means a judge has to pay attention to various conditions affecting meet conduct, such as wind levels and directions, haze and clouds, and ground-to-air communications, among other things.

A judge must work well with other staff members, must know rules and how to brief competitors, tally scores, handle protests, and deal with irate competitors. Last, and certainly not least, a judge must know to "make a call" pertaining to whichever event is being judged.

Someone interested in being a judge generally starts by helping a meet judge in any number of ways. Watching nonmeet aerial maneuvers will help develop familiarity with a telemeter; recording the comments of a judge while a freefall style competitor is executing turns and loops or as a four-person relative work team makes a formation will be another lesson learned. Helping a judge and other meet personnel will be an interesting experience and excellent training toward the first step in becoming a USPA-rated Judge.

To become a USPA-rated Conference Judge a candidate must have been a USPA member for one year, judged three local meets, one being a Conference Championship, and obtained approval from a Conference Director.

To achieve a National Judge rating a candidate must participate in the National Judge Certification Program (NJCP). To attend an NJCP a candidate needs a current Conference Judge Rating, must have been a USPA member for two years immediately preceding NJCP participation, must have judged at least one conference meet with certified events (e.g., Style/Accuracy, Relative Work) within the previous two years, and must further obtain a Conference Director's approval. A candidate attending an NJCP will be working with highly skilled, experienced judges happy to pass on their expertise.

The pinnacle of parachute judging is an FAI International Judge rating. After judging three National Championships and maintaining a proficiency level prescribed by the FAI Sporting Code, plus obtaining the approval of three current FAI Judges, a National Judge can apply for an FAI Judge rating. An FAI Judge can certify World Records and judge World competitions.

Judging a meet can be personally satisfying, and competitors benefit immensely when they know they have been fairly and skillfully evaluated.

BECOMING A PARACHUTE RIGGER

This section is not brief—but it should be read attentively for more than one reason:

- So you will have a full appreciation of yet another level of sophistication that exists in the world of skydiving, a level intended to provide the fullest measure of protection and safety to users of parachutes—the distinctly related field of parachute rigging.

- So you will have greater confidence in the equipment used in making sport parachute jumps.
- To provide motivation for striving toward another goal in parachuting that would help a participant in the sport become a "compleat" skydiver.

A Federal Aviation Regulation (FAR) states that (with one exception related to sport parachuting) all parachutes to be put into civil (that is, *nonmilitary*) service must be packed by someone who is an FAA-certificated (the FAA uses "certificated," not "certified") AND appropriately rated parachute rigger. (Ratings are issued for back, chest, and seat types of parachutes for personnel use.)

The FAR is straightforward in its intent, and words used are specific in meaning: *All* means all; *must* means must; *certificated* means certificated, "*ticket in hand* does *not* mean someone who is in training for certification and is legally packing parachutes under the supervision of an FAA-certificated Senior or Master Parachute Rigger; and "put into service" means carried aboard a civil aircraft for the purpose of providing emergency equipment; also meaning, with regard to sport parachuting, being used by a person making an intentional parachute jump using a dual parachute system with a main parachute and an auxiliary parachute.

(A reasonable simile pertaining to specific wording is a traffic sign that says STOP: It does little good to argue with a police officer if you have rolled through an intersection posted with a STOP sign, no matter how slowly you did it, no matter—as you attempt to rationalize with the police officer—how ever so slowly and carefully you did it. The officer will decide that you have violated the law, because STOP means STOP, nothing else!)

FAA parachute rigger certification requires substantial effort and time on the part of a rigger candidate. First, a candidate must, under rigger supervision, have packed a minimum number of parachutes of the type for which a certificate/rating is being sought. Concurrent with packing practice, the candidate must also learn information detailed in FARs pertaining to parachutes and parachuting. A third preliminary step, after completing the minimum number of packings, is obtaining a letter from an FAA-certificated Senior or Master Parachute Rigger affirming that the candidate has indeed met the packing requirement for each rating wanted. (A rigger candidate lists each of at least 20 parachutes inspected and packed in a "Parachute Technician's Log" and has the entry countersigned by an FAA rigger with an appropriate rating.) The letter writer must also state satisfaction that the candidate is well versed in specific FARs. All this is in preparation for applying to the FAA to sit for the parachute rigger written examination.

Rigger candidates must report to an FAA testing center, or an FAA Written Test Examiner's location, or another designated place in order to take an airman's written examination. (The FAA, unfortunately, has not yet rid its official language of sexist references, as in *airman*. Both men and women are eligible for FAA-certification as a Senior or Master Parachute Rigger and for appointment as a Designated Parachute Rigger Examiner (DPRE).)

At the designated place a candidate will be given a copy of the FAA *Parachute Rigger Question Book* (FAA-T-8080-9), a 50-item "question selection sheet" that lists specific questions chosen from 8080-0 to be answered by the candidate, and an *Airman Written Test Application* (AC Form 8080-3). Multiple-choice questions presented in the written test are based on information from a variety of readily available resources. Also, the question book contains supplementary material (e.g., drawings) to aid in answering questions. A maximum time of two hours is allowed for the written test. (There is a special "military competency" written examination for military personnel seeking FAA certification as a parachute rigger. That specific exam has to do only with FAA regulations and allows only one hour for completion.) In either case, there is plenty of study material available to rigger candidates (see this book's Bibliography), and the time allowed for the written examination is quite sufficient.

The answer form is sent by the testing center (or the Designated Written Test Examiner) to the Monroney Aeronautical Center at FAA headquarters in Oklahoma City, Oklahoma.

The test is scored by computer, and a minimum score of 70 (of a possible 100) is required for a passing grade. Soon after scoring, the FAA will send the rigger candidate an *Airman Written Test Report* (AC Form 8080-2), listing the test score and identifying the test questions answered incorrectly.

A rigger candidate with a passing grade may then present the AC Form 8080-2 to an FAA office or to an FAA-Designated Parachute Rigger Examiner (DPRE) to arrange taking an oral and practical examination pertaining to one or more of the three ratings available (back, chest, seat).

A candidate who receives a failing grade may apply for retesting and has two options for doing so: (1) After thirty days following the date the applicant failed the written test; or (2) before the thirty days have expired by presenting a signed statement from someone with FAA parachute rigger certification and (appropriately rated—i.e., back, seat, chest—to match the rating sought by the candidate) stating that the applicant has received additional instruction in each failed subject and that the FAA-certificated rigger considers the applicant prepared for retesting.

An oral and practical examination requires that a rigger candidate demonstrate basic skills to an FAA Inspector or to a DPRE, skills such as inspection, packing, repairs, and use of tools and equipment. Furthermore, knowledge of techniques and materials is verified by the examiner's questioning during the course of practical testing. Properly administered, a practical examination for a single rating can be a lengthy process. Applying for a second, and perhaps a third, rating at the time of the practical exam will easily extend the time needed to complete testing.

With issuance of a Senior Parachute Rigger certificate, listing a rating or ratings, the new rigger is assigned a "seal symbol." This symbol—usually a set of three letters, or perhaps letters and numbers—is inscribed on the dies of a "seal press," a hand-held device (made of lead), used by a parachute rigger to identify the ripcord safety seal when packing is completed. In addition to the safety-tie thread/seal combination, a rigger must also sign a packing ticket that is stored in a container pocket accessible for verification of packing date and other information. A parachute intended for emergency use by a pilot, crew member, or passenger must have been packed within the previous 120 days before a flight. The auxiliary (reserve) parachute of a dual sport parachute assembly must also meet the 120-day repack criterion. In the case of a sport parachuting/skydiving main parachute intended for use in an intentional parachute jump, the 120-day repack criterion also applies, though no packing data card is required to be completed for the sport main parachute.

Certification is the time-consuming process it appears to be, but acquiring certification certainly has its rewards: a sense of accomplishment; important knowledge; respect; opportunities for employment; income to cover costs of making jumps and acquiring equipment; another credential toward becoming a highly qualified skydiver, and so on.

4

How Parachutes Work

A parachute is a simple mechanical device, and in 99.44 percent of cases it is absolutely reliable. Thus, it's a wonder that there are so many pilots who have no faith in a parachute as a lifesaving device. You might have met the type—"I can fly the *crate* my airplane came in! "

It's not a modern-day boast, though; it dates back to World War One, when disassembled and crated JN-1 "Jenny" aircraft were transported by ship and rail to air bases in France. The bravado of those first wartime aerial combatants, some with as few as 20 or so hours of flying time, was perhaps needed badly at the time to counteract the frightening conditions of combat and the often frightful ordeal of just ordinary flying.

Pilots since those days who believed in parachutes are still around to tell of their flying and lifesaving parachuting ventures. One of the old-timers once sent a telegram to Leslie Irvin, founder of the Irving Air Chute Company: "PLANE FAILED—CHUTE DIDN'T. " It was signed by Jimmy Doolittle.

Understanding how a parachute works makes it easy to have confidence in equipment, and that, in turn, makes skydiving enjoyable.

To start understanding means knowing, among other things, what components go into creating a parachute assembly. Since this book is not intended to be an encyclopedia of every item of parachute equipment, only basic parts and systems will be examined. Specific information about the latest in sport parachute equipment can be acquired from parachute riggers, experienced sport parachutists, equipment retailers, direct contact with manufacturers, and current periodical skydiving publications.

Start with a standard manually operated freefall parachute system, dating back to 1919 and from which sport parachuting equipment evolved.

Shown in FIG. 4-1 are all the parts of a parachute except the container, which is hidden behind the jumper. Such parachutes were normally used in emergency aerial situations, but in the 1920s and 1930s they were used extensively by barnstorming parachutists to make exhibition jumps. The same type was used often in World War Two for wartime clandestine missions that began with a parachute jump behind enemy lines.

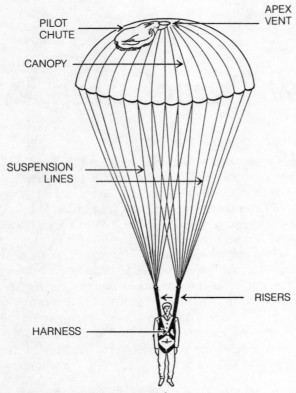

Fig. 4-1. *Parts of a basic emergency parachute system.*

A truly basic item of a parachute assembly is the harness. The principal purpose of a harness is to form a *sling* (liken it to a *swing* seat) in which a user can sit without danger of separation from the parachute at a moment of strain. It is an arrangement of webbing in a configuration conforming to the shape of a load to be carried in such a manner so as to properly safeguard the load and to evenly distribute forces and weight during opening and throughout descent. Military and nonsport harnesses today are much like those of early designs.

FIGURE 4-2 is a harness of the 1940s that includes D-rings at the front of the assembly for attaching an auxiliary (reserve) parachute if a user is to make an intentional jump, for example, as part of training.

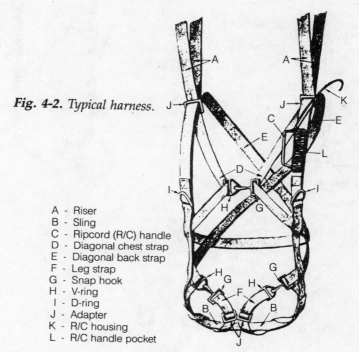

Fig. 4-2. *Typical harness.*

A - Riser
B - Sling
C - Ripcord (R/C) handle
D - Diagonal chest strap
E - Diagonal back strap
F - Leg strap
G - Snap hook
H - V-ring
I - D-ring
J - Adapter
K - R/C housing
L - R/C handle pocket

A diagram of an early sport parachute closely resembles a standard freefall parachute; compare FIGS. 4-1 and 4-4. However, the *sport* rig additionally has a *deployment sleeve* (an inflation retardation device) and a *sleeve retainer line* (for keeping an expensive accessory from being lost).

The "conventional" round sport canopy shown in FIG. 4-5 was supplanted by an American-made, high-performance canopy—the Para-Commander (abbreviated *P-C*). It was classified as a *round* canopy, but there the resemblance ended. (See FIGS. 4-5 and 4-6.)

The PC's performance and handling characteristics soon brought about the disappearance of conventional round canopies from DZs, except as a means of training students. However, packing and deployment/inflation was much the same as for other round sport main canopies.

A sleeve (or *bag*, or *POD*, etc.) is undoubtedly the single item of sport parachuting equipment that helped skydiving become a widespread recreational activity. Use of such a retardation device made it possible for *line-first* deployment of a sport main parachute system and greatly eased opening shock. It was a simple piece of equipment that was a long time in being developed.

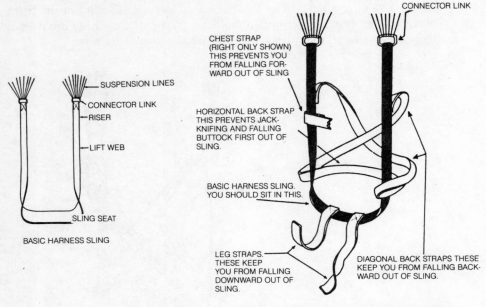

SUSPENSION LINES
CONNECTOR LINK
RISER
LIFT WEB
SLING SEAT

BASIC HARNESS SLING

CONNECTOR LINK

CHEST STRAP
(RIGHT ONLY SHOWN)
THIS PREVENTS YOU
FROM FALLING FOR-
WARD OUT OF SLING

HORIZONTAL BACK STRAP
THIS PREVENTS JACK-
KNIFING AND FALLING
BUTTOCK FIRST OUT OF
SLING.

BASIC HARNESS SLING.
YOU SHOULD SIT IN THIS.

LEG STRAPS.
THESE KEEP
YOU FROM FALLING
DOWNWARD OUT OF
SLING.

DIAGONAL BACK STRAPS THESE
KEEP YOU FROM FALLING BACK-
WARD OUT OF SLING.

BASIC HARNESS SLING WITH SUPPORT STRAPS ADDED

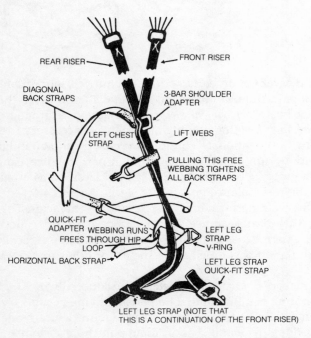

REAR RISER
FRONT RISER
DIAGONAL
BACK STRAPS
3-BAR SHOULDER
ADAPTER
LEFT CHEST
STRAP
LIFT WEBS
PULLING THIS FREE
WEBBING TIGHTENS
ALL BACK STRAPS
QUICK-FIT
ADAPTER
WEBBING RUNS
FREES THROUGH HIP
LOOP
HORIZONTAL BACK STRAP
LEFT LEG
STRAP
V-RING
LEFT LEG STRAP
QUICK-FIT STRAP
LEFT LEG STRAP (NOTE THAT
THIS IS A CONTINUATION OF THE FRONT RISER)

SLING AND LIFT WEBS (AND RISERS) WITH SUPPORT STRAPS ADDED

Fig. 4-3. *Harness construction.*

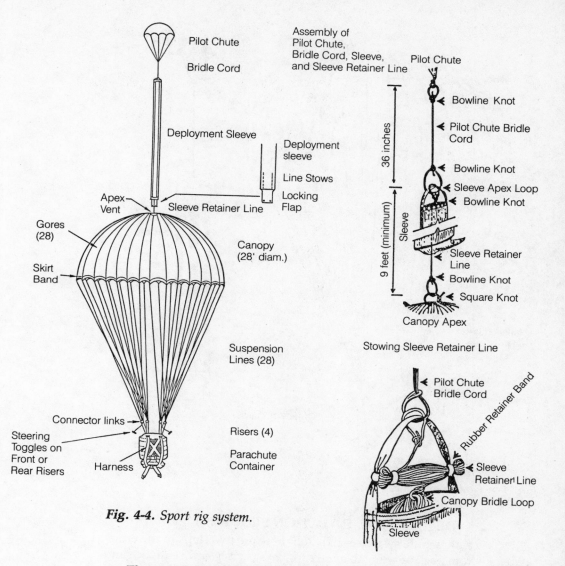

Pilot Chute

Bridle Cord

Deployment Sleeve

Assembly of
Pilot Chute,
Bridle Cord, Sleeve,
and Sleeve Retainer Line

Deployment sleeve

Line Stows

Locking Flap

Apex Vent

Sleeve Retainer Line

Gores (28)

Skirt Band

Canopy (28' diam.)

Suspension Lines (28)

Connector links

Steering Toggles on Front or Rear Risers

Harness

Risers (4)

Parachute Container

Pilot Chute

Bowline Knot

Pilot Chute Bridle Cord

Bowline Knot

Sleeve Apex Loop

Bowline Knot

36 inches

9 feet (minimum)

Sleeve

Sleeve Retainer Line

Bowline Knot

Square Knot

Canopy Apex

Stowing Sleeve Retainer Line

Pilot Chute Bridle Cord

Rubber Retainer Band

Sleeve Retainer Line

Canopy Bridle Loop

Sleeve

Fig. 4-4. *Sport rig system.*

The retardation technique was simply a matter of encasing a canopy so that it could not inflate until all suspension lines were extended fully. At that point the pilot chute could then remove the sleeve from the canopy, which could inflate in orderly fashion. Suspension lines were stowed on the base of the sleeve, with two suspension line stows used to keep the sleeve in place on the canopy during the sleeve/canopy deployment stage. (See Fig. 4-7.)

A parachute system starts to deploy when a container is opened, and a pilot chute commences to provide drag as a parachutist continues to fall. The diagrams in FIG. 4-8 illustrate the beginning of a "sleeved" canopy deployment.

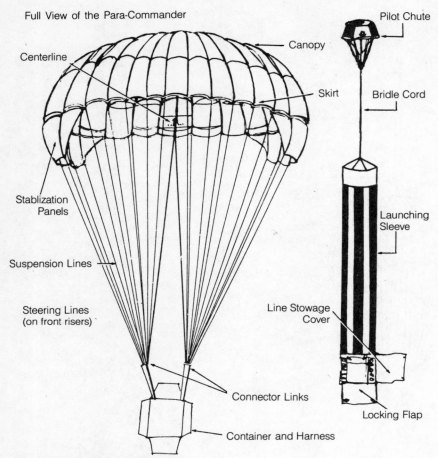

Full View of the Para-Commander

Centerline

Canopy

Skirt

Pilot Chute

Bridle Cord

Stablization
Panels

Suspension Lines

Steering Lines
(on front risers)

Launching
Sleeve

Line Stowage
Cover

Connector Links

Locking Flap

Container and Harness

Fig. 4-5. *Para-Commander (P-C).*

DEPLOYMENT/INFLATION SEQUENCES

When a parachute system is actuated there are two steps in the entire
sequence from pack opening to a full canopy—a *deployment* sequence and
an *inflation* sequence. The sequences are alike whether a parachutist is
making a "fun" skydive or an emergency jump, and the dual sequences
occur with cargo loads also (e.g., trucks, artillery pieces, space vehicles).

For sport parachuting use, time delays are added deliberately for
comfort of the parachutist and to make it possible to make several jumps
a day. A standard emergency parachute is designed to be inflated fully
within 1.5 seconds after a ripcord pull that opened a container. That's
fast—and could be hard on a person's body, even injurious, depending
on the jumper's body position and other factors (e.g., harness adjustment) at the time of opening shock.

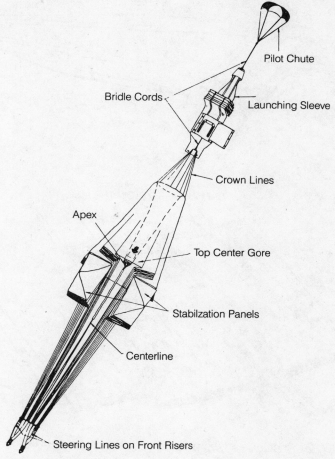

Pilot Chute

Bridle Cords

Launching Sleeve

Crown Lines

Apex

Top Center Gore

Stabilzation Panels

Centerline

Steering Lines on Front Risers

Fig. 4-6. *Para-Commander (P-C).*

How a Round Canopy Works

Look at FIG. 4-9 depicting the inflation of a standard round canopy attached to a test load.

FIGURE 4-9 might seem a curious-looking depiction of a deployed, inflating canopy. But keep in mind that when a parachute-equipped object separates from an aircraft, the object continues briefly in the same direction as the airplane had been traveling.

Simply stated, a body in motion tends to remain in motion until affected by other, greater forces. Thus, once an object leaves an aircraft, its path approximates that shown in FIG. 4-10. Gravity is instant; horizontal movement is quickly slowed and becomes vertical.

SLEEVE IN PLACE OVER ENTIRE CANOPY.

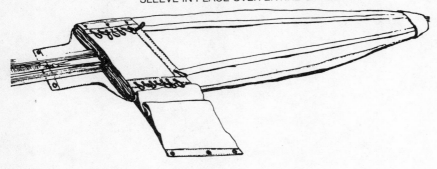

PREPARING TO STOW THE LINES.

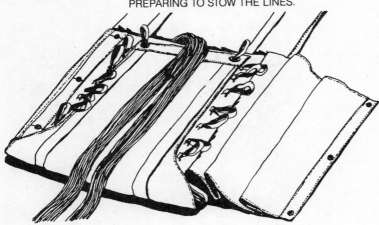

FIRST TWO STOWS THROUGH LOCKING FLAP RETAINERS.

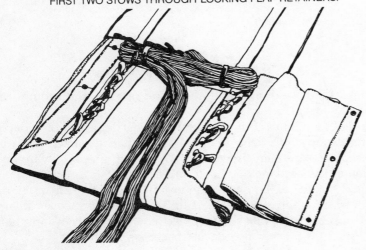

Fig. 4-7. *Line stowage.*

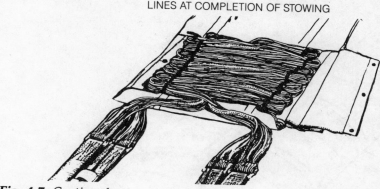

LINES AT COMPLETION OF STOWING

Fig. 4-7. Continued.

If a parachute is deployed in one to three seconds after an object leaves an aircraft, with the object still having brief horizontal movement, the deploying and inflating canopy will approximate the changing attitudes shown in FIG. 4-9.

A basic sport parachute system of the sort used from the mid-1950s through the early 1970s (though still in use at some DZs in this country and other places about the world) functioned in much the same manner except that the addition of a "sleeve" as an inflation retardation device slowed the mandated fast opening of about 1.5 seconds (sometimes faster!) to a comfortable two and a half to three seconds. FIGURE 4-11 illustrates the deployment/inflation sequence of a sleeved round canopy sport parachute system.

In other sport systems, a "bag" was used in place of a "sleeve," but the two items served the same purpose—to slow the opening speed of a sport rig. Another form of a *bag* was a para-opener device (POD), which permitted a different method of stowing a canopy. (See FIG. 4-12).

When ram air canopies evolved into the "main" parachute for skydivers, a *bag* and POD-like containers became the primary means for stowing a packed canopy. In these days, however, a sleeve is rarely seen (a *sleeve* is never used with a ram air canopy). (See Chapter 5.)

How a Ram Air Canopy Works

A ram air canopy deployment/inflation sequence is basically the same as for a round canopy:

1. Pilot chute out (hand-deployed or by ripcord), providing drag.
2. Skydiver continues to fall; suspension lines extend from stowage bands on deployment bag; stowed canopy streams out of bag, with slider retarding canopy from fully opening, resulting in a progressive canopy inflation rate and achieving a greatly lessened opening shock.

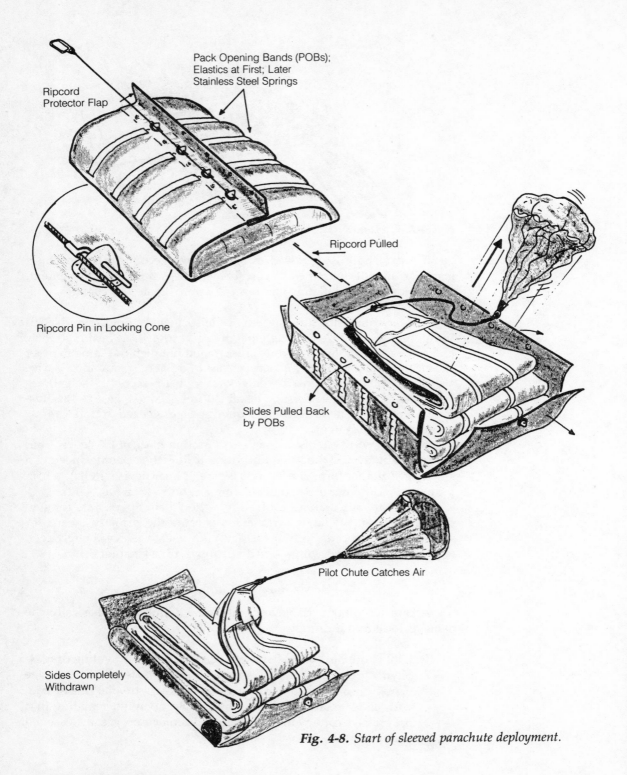

Ripcord
Protector Flap

Pack Opening Bands (POBs);
Elastics at First; Later
Stainless Steel Springs

Ripcord Pin in Locking Cone

Ripcord Pulled

Slides Pulled Back
by POBs

Pilot Chute Catches Air

Sides Completely
Withdrawn

Fig. 4-8. *Start of sleeved parachute deployment.*

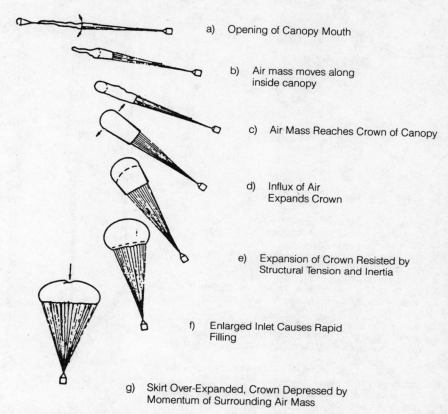

a) Opening of Canopy Mouth

b) Air mass moves along inside canopy

c) Air Mass Reaches Crown of Canopy

d) Influx of Air Expands Crown

e) Expansion of Crown Resisted by Structural Tension and Inertia

f) Enlarged Inlet Causes Rapid Filling

g) Skirt Over-Expanded, Crown Depressed by Momentum of Surrounding Air Mass

Fig. 4-9. *Stages of parachute inflation. (Time=0-1.5 seconds; ripcord pull to full inflation)*

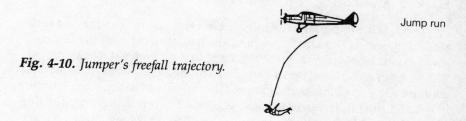

Jump run

Fig. 4-10. *Jumper's freefall trajectory.*

3. Cells inflate, expanding the size of the canopy, forcing the slider away from its stowed location at the base of the folded canopy and down the suspension lines.

4. Cells continue inflating, with the slider resisting too rapid filling of the cells.

5. With all cells inflated, slider moves fully down suspension lines, resting on connector links at top of risers. Pilot chute and deployment bag rest on top of canopy (or trail slightly behind canopy, depending on canopy design).

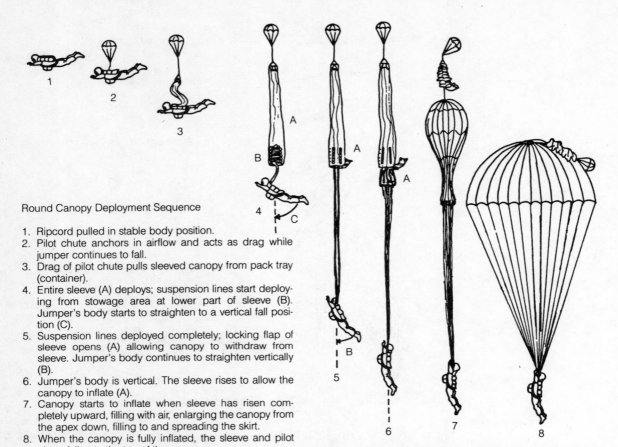

Round Canopy Deployment Sequence

1. Ripcord pulled in stable body position.
2. Pilot chute anchors in airflow and acts as drag while jumper continues to fall.
3. Drag of pilot chute pulls sleeved canopy from pack tray (container).
4. Entire sleeve (A) deploys; suspension lines start deploying from stowage area at lower part of sleeve (B). Jumper's body starts to straighten to a vertical fall position (C).
5. Suspension lines deployed completely; locking flap of sleeve opens (A) allowing canopy to withdraw from sleeve. Jumper's body continues to straighten vertically (B).
6. Jumper's body is vertical. The sleeve rises to allow the canopy to inflate (A).
7. Canopy starts to inflate when sleeve has risen completely upward, filling with air, enlarging the canopy from the apex down, filling to and spreading the skirt.
8. When the canopy is fully inflated, the sleeve and pilot chute fall onto the top of the canopy.

Captions: Included at points in drawings. See wording in illustrations.

Fig. 4-11. Round canopy deployment sequence.

There is an important distinction between round and ram air canopies (also termed "square" canopies, the latter the expression most commonly used by skydivers when referring to a ram air parachute).

As soon as a round sport canopy (whether a conventional steerable configuration or a high-performance canopy such as a Para-Commander) is inflated, it is fully ready to be directionally controlled (steered) using canopy control lines. All a parachutist needs to do is reach up and grasp a right and left steering toggle in each hand and commence manipulating the canopy toward a target area. However, it is a different matter with a ram air/square canopy.

Part of the packing procedure of a ram air canopy is to shorten the length of both steering (control) lines and to maintain the shortened length throughout the canopy deployment/inflation sequences. This is done to prevent the high-performance canopy from starting to fly at the instant it becomes fully inflated. To keep the "snubbed" control lines in position until the parachutist wishes to have the canopy in a full flight

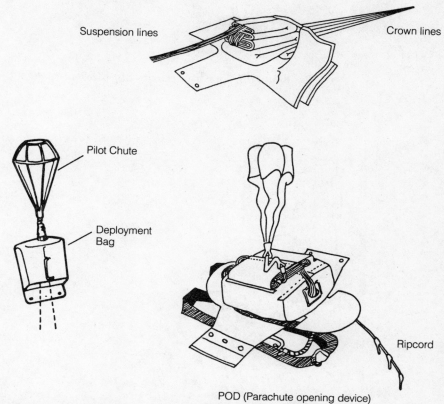

Suspension lines

Crown lines

Pilot Chute

Deployment Bag

Ripcord

POD (Parachute opening device)

Fig. 4-12. *Bag/parachute opening device (POD) illustrations.*

mode, the pulled-down control lines are temporarily "locked" in place on the risers by the parachute packer. In effect, the trailing edge of the canopy is packed so that the parachute is in a "half brake" flight mode when the canopy fully inflates; thus forward speed on opening is greatly diminished. The minimal forward speed that does develop is comparable to that of a high-performance *round* canopy, such as a Para-Commander. Excessive stowage of control/steering lines will adversely affect desirable canopy opening characteristics—that is, opening in a "stall" mode, with the canopy not having any forward speed at all.

A basic reason for the half-brake configuration is safety when there are multiple canopies deploying at approximately same levels and within relatively close distances to one another. Ram air canopies have "no wind" forward-motion flying speeds ranging from more than 20 to nearly 30 miles an hour, depending on various canopy designs; *no wind* meaning that in an unlikely situation of there being no natural air movement, a ram air canopy would fly at its designed forward speed. However, natural air movement—wind—only affects the actual speed across the ground (aircraft pilots think in terms of airspeed and ground speed).

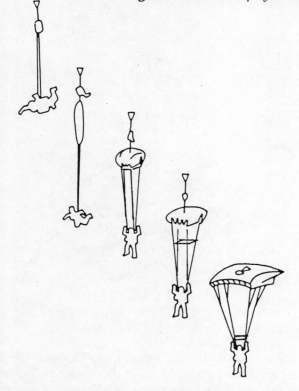

Fig. 4-13. *Ram air deployment/inflation sequence.*

The design speed of the canopy is called *flying speed* and is constant throughout flying upwind, crosswind, or downwind. The only change in flying upwind or downwind will be a change in *ground speed* (often mistakenly thought of and defined as *airspeed* by nonaviation-trained persons).

A 20-mile-an-hour ram air canopy will actually have a ground speed of 40 miles an hour when running with a 20-mile-an-hour wind. Conversely that canopy will have only a 10-mile-an-hour ground speed when holding against the 20-mile wind. With just a little imagination, it can be seen, for example, that four "unbraked" ram air canopies opening in proximity to one another could be involved in a risky traffic jam, even in an unlikely no-wind condition. There is simply no guarantee as to what direction a canopy will be facing when deployment/inflation is completed.

A "Square" Canopy?

Square has for a long while been a misnomer for describing the appearance of a ram air canopy, but it is a term solidly in place in sport parachuting jargon. When the ram air canopy was introduced it had the look of being nearly square in shape when observed from below or above. It was not square, but it was close enough to quickly earn the nickname. Though ram air canopies soon got larger and were clearly rectangular in form because of increased span, the square description remained. It was much like *scotch tape* becoming a term everyone used for pressure-sensitive transparent tape, although "Scotch" is a brand name.

PARACHUTE STEERABILITY

Steering a canopy—getting it to go where the parachutist wants—has progressed from kicking, thrashing, body twisting, *slipping*, and making *riser turns* to sophisticated arrangements of steering lines and control lines *cascades*, canopy line attachments, *braking, stalling, backing up, off-hand turns,* and *flaring*.

In 1955, at the National Air Races in Philadelphia, sport parachutists of the time competed in an accuracy contest. Under an open canopy—one without any steerability function built into it because such capability was not yet known—a competitor's target was a straight line some 100 feet long. Accuracy was measured by how far the jumper landed from the line, at any point along the length. It was possible for first- and second-place winners to have recorded scores within inches of each other but to have actually landed at opposite ends of the hundred-foot-long target line. A contestant had to rely a lot on physical strength and stamina in pulling downward on groups of suspension lines and pulling down the skirt to get the canopy to "slip" sideways and gain some horizontal movement across the ground and get closer to the target area. If a competitor wanted to lose altitude quickly to avoid overshooting the target area, then a "glissade" would be performed.

Glissade is a French term for an action in which a parachutist pulls down a canopy's front suspension lines and/or risers for more than three feet in order to partially collapse the canopy, thereby increasing rate of descent. Competition accuracy jumpers sometimes resorted to more than one glissade during a descent, some glissades lasting until nerve gave out as an extreme measure to lose altitude rapidly.

When sport parachuting started taking hold it didn't take long for some participants to put their heads and hands to work at discovering what made parachutes work. As a result keen inquiring minds started calculating how to alter original canopy configurations and came up with *thrust slots, turn windows, steering lines,* and other features. Canopy oscillations practically disappeared, making a descent more enjoyable, for one thing, and horizontal movement and quick turns became the order of the day. As experimentation continued, horizontal movement increased, turns became quicker, rates of descents lessened with improvements in canopy fabric permeability, and landings got less thumpy—and less injurious.

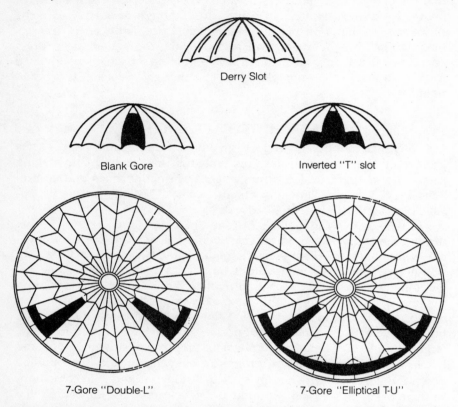

Derry Slot

Blank Gore

Inverted "T" slot

7-Gore "Double-L"

7-Gore "Elliptical T-U"

Fig. 4-14. Above—*Frank Derry was issued a U.S. Patent in 1945 for his rudimentary but effective design for steering a parachute canopy. This configuration was used for a long while by ''smokejumpers'' of the U.S. Forest Service. Below—Four early common canopy modifications for improved maneuvering. A canopy with an ''elliptical T-U'' configuration was considered a high-performance canopy of the 1960s and early 1970s.*

Accuracy improved greatly for ordinary fun-jumpers and for serious-minded accuracy competitors. By the time of the Sixth World Parachuting Championships, for the first time held in the United States (1962, Orange Sport Parachute Center, Orange, Massachusetts), the best accuracy competitors from 26 nations throughout the world were being scored to within 100 feet of the target's center, most of them easily landing within 10 feet or so of the ten-inch, orange-painted, inverted cardboard pie plate serving as the dead center disc.

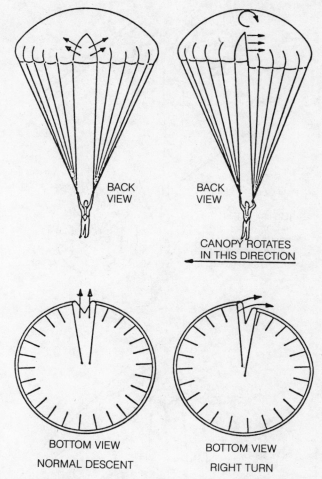

Fig. 4-15. *Back and bottom view of parachute in a normal descent and in a right turn.*

With the Para-Commander on the sport parachuting scene in the mid-1960s dead centers began to be more readily achievable. As they became a fairly regular occurrence for the really good competitors, the target disc got steadily smaller, finally decreasing to 10 centimeters (four inches).

The Para-Commander differed remarkably from the best of the conventional round canopies and was far superior in every respect. It flew farther and faster; oscillation was negligible; and rate of descent was less, so landings got to be more enjoyable and injuries were fewer. FIGURE 4-16 illustrates how the P-C reacted to a parachutist's handling.

A French parachute manufacturer introduced a "Papillon" canopy (papillon meaning butterfly). Although it was intended primarily for

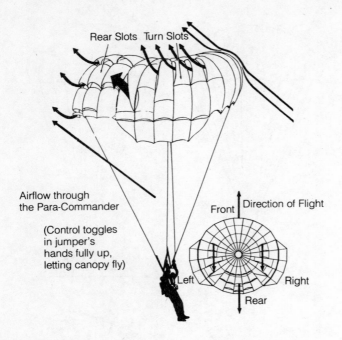

Rear Slots Turn Slots

Airflow through
the Para-Commander

(Control toggles
in jumper's
hands fully up,
letting canopy fly)

Front   Direction of Flight

Left

Right

Rear

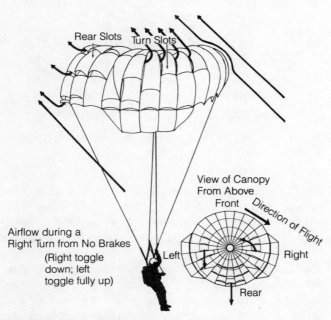

Rear Slots   Turn Slots

Airflow during a
Right Turn from No Brakes
(Right toggle
down; left
toggle fully up)

Left

View of Canopy
From Above
Front   Direction of Flight

Right

Rear

Fig. 4-16. *Three Para-Commander canopy modes.*

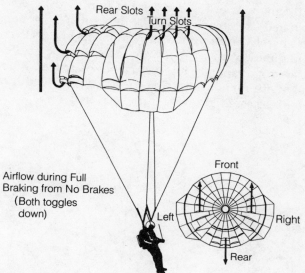

Rear Slots

Turn Slots

Airflow during Full
Braking from No Brakes
(Both toggles
down)

Front

Left

Right

Rear

Fig. 4-16. *Continued.*

accuracy parachutists, it was widely used. It resembled a Para-Commander in appearance, but aerodynamically it was a notable improvement for serious accuracy competition because of its more controllable "sink rate." Using various braking modes, a skilled accuracy jumper could better control rate of descent, particularly in the last moments of an approach, and thereby gain extra seconds and fractions of seconds to strive for a ten-centimeter disc. But a *Competition Para-Commander*, improved aerodynamically for competition accuracy, soon appeared on the market, answering the Papillon challenge. Though other canopies, some radically different in design from rounds, were introduced in the constant search for improvement, the Para-Commander and Papillon dominated skies over drop zones everywhere for a long while.

But a truly remarkable improvement was over the horizon.

A SQUARE WILL GET YOU THERE!

The giant step for parachutists was development of the ram air parachute canopy. There were several other canopy designs produced between ubiquitous rounds and the first production "squares," and several types were seen at DZs here and there for two to three years. However, nearly all of them failed ultimately to meet the criteria for an "all-purpose" parachute canopy suitable for the range of experience levels found at every sport parachute operation. The exception was the ram air canopy.

A ram air canopy is of cellular construction, with upper and lower surfaces separated laterally with cell dividers (ribs). In general descriptions, *squares* are referred to primarily by numbers of cells that constitute the final configuration of a canopy. A more specific size description includes the area of a canopy's top surface in square feet. When the canopy is inflated with ram air (entering the open front width of the canopy), a pressurized semirigid wing form is created.

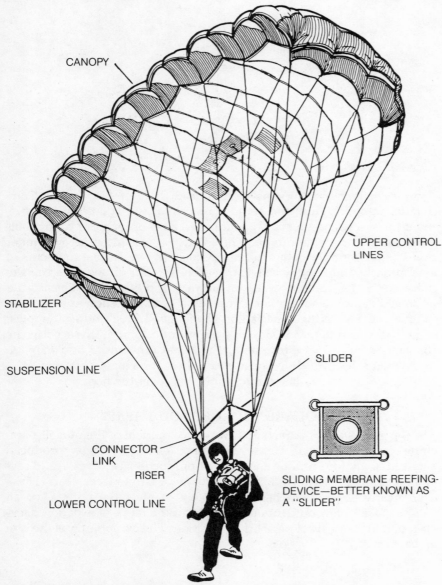

CANOPY

UPPER CONTROL LINES

STABILIZER

SLIDER

SUSPENSION LINE

CONNECTOR LINK

RISER

SLIDING MEMBRANE REEFING-DEVICE—BETTER KNOWN AS A "SLIDER"

LOWER CONTROL LINE

Fig. 4-17. *Typical ram air canopy/slider.*

Flight—as thought of with gliders and powered aircraft—with a ram air parachute canopy is accomplished because the aerodynamically formed fabric airfoil—shaped much like an aircraft wing—generates "lift " due to forward movement through air, brought about by the lowered pressure across the curved top surface of the canopy, just as in a conventional aircraft. (A standard, unmodified *round* canopy produces no lift, providing drag only, as intended by design. However, a round canopy modified to a steerable configuration gains forward movement provided by thrust from slots formed by removed canopy fabric. The forward movement creates airflow over the top of the canopy and that airflow provides a degree of lift, helping reduce rate of descent. A *round* canopy of the Para-Commander class produces greater thrust and correspondingly greater lift, slowing the descent rate even more.)

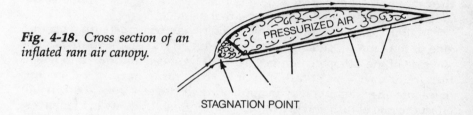

Fig. 4-18. *Cross section of an inflated ram air canopy.*

A specific angle of attack is maintained throughout descending flight by varied lengths of load-bearing suspension lines attached to the canopy. Line lengths are such that the leading edge of the canopy in flight is lower than the trailing edge. The result is that the canopy airfoil moves through the air and develops lift so necessary in reducing rate of descent.

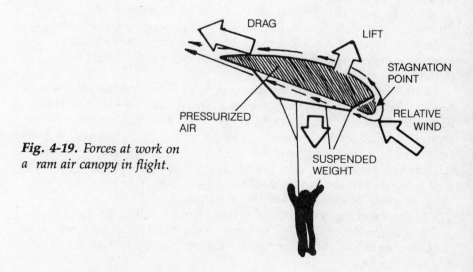

Fig. 4-19. *Forces at work on a ram air canopy in flight.*

MANEUVERING A RAM AIR CANOPY

Airspeed of a ram air canopy is parachutist-controlled by means of the canopy's braking system, using control lines (often termed *steering* lines) and toggles. (Toggles were initially small lengths of wood, plastic, or light metal secured to the ends of control/steering lines and were gripped in a jumper's hands as a means of firmly handling control/steering lines while guiding a canopy throughout descent from opening to landing. Large fabric loops made of light, narrow webbing are now used generally with ram air/square canopies because more positive control is achievable. The use of toggles in the text applies to whatever device is attached to control/steering lines.)

In a "hands-off, toggles-up" flight mode the ram air canopy will move forward at its maximum airspeed. Moving right and left toggles/loops downward will pull down the respective side of the trailing edge of the canopy. The greater the amount of downward toggle movement, the greater the angular deflection of the trailing edge.

Pulling down one side of the trailing edge will create drag on that side of the canopy, causing loss of airspeed on that side—but the opposite side of the canopy continues flying at its speed and the canopy will turn (right drag = right turn; left drag = left turn). Varying the amount of trailing edge deflection by manipulating the toggles up and down will affect the rate of turn and give a parachutist great flexibility in maneuvering a ram air canopy. The following illustrations show representative manipulations of control lines and canopy surfaces used in flying a ram air canopy.

Full Glide. Toggles fully up; maximum airspeed forward flight, ranging from 20-30 m.p.h. (dependent on varying factors); approximate 13-17 f.p.s descent rate, dependent primarily on canopy size and jumper weight.

Half Brakes. For slowing forward speed of canopy; also increases rate of descent; pulling down trailing edge of canopy produces drag (as in an aircraft wing); lowering toggles to chest area slows forward speed to approximately 10-12 m.p.h. and vertical descent to about 10-15 f.p.s. (feet per second).

Full Brakes. Achieved by lowering toggles to approximate area of hips, substantially reducing forward speed and somewhat further increasing descent rate; airspeed is about 4-5 m.p.h., and descent rate increases to about 11-16 f.p.s. Braking further by depressing toggles below the hip area results in the canopy reaching a stall state, with loss of all forward movement. The parachutist experiences a mushy-feeling, and perhaps wobbly, sinking action. Toggle control requires extremely close attention at this stage of canopy handling.

Right Turn/Left Turn. Usually done from a full glide flight mode; will result in wide arcs while changing direction; done by lowering either toggle while leaving opposite toggle fully up; canopy will bank and dive

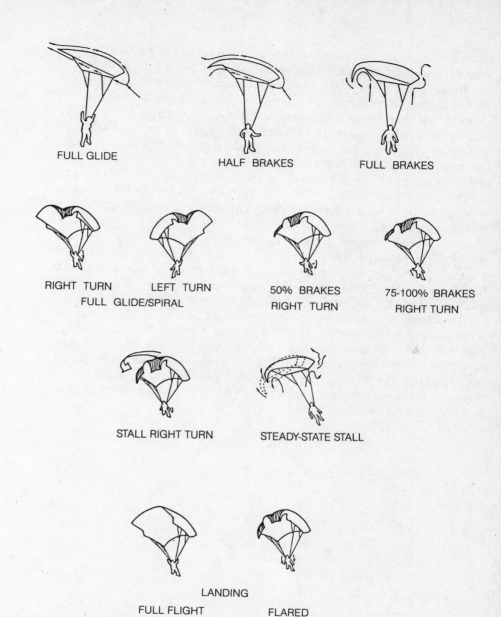

FULL GLIDE   HALF BRAKES   FULL BRAKES

RIGHT TURN   LEFT TURN

FULL GLIDE/SPIRAL

50% BRAKES
RIGHT TURN

75-100% BRAKES
RIGHT TURN

STALL RIGHT TURN   STEADY-STATE STALL

LANDING

FULL FLIGHT   FLARED

Fig. 4-20. Ram air canopy modes.

depending on parachutist's amount of toggle manipulation. A spiral turn is essentially the same maneuver as a full glide turn but in a spiral turn the toggle is held down steadily as the canopy rotates more than 360 degrees. A spiral turn starts relatively slowly, with a shallow banking angle, but increases quickly as toggle depression is maintained. A sharp spiral turn will cause excessive diving speed and extremely rapid loss of altitude. The latter maneuver can be useful at times but should be used with care and should be avoided below 500 AGL (above ground level).

Brake Turns. Turns in a "braked" canopy flight mode are quicker and smoother, have minimal banking, and incur a smaller increase in descent rate than those made from full glide. Brake turns are made by simply further lowering either toggle. With toggles in the 75-100% control range a jumper achieves extremely fast responses and must remember that the canopy is being manipulated near the stall range, where there is negligible forward speed, and momentary uncontrollability can result—with a potentially unfortunate result for an accuracy jumper in the final seconds of an otherwise perfect approach to a dead center on a five-centimeter target disc.

Stall Turns. These are made in the 90-100% brake range and are rarely done. However, they can be a "salvage" technique for a skilled accuracy jumper. A stall turn produces a quick pivoting movement, and the stalled side of the canopy flies backward to some degree, with increased descent rate. Stall turns should be used with extreme caution.

Landings. A ram air canopy should always be landed facing into the wind and can be brought easily to the ground in its full flight mode (toggles fully up). On final approach the canopy is flown at 50-75% brakes and then, with only seconds until touchdown, final braking is added until landing. The ground speed of landing will depend on the speed of the wind into which the canopy is being landed and the amount of final braking used by the parachutist.

5

Equipment
Used in Skydiving

Basic equipment for all skydivers is *two* parachutes—a *main* parachute, the primary parachute intended for use on each skydive, and a *reserve* (also termed "auxiliary" in formal or technical descriptions) parachute, a secondary parachute for use in emergency situations.

There are many people outside the sport who think that jumpers use only one parachute, and that belief contributes to their perception that parachuting is extraordinarily risky, something not worth doing as a recreation or a sport. It is not uncommon to hear a spectator at an exhibition jump site say something akin to "Oh, really?" or "Is that so?" or "I didn't know that" when a demo jumper answers questions and points out the reserve parachute and explains that it is standard equipment for every skydiver. (However, before sport parachuting was developed in the 1950s, many parachutists did use only a single rig for making jumps because "dual" harnesses for using two parachutes were not commonly available. U.S. military paratroopers throughout World War Two and thereafter had dual harnesses as standard equipment, but they were not available to civilians.)

The previous chapter started by claiming that "a parachute is a simple mechanical device, and in 99.44 percent of cases it is absolutely reliable." It is because a sport main parachute is not perfect, not a full 100 percent reliable, that a second parachute is mandatory for skydiving—by federal government fiat, in accordance with USPA basic safety requirements, and by the aviation regulations of most states. In general, most common skydiving malfunctions are the result of human error—for example, poor packing procedures, inadequate inspection practices ("equipment safety check") before boarding an aircraft, improper body position when the main canopy is deployed.

In general, most skydivers pack their own sport main parachute, a basically easy task, but the reserve parachute must, by federal law, be inspected and repacked every 120 days by an FAA-certificated parachute rigger. An FAA rigger is specially trained and has substantial knowledge and experience.

PRIMARY PARTS OF MAIN AND RESERVE PARACHUTES

The primary components of a sport main parachute include the following:

- Pilot chute, with bridle (a connecting line between pilot chute and deployment device (e.g., bag, sleeve), or canopy).
- Deployment device (sleeve, bag, "diaper").
- Canopy; including suspension lines, risers, slider (if appropriate to canopy type), control (steering) lines.
- Harness, including hardware, ripcord pocket, ripcord housing, etc.
- Container.
- Actuation device: ripcord, static line, pull-out pilot chute, throw-out pilot chute, etc. (Also see Chapter 4.)

The principal parts of a sport *reserve* parachute include the same items, except a harness. The configuration in which main and reserve assemblies can be used together can vary.

For many years the "conventional" sport parachute rig consisted of two separate and complete systems combined on a single harness at the time a jump was to be made. The *main* parachute was a back-mounted type packed into a container secured to a harness, and the entire assembly was informally considered to be a jumper's "basic rig." To make the rig ready for skydiving called for simply securing a separate *reserve* parachute assembly to D-rings on the front of the harness of the *basic rig*, further securing the reserve more tightly to the jumper's body by means of tie-down straps with adjustable fittings that mated to fittings on the back parachute container.

Such combinations of front-mounted reserve parachutes and back-mounted main parachutes are still in use at skydiving DZs in the U.S. and throughout other parts of the world, but they are steadily disappearing, replaced by state-of-the-art piggyback main/reserve parachute systems. In 1990 the USPA has mandated sole use of tandem parachute systems for student instruction for all its "Group Member" affiliates.

Fig. 5-1. *A student of the 1970s (in white), equipped with a static line-deployed main parachute on his back and a reserve parachute on the front of his harness, prepares for a sport parachute jump. The jumpmaster is doing one of the many steps in completing an equipment safety check, prior to discussing procedures with the novice parachutist. The jumpmaster is equipped with a piggyback system, with both the main and reserve parachutes mounted one above the other and worn on the back.*

PARACHUTE DEPLOYMENT

A main or reserve parachute canopy is put into use by initiating parachute deployment through means that permit a pilot chute to provide drag (resistance) and assist in the deployment/inflation sequences as a parachutist continues to fall.

ACTUATION DEVICES

Once a freefalling skydiver has determined it is "pull time" (also termed "pull altitude"), the parachute rig's actuation device is what gets things going. The device can be a manually-operated ripcord, a "pull-out" pilot chute, or a "throw-out" pilot chute.

In the case of a static line student, pull time is immediately on exit when a static line (controlled by a jumpmaster) attached between a student's main container and the aircraft opens the container and extracts the pilot chute. The static line then separates from the parachute and remains with the aircraft.

The earliest freefall actuation method was by means of a ripcord. In either a conventional parachute system—one with a back-mounted main parachute and a front-mounted ("chest-mounted") reserve parachute—or a piggyback system, a manually operated ripcord is used to open a container so a spring-loaded pilot can escape, inflate, and provide drag throughout deployment and inflation of the main canopy. After inflation, the pilot chute, secured to the deployment device (or to the canopy itself for emergency parachutes) simply rests on the canopy or trails behind it.

The "pull-out" actuation method can be said to be a "cousin" to the ripcord technique; a handle in the form of a miniature, squarish fabric pillow is held in place on the lower right-hand corner of a main parachute container. The handle connects directly to a straight metal ripcord pin that is on an eight to ten inch line that passes through a container locking loop/grommet configuration that aids in holding the main container closed until it is ready to be opened. The locking loop is fastened directly to the base of a springless, collapsed pilot chute stowed inside the main container. When the pull-out handle is pulled a short distance, the metal pin clears the locking loop and the container is opened. Continuing the pull extracts the pilot chute from the container. The skydiver then releases the handle/pilot chute into the airflow and deployment/inflation of the main parachute system commences.

There is a third means of getting a pilot chute into the air to start deployment at *pull-time*—the "throw-out" method. In some piggyback systems the pilot chute is first to be deployed, in turn opening the container, then providing drag as the skydiver continues to fall. As the pilot chute provides resistance, the canopy deploys, then inflates. The handle of the device (generally a one-inch-diameter piece of brightly colored, strong plastic tubing about two inches long) is mounted to the top of a springless, collapsible pilot chute. The pilot chute is folded and rolled and stowed in an accessible location on the harness assembly. At pull time, the skydiver grasps the handle firmly, pulls the collapsed pilot chute from its pouch, and throws it to the side vigorously. The upside down pilot chute rotates to a right-side-up position and inflates, starting the main canopy deployment/inflation sequences.

It is estimated that about 90% of experienced skydivers use the throw-out pilot chute actuation method and some 10% use the pull-out technique. Included in the latter figure are those who still rely on the old stand-by: the ripcord/spring-loaded pilot chute combination.

A sport main canopy, being equipped with a "deployment/inflation retardation device," such as a sleeve, bag, or diaper, will take about three seconds to open fully. A sport reserve canopy, designed for quick opening in emergency situations, will take less than half that time for full opening.

PILOT CHUTES

Pilot chutes are important to enjoyable skydiving. Although they don't need a lot of special attention, they should not be abused or ignored. To do so might create some uneasy moments at the wrong time, perhaps at the time of unintentional lower-than-permissible opening altitude, when a pilot chute is "sniveling," for example, because of excessive fabric permeability brought on simply by age. Regular inspection should be made of the item that is an important, often crucial, step in the train of every parachute opening. If something is suspect, replacement is better than apprehension or worry.

BRIDLES

The term *bridles* refers to lengths of fabric used as "connectors" (connecting devices) for a variety of purposes in parachuting. Primarily, they serve as connections between a pilot chute and a deployment device such as a sleeve or a bag, but sometimes they attach directly from pilot chute to canopy (some sport main canopies and most emergency-type canopies). Bridles can be any length and can be made of various strengths of any kind of durable, flexible material—in essence, whatever it takes to do a job.

DEPLOYMENT DEVICES

There are various types of deployment devices in use for sport main parachutes; also there is more than one type used with canopies intended for emergency use—a sport reserve, or a standard emergency back-type or seat-type emergency parachute used by pilots, crew members, and passengers.

A primary, basic benefit to pioneering skydivers starting with military surplus equipment was that deployment devices slowed the speed at which a parachute deployed and inflated after a container was opened, whether a parachutist was making a static line or freefall jump. A standard, federally mandated full-opening time of 1.5 seconds for an "approved," unmodified, emergency-type canopy was extended to just about three seconds. Now a jumper was not limited to one jump a day, perhaps two, because of severe physical discomfort. Another important benefit was that such a device aided greatly in orderly deployment, resulting in far less possibility of malfunction.

Before the advent of the *sleeve* in the early 1950s, several things were tried to reduce the body-jolting, often injurious opening of a parachute canopy. One common technique was grouping suspension lines tightly and holding them together immediately below the skirt of the canopy with a sturdy rubber band; but one rubber band was the same as having none. Two were tried. No better! A terminal velocity opening in excess of

100 miles an hour still rattled a jumper about in a harness; even subterminal openings brought little additional comfort. Three rubber bands brought about no change for the better. "Hell—let's try four!"

Fortunately, the test jumper was equipped with a dual harness and a chest-mounted reserve. Four rubber bands worked altogether too well, and the test jumper had to deploy a reserve parachute past a fast-moving, streaming main canopy fluttering wildly and noisily above his head. Dame Fortune smiled, and he landed without further incident.

While such experimentation was going on, the *deployment sleeve* was brought to the U.S. and promptly got into widespread use. Civilian jumpers then modeled a sport-type *deployment bag* after military equipment used by paratroopers and various models were also soon in use at DZs everywhere. A particular advantage of a *bag* was that its size could be made to greatly reduce the bulk of a stowed canopy, thereby making it possible to reduce the size of main containers, contributing to skydivers' comfort in the cramped confines of small airplanes.

Both types of deployment devices are still in use, though with the growing use of ram air canopies and piggyback container/harness rigs, it very likely won't be too long before sleeves become museum pieces and a footnote in history.

A "diaper" is another inflation retardation device that aids in reducing bulk and contributes to orderly deployment. A piece of fabric is sewn to a canopy in such manner that when the canopy is reduced in bulk by pleating, folding, stacking, etc., the fabric is then "wrapped" about the base of the canopy and held in place by portions of the upper suspension lines to "lock" the diaper in place until suspension lines are extended fully. When all lines are completely deployed the *lock* is "opened," the diaper unwraps, and the canopy starts its inflation stage. A like method is used with reserve parachutes in sport use and with emergency parachutes used in general aviation. A similar technique—except that a "wrap" takes place about the suspension lines immediately below the canopy skirt, much as in the rubber band method explained above—is used for both sport reserves and general aviation emergency parachutes. This technique, the "Reuter Wrap," was named for the then Chief Engineer of Pioneer Parachute Company, Jim Reuter.

HARNESSES AND CONTAINERS

A large variety of harness and container configurations are used in sport parachuting. Customized gear is readily available, with cost being based on how much a user wants to spend. However, there are many off-the-shelf combinations, and personal choice can be wide-ranging. More and more today all that is seen on most DZs in the U.S., and probably throughout the world, are piggyback rigs, the state-of-the-art in harness/container configuration.

In the case of "conventional" skydiving gear (back-type parachutes and front-mounted (chest-mounted) reserve parachutes), though less and less of it is seen at DZs, it is still being produced by manufacturers on a limited basis.

Numerous commercial firms produce harnesses, containers, and piggyback harness/container systems, and most of them provide descriptive literature describing the features and benefits of their products.

Information about basic harness construction can be found in Chapter 4.)

CANOPIES

Ram air canopies of every size, many design configurations, and just about any combination of colors imaginable, limited only by what fabric manufacturers are producing, are about the only type of sport parachute seen in the skies over much of the globe today. They are highly sophisticated, flexible wing "flying machines" with a wide range of characteristics. There are ram air canopies suitable for every skydiver weight, from ultralightweights right through the range of superheavyweight "flying anvils."

In addition to ram air main canopies, reserve parachute systems are produced in ram air canopy configurations.

The endless variety of model names is just as confusing as trying to figure out which manufacturer makes which car model and what a color's name is. Ram air main canopies go by such model names as Challenger, RW Challenger, Cruiselite, Cruiselite XL (for extra large), Nimbus, Nimbus Beta, Cloud, XL Cloud, Pursuit, DC-5, Strato Cloud Delta, Jalbert Parafoil 232 (representing canopy top surface area in square feet; also 252, 272, 282, 302), Raven, Super Raven, Falcon, Spirit, Wizard, Mightymak, Robo, Bogy, Astrobe, Excalibur, Cricket, Firelite, Maverick, Fury, Sharpchuter, so on and so forth. Befuddling array, isn't it?

Color patterns are just as mind-boggling: Silverado, Midnight Blues, Night Rider, Firestream, Desert Sand, Rainbow, Snowbird, Firefly, White Rainbow, Black Rainbow, Waterfall, Independence, Monarch, Snowflake, Moonlight, Stars and Stripes, Red Wine, et cetera, et cetera.

Luckily, all the manufacturers produce specification sheets for their products with such information as wing area in square feet, pack volume in cubic inches, canopy weight in pounds, maximum gross/suspended weight (re: jumper weight), number of cells, airfoil technical description, span (side-to-side measurement) in feet, chord (front-to-rear measurement) in feet, aspect ratio, construction type, crossport data, canopy fabric weight in ounces, type of reefing system, suspension line type and tensile strength, models, colors, plus copious performance data concerning forward speed, rate of descent, turn rate, and much more.

HEADGEAR

There are several types of headgear used by skydivers—but some of them use no head protection at all. Parachutists who reach a certain advanced level of experience are no longer required to wear headgear.

Full coverage helmets, such as those made by the Bell Helmet Company, are desirable for beginning student use because of the extensive head protection they provide. The type of full coverage helmet favored by motorcycle riders that has protective areas covering the mouth and chin and limits peripheral vision is not permitted for sport parachuting. Hockey-type helmets are also acceptable for student and experienced jumper use. Many skydivers wear a soft leather, snug-fitting, helmet-shaped cap that has several protruding "cushioning ribs" that are intended to provide some degree of protection—if one is not knocked in the head too hard.

FOOTWEAR

Gone are the days of calf-high, tightly laced paratrooper boots; gone are the days of thick-rubber soled "French boots" (developed by French parachutists and imported from France). Today, with slow canopy rates-of-descent and generally soft, easily tolerated landings, even first-jump students can wear only jogging-type shoes on every jump. Many experienced relative work skydivers have taken to wearing lightweight sandals because greater quickness of leg and foot movement can be had while doing sequential freefall maneuvers, yet there is still *some* foot protection when landing. Still another number of RW parachutists jump barefoot, seeking what they perceive to be the ultimate in foot-movement quickness. There are even dedicated accuracy jumpers who jump barefoot in competition to achieve ultraquickness of movement in a final split-second of an approach to a five-centimeter disc.

The point of detailing no foot protection whatsoever is that earth-shaking landings as a normal occurrence are a thing of the past. Ankles no longer need be stringently braced; footwear does not need an inch of rubber cushioning. Bare feet can readily withstand landings under current main parachute canopies.

However, having adequate foot protection should get a jumper's earnest attention because an unusual circumstance can happen on any jump—a ride under a nonsteerable reserve canopy; a high or low opening on a main canopy, possibly resulting in landing long or short of a target area; unanticipated and radical wind shifts, with the same results. Such an unexpected development could result in an unusual landing site for an unshod skydiver, say in a town dump or some such other locale.

ALTIMETERS

An altimeter is a "flight instrument" accessory carried by skydivers that shows height above the ground. Altimeters are manufactured in varied sizes and are extremely reliable. Jumpers locate them on a harness chest strap, on a harness main lift web, on a wrist, or on the back of a hand. It makes little difference and is a matter of personal preference, as long as they are always visually accessible.

Returning to the days of yesteryear in sport parachuting, jumpers used to carry an instrument panel mounted on a front-mounted reserve parachute, positioned so the faces of a stopwatch and an altimeter could be readily observed in freefall. The thinking in those days was that a surplus aircraft altimeter would not accurately show a height above the ground because its mechanism wasn't designed for rapid changes in altitude. At least that was what the talk was among parachutists of the late-'50s and early-'60s. And there was not an easy way to prove or disprove the claim. So, as a backup instrument, a stopwatch was included on the instrument panel. Figures had long since been calculated as to how far a jumper would fall for times as long as 60 seconds, and on each jump a parachutist would know, timewise, how long a freefall should be made from a specific altitude in order to open a parachute at a prescribed altitude. The watch was started at exit and both instruments were regularly observed during freefall, the watch for how long a jumper had been falling, the altimeter to show how high above the ground the jumper was. The two instruments sometimes caused great confusion to students, and in the mid-'60s, when specially designed skydiver altimeters were developed, stopwatches stopped being used.

AUTOMATIC ACTIVATION DEVICES (AADs)

Automatic activation device (AAD) is a generic term for a self-contained device to remove ripcord pins from closure devices that keep a reserve parachute closed. The automatic opening feature can be based on preset altitude, time, percentage of terminal velocity, or a combination thereof. Development for sport parachuting use began in 1959, and the first such device was patented the following year. Over many years many lives were saved using AADs. An AAD is a personal preference item that many experienced skydivers opt not to include with their gear because of concern about premature operation, particularly during freefall relative work (RW). However, many drop zones have an AAD installed on all student reserve parachutes.

(At one time an AAD was known as an *automatic opening device*; but that term was sometimes misconstrued as meaning *canopy* opening rather than the intended meaning of *container* opening. Manufacturers took to referring to their product as an *automatic activation device*, further reinforcing explanations in instructions that an AAD was merely intended to activate (begin) the opening sequence of a container under prescribed conditions.)

Any AAD is a backup device for a skydiver's own senses and actions, and problems occur when a skydiver puts total reliance on the backup device and carelessly does not pay constant attention to altitude, especially how much there is below. AADs have a good long-term reliability record, but they have occasionally malfunctioned under a variety of conditions (like any other mechanical device in any other field). Therefore, they should always be treated simply as they are intended to be—something that could give a skydiver an edge in the worst of times.

ALTITUDE WARNING DEVICES

There are several models of "beeper" instruments that are worn on a jumper's helmet that will trigger alert warnings at a preset altitude. Such devices can be most useful when a jumper's attention in freefall is on performing relative work maneuvers and rapt absorption affects total awareness, especially altitude awareness. Such instruments are easily adjustable to DZ altitude from one region to another and are becoming increasingly popular. One of the latest devices is billed as a "speaking altimeter": "Hear your altitude spoken in your ear DURING YOUR SKYDIVE. User-selected even- or odd-thousand-foot altitude announcements and alarm points. Verbal warning for internal malfunction or low battery. Available in any spoken language." High technology continues to produce remarkable skydiving products.

But, again, *beepers* and *talking altimeters* and whatever similar devices crop up in the marketplace in the future should always be thought of and put to use as a backup to a skydiver's own senses and awareness.

GLOVES

A good set of gloves is another item of personal equipment that is often overlooked as a form of protection—overlooked especially in warm weather conditions.

There are numerous other skydiving accessories, some with definite safety advantages. Numerous catalogs, folders, booklets, pamphlets, fliers, and various other sales material describe features and benefits, and manufacturers are happy to send promotional and specification information to those with inquiring minds.

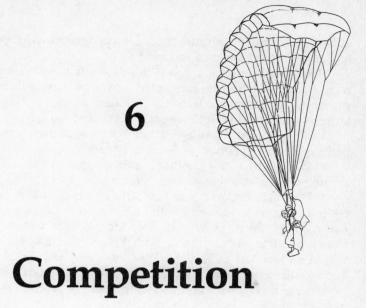

6

Competition

Most humans have a competitive streak somewhere in their complex make-up, with degrees of competitiveness ranging the gamut of possibilities. More than 60 years ago, once people got to a point of fairly well mastering the complexities of parachutes and parachuting, they sought ways of making the jumping part a tad more interesting, more challenging. Competition was one of the answers.

Since the most that nearly all early jumpers knew about parachuting was basic canopy maneuvering as a hopeful means of avoiding obstructions and hazards on the ground, it was natural for one jumper to finally bet another jumper as to who was able to get closest to a specified target.

Then, as parachuting for recreation and sport grew in popularity (there are those who consider that an activity is not a *sport* unless some aspect of competition is included), competition evolved from accuracy only to the new skydiving activities also—"style" (aerial maneuvers in freefall); RW, formations in freefall by two or more skydivers; CRW, canopy relative work, flying open canopies in formations; and para-skiing, combining skills in separate *accuracy parachuting* and alpine *giant slalom ski racing* events resulting in a combined score for a wintertime competition.

BRIEF CHRONOLOGY OF PARACHUTING COMPETITION

1926. Joe Crane, a pioneer barnstorming parachutist and parachute rigger, suggested a change to the organizing committee of the Pulitzer Races (forerunner of the National Air Races). Parachute demonstration jumps were to be part of the major aviation event, held in Philadelphia, and Crane thought a "spot jumping" contest would have more spectator appeal and draw more jumpers. That meet appears to have been the first recognized parachute competition.

1930. The Russians, a sports-minded nation with a vast number of recreational parachutists, conducted a parachute meet during one of the country's many sports festivals. Civilian amateurs competed to determine who could land closest to a designated target.

1932. Joe Crane organized a nationally sanctioned parachuting competition for the National Air Races at Roosevelt Field, New York.

1951. Five European countries participated in the First World Parachuting Championships in Bled, Yugoslavia.

1954. The U.S. participated in its first international parachuting competition, but with only one entrant: Sergeant Fred Mason, of the U.S. Army. The event was the Second World Parachuting Championships at St. Yan, France, with seven countries taking part. Sgt. Mason ranked 21st of 31 competitors. An international committee then decided that world parachuting championships would be held biennially in even-numbered years and that sites would be selected by sponsor bidding.

1955. The National Air Races in Philadephia had a "jump-to-the-line" contest. The target for competitors was a straight line measuring 100 feet long. A contestant was scored by distance from the line *anywhere along its length!* Two competitors separated by inches on the scoreboard could have been as much as one hundred feet apart along the line.

1956. A U.S. parachute team—the first—using borrowed equipment, took part in the Third World Parachuting Championships in Moscow, Russia. Twelve of the limited number of recognized parachutists in the country were contacted to take part in tryouts. Six responded, and trials began early in the year. Team members were selected by Jacques Istel, the guiding force behind a team formed with private sector support only. At the close of the world meet, the team ranked sixth of the 10 competing countries, not bad for a group that had never been in competition, and one of its members had fewer than 10 jumps at the start of tryouts.

1957. *April*: The first intercollegiate parachute meet was held at a farm in Woodbury, Connecticut. A several-page document detailed the specifics of competition regarding several aspects of an accuracy event and further introduced a "Style"event, replete with its own complex scoring details, though maneuvers were only rudimentary. The number of individuals representing various colleges and universities was limited and scores were wide-ranging. A second, larger meet was held in October.

August: Fifty-one male and female parachutists from 10 countries took part in the First Adriatic Cup Invitational Parachuting Championship held in Tivat, Yugoslavia. Five men constituted the U.S. Team, and Joe Crane was on the three-member judging staff. (After a layoff of 20 years, Crane made his 689th jump, into the Adriatic Sea.)

October: The second intercollegiate meet, now sponsored and supervised by the newly named and reorganized Parachute Club of America (PCA), had 19 competitors representing 11 collegiate schools.

1958. Tryouts for the U.S. Parachute Team were held in Vancouver, British Columbia, Canada during June. During this time, "relative work"(RW) was conceived when two Americans accomplished the first "baton pass", one jumper passing a short length of wood to another jumper during freefall. Later in the year, two American college students made the first baton pass in the U.S. Twenty-one civilians and 11 military personnel were selected to train for and participate in elimination competitions to make up the final American parachute team and alternates. The U.S. Army had approved support of sport parachuting, and the team included civilian and military members. The U.S. competed at the Fourth World Parachuting Championships in August at Bratislava, Czechoslovakia, finishing sixth of 14 nations taking part. Competition rules became more complex, with the Official Rules and Regulations of the world meet having 77 items defined. The quality of judging improved steadily as more competitions took place at every level in every country.

1959. The Parachute Club of America (PCA) developed a 22-part set of official regulations for PCA-sanctioned competitions.

1960. U.S. Parachute Team tryouts were held at Fort Bragg, North Carolina, with 13 civilians also competing. U.S. Army parachutists ultimately made up the entire seven-member team, including, for the first time, two women. The U.S. competed at the Fifth World Parachuting Championships at Sofia, Bulgaria. Jim Arender won the first Gold Medal for the U.S. as World Champion of Style, and the first "dead center" in a world championship was scored by American Dick Fortenberry.

1962. The U.S. hosted the Sixth World Parachuting Championships. They were held at Jacques Istel's Orange Sport Parachute Center in north-central Massachusetts. Twenty-four nations competed, and for the first time, the U.S. fielded a full team of women. "Round"canopies were still state-of-the-art equipment, but by now commercially produced "calendared" parachute fabric was being used to make a low porosity (LoPo) canopy. The result was a noticeably slower rate of descent and a much improved (flatter) glide angle, both features of substantial benefit to U.S. Team accuracy competitors. Though accuracy ("precision landing" by international competition definition) had improved through skill betterment and equipment advances, officials still set the maximum measurable distance at 100 feet.

The winning time for a full *style series* was just under nine seconds, with most times in the 10- to 12-second range. American parachutists's skills had improved considerably; the U.S. Team won 10 medals of the 27 awarded for individual and team events. Americans Muriel Simbro and Jim Arender were Overall World Champions.

Fig. 6-1. *A European competitor misses the "dead center" disc during the 6th World Parachuting Championships held in Orange, Massachusetts in August 1962. The distance is considered "really close" for those times. The dead center disc was about 10 inches in diameter and competitors were measured to a distance of 100 feet.*

1964. The Para-Commander, a high-performance round canopy of radical design, had been introduced and refined since the 6th WPC. The U.S. Team selected it for accuracy use and dazzled spectators and participants at the Seventh World Parachuting Championships, in Leutkirch, West Germany. Thirty-one countries sent 170 competitors, including 39 women. Americans Dick Fortenberry and Tee Taylor were Overall World Champions. Taylor was also Women's Style Champion. The U.S. Team brought home seven medals. A high point of the U.S. Team achievements was the First Place national standing of the Women's Team.

1966. For political reasons, the U.S., as well as other nations, did not compete in the Eighth World Parachuting Championships. However, 109 contestants (36 of them women) from 18 countries did enter the meet, held in Leipzig, East Germany.

1968. With quiet on political fronts, the Ninth World Parachuting Championships returned to widespread international participation. Twenty-six nations sent 129 men and 53 women to the meet in Graz, Austria. Competition was tough, and the U.S. Team garnered only five medals. However, national standings were impressive for the U.S.— Men, First Place; Women, Second Place.

1970. Four-way ("four-person") relative work (RW) was introduced as a competitive event at the U.S. National Parachuting Championships at Plattsburgh, New York. The object of four-way was to form a circle (a "speed star") as quickly as possible, timed from exit of the first skydiver from the plane until the last person entered the formation. In the Tenth World Parachuting Championships at Bled, Yugoslavia, 28 nations competed (with 129 men and 54 women entrants), and American Don Rice became the men's World Accuracy Champion. An American RW team made demonstration jumps at the 10th WPC and RW was on its way.

1972. Ten-way relative work became a competitive event at the U.S. Nationals in Tahlequah, Oklahoma. The objective was a *speed star*, timed like a four-way formation described above. The U.S. hosted the Eleventh World Parachuting Championships, this time in Tahlequah, Oklahoma. There were 187 competitors (including 42 females) representing 31 nations. U.S. Team member Clayton Schoepple became Absolute World Champion (Men).

1973. The Commission Internationale de Parchutisme (CIP) accepted RW as an event for international sport parachute meets.

1974. In the Twelfth World Parachuting Championship, which was held in Szolnok, Hungary, 30 nations competed, with 221 contestants, including 70 women. Europeans fared best in individual events, winning most of the medals. The U.S. Team (Men) won a Bronze Medal for team accuracy. In national standings, the U.S. Team (Men) was second. Later in the year, a new activity was added to skydiving; the first para-ski meet was held at Steamboat Springs, Colorado.

1976. Canopy relative work (CRW) demonstrated at the U.S. Nationals in Tahlequah, Oklahoma, as a form of "stunt flying" with parachutes.

More than a hundred 10-way teams entered an RW meet, which was held in Zephyrhills, Florida.

1977. The CIP adopted eight-way *sequential* RW as an event for international sport parachute meets.

1980. The United States Parachute Association (USPA) adopted rules for National Para-Ski Championships, after having been annual events at local and regional levels for several years. Biennial para-ski world championships were planned as a regular international event.

1981. An RW World Parachuting Championships was hosted by a commercial DZ in Zephryhills, Florida.

1982. CRW was introduced as an event at the U.S. National Parachuting Championships. CRW had its first World Cup competition this year.

1988. A select team of skydivers participated in an artfully presented eight-minute segment of the opening ceremonies of the Olympic Games held in Seoul, Korea. Skydivers everywhere were elated by the prospect that skydiving would become a demonstration sport in the 1992 Olympic Games and ultimately become a full-fledged Olympic sport.

STARTING IN COMPETITION

Competition is an important part of skydiving, though there are many parachutists who find little appeal in the pressure of competing with someone else or even against a given standard, such as striving for an achievement award. Students particularly often would, at least early on, prefer to make a *fun* jump without the stress of being evaluated. After all, a student recently approved for jumping on his or her own has been through an arduous spell of evaluation, criticism, correction, and more evaluation. A break is needed, a time to enjoy the fruits of long labor; however, many clubs and commercial DZs run special low-key novice competitions and encourage participation, knowing full well that a touch of competitiveness helps bring out the best in a novice's abilities, with resultant improved skills.

THE SCOPE OF COMPETITION

As noted at the beginning of this chapter, there is an element of competition in every aspect of sport parachuting: individual accuracy, team accuracy, style, RW, CRW, and para-skiing.

Individual Accuracy

Individual accuracy was the first competitive parachuting event, going back to the 1930s, and even today is the mainstay of most parachuting competitions. One reason is it requires the least amount of altitude to carry on a meet, ranging from a low of 2,000 feet for USPA "D" license holders to 2,800 feet for static line students. A second reason is that jumps from lower altitudes cost less. Many accuracy contests often permit students on static line training to be in the novice event of a meet.

Accuracy is simple to practice—it can be done on every jump. Even if a customary target area cannot be reached (perhaps because of a spotting error, or because of a wind shift), an accuracy-minded jumper finds an alternate target (*anything*) and goes for it.

At many DZs, serious accuracy jumpers often get a mini-meet going among themselves, usually in preparation for an upcoming formal competition, losers paying a dollar or so to the winner or buying the winner's beer at the local watering hole after the jumping day is over.

The beginning objective of accuracy is not to "stomp the dead center disc," but simply to get proficient enough to achieve consistency in getting close to a target area ("the pit"). The next goal is consistently getting *into* the pit, followed by consistently touching down in the immediate vicinity of a scoring pad (usually one with a five-centimeter disc in the center of a thirty-centimeter target). With contact on a scoring pad being regularly made, it's then time for utmost concentration and exercise of skills recently learned, time to press harder, to go for the minuscule five-centimeter disc. Currently, a five-centimeter disc on a thirty-centimeter electronic scoring pad is used at the annual U.S. National Parachuting Championships, and five centimeters is the standard dead center disc size in international competitions also. However, in training at many home DZs, dedicated accuracy parachutists practice with a three-centimeter disc. Except for novice and intermediate events, the maximum distance measured for scoring in most meets is five meters (a bit over 16 feet). Anything beyond that is considered an "OUT."

Getting dead centers or staying in close range consistently is not a simple accomplishment. It is not learned in two or three jumps, or in a dozen. It might require 25 to 50 jumps, or more. A parachutist striving for success in accuracy competitions must master his or her particular canopy, learning the ultrafine points of its handling characteristics. A great number of jumps must be made under varying conditions and in the shortest possible amount of time. "Trimming" the canopy for best performance has to be learned, as does discovering at what point the canopy stalls and loses forward movement—and how well and quickly it recovers. In addition, learning how to achieve maximum "sink" without losing canopy control is most important to a consummate accuracy performer.

Understanding wind velocity (velocity refers to speed *and* direction, not speed *only*) is critical to an accuracy jumper's success. If the wind is not understood, there is little hope for a disc strike. Wind conditions in an accuracy meet can vary widely—ranging from light and variable winds without definite direction to suddenly stronger winds, gusts, wind shears (a point at which winds sharply change direction, often to a great degree), thermals (causing unwanted lift), and several direction variances between opening altitude and the target area.

Fig. 6-2. Judges in a training session watch a simulation of an accuracy competitor's "first point of body contact." The scoring pad shown is about 12 inches in diameter, and the "dead center" disc is 10 centimeters across. However, the dead center disc has been reduced to five centimeters (two inches) in diameter, the size used in national and international competitions. Many accuracy jumpers practice with a three-centimeter disc (just over one inch across.)

Nonetheless, good accuracy jumpers—even in small, local competitions, even in practice—can step on the disc time after time. At one National in recent years, two jumpers were tied at 10 dead centers each at the end of the scheduled 10-jump accuracy event. A "jump-off" was started and more than a dozen more consecutive dead centers were registered by each competitor before a Men's National Accuracy Champion was determined when one competitor scored four centimeters, immediately followed by the incoming jumper scoring only three centimeters.

Team Accuracy

Team accuracy is simply an extension of individual accuracy, with a team's score being the total distance from target center for all team members. A team can have any number of jumpers on it, but customary formal competitions call for four-member teams, each with a team captain. All jumpers exit an aircraft on the same jump run, usually at an altitude of 3,500 feet, spacing exits and canopy deployment times to achieve a "stack" of canopies at different altitudes (e.g., first jumper, 10-second

Fig. 6-3. *Judges at a formal competition move in to mark an accuracy competitor's contact as he maneuvers his Para-Commander continuously until landing.*

delay; second jumper, 6-second delay; third jumper, 3-second delay; fourth jumper, jump-and-pull). Freefall times can vary, based on individual jumper weights, types of canopies used, and so forth, with team members responsible for determining their stack, designed to avoid interference among team members during the descent and on final approach to the target area and the disc. Competition rejumps are not allowed due to canopy conflict among team members while landing. During one recent practice session, a five-member team scored a total distance of two centimeters—four dead centers and a two-centimeter jump.

Needless to say, such results are the product of superior individual skills plus team members often jumping together as a unit.

Style

"Style" refers to the manner in which a competitor can perform a set of six turns while in freefall. The objective of a style jump is to complete the series of simple maneuvers as quickly and precisely as possible.

Fig. 6-4. *Veteran skydiver John Spear does a fine job demonstrating accuracy on an exhibition jump. Subsequently this skilled parachutist captured the 1989 Men's Individual Accuracy Champion title at the U.S. National Skydiving Championships in Muskogee, Oklahoma in August 1989. Spear's total distance from the five-centimeter target on 10 successive jumps from approximately 2,500 feet was only two centimeters (0.00; 0.00; 0.00; 0.01; 0.00; 0.00; 0.00; 0.00).*

A style jump consists of a skydiver exiting an aircraft, tucking into a tightly compressed diving position ("fall-away") so as to build speed rapidly, then performing two 360-degree horizontal-plane turns, then a backloop (a 360-degree vertical-plane turn), followed by two more 360-degree horizontal turns, and concluding with a second backloop.

"International series" are the basis for national and international competitions and are also prescribed for many lower levels of competitions as a means of preparing for the higher-level meets. There are three categories of international series:

- Right Series RT-LT-BL-RT-LT-BL
- Left Series LT-RT-BL-LT-RT-BL
- Cross Series RT-LT-BL-LT-RT-BL

Imagine what it would be like to leave a plane at 6,600 feet to do a right series. Get into a fall-away position for eight to ten seconds until you reach a speed of 120 miles or so an hour. Start your maneuvers. Next, a 360-degree turn to the right, *stopping on heading.* Don't overshoot, it costs time; don't undershoot or penalty points are assessed. Make a similar turn to the left, again *on heading,* Backloop; and come out of it smoothly into a left turn, stop *on heading.* Make a quick right turn, and stop *on heading;* now, another backloop. Coming out of the loop, start out of the tightly tucked body position, then flare to slow your speed and ease the force of opening. Deploy your parachute.

All this takes place in far less time than taken to read this. World records have times of less than six seconds. When style was first performed in international competition a set series of ground panels were used to signal a jumper in freefall as to which style set series was to be performed. When a competitior had reached the tenth second of freefall, signal panels would be shown for five seconds, at which point the style jumper would commence aerial maneuvers.

Many problems were encountered with this method, for competitors and judges alike, and it simply became a matter of deciding beforehand which series was to be done for each style round. Jumpers would then go to altitude and exit, and judges would be observant from the exit throughout the canopy opening.

Judging style was difficult at first, but it was gradually made easier as equipment was modified and developed to make observation and decision-making easier. It got its start by a judge sprawled on his or her back, peering upward through hand-held powerful binoculars at a small figure more than 6,000 feet overhead as it left a plane and fell.

The figure took a predesignated heading, and the judge had to observe turns, noting overshoots (which cost the competitor time) and undershoots (which cost the jumper penalty points for incompleteness); and points were assessed for exceeding a 25-second working time allowance (to avoid letting a jumper get into a low-altitude opening situation).

In time, tripod-mounted telemeters (high-powered binocular optics) came into use, offering superior observation.

Methods of judging improved through evolution, and very often today, as at the annual U.S. National Championships, style maneuvers

Fig. 6-5. *In the early 1960s ''style'' judging was primitive: a stopwatch taped to binoculars to time maneuvers in freefall; a second hand-held stopwatch to clock amount of a competitor's freefall time from aircraft exit to pilot chute deployment, checking for violation of a 25-second time limit; a supine position on the ground for the judge; something for a headrest; plus a recorder to write notes about a judge's penalty calls and other comments.*

are videotaped, using ground-to-air equipment. This enables the judging staff to more carefully evaluate and reexamine a competitor's freefall work.

Relative Work

Jumpers work together in freefall to perform RW formations—from a simple round-shaped "star"(See #1 in FIG. 6-7) for beginning RW parachutists, advancing, with experience, to complex shapes ("stair step," "arrowhead," "donut," "double diamond," and many others, numbering many jumpers). The current world record for largest freefall formation had 144 male and female jumpers on it. It was accomplished in August 1988, after multiple attempts over several days, using a C-130 Hercules aircraft.

Other skydivers prefer "sequential" maneuvers, where jumpers falling at about 120 mph (approximately 175 feet per second) move swiftly from one shape to another to another to another, rapidly changing the formation's configuration. Each completed formation is considered one point, and RW groups strive for as many points as possible in a specified

Fig. 6-6. *A judge uses a telemeter to observe a ''style'' jumper's freefall maneuvers and calls them out to a recorder who records turns made, times, penalties, and other judge's comments. The judge is also using a portable tape recorder (note cable, recording device, and microphone secured to the tripod) as a backup for the written notes.*

amount of working time, based on exit altitude and safely spaced, predesignated individual canopy openings from 3,500 feet down to 2,500 feet, depending on the number of skydivers in the group.

Canopy Relative Work (CRW)

Canopy relative work (CRW) is intentionally flying two or more ram air canopies in proximity or in actual contact from canopy opening and during descent.

CRW started as something for freefall RW jumpers to do after deploying parachutes. To them it was simply an extension of what they had been doing in freefall. CRW soon had a growing number of adherents, and manufacturers came to their aid by producing canopies with special flying characteristics to suit CRW conditions. Experienced CRW parachutists can fly tightly spaced parachute canopies one above

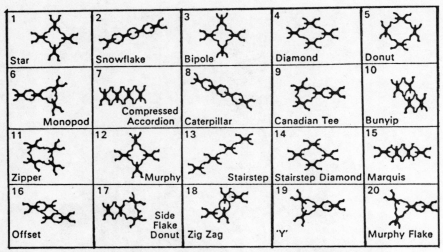

Fig. 6-7. *Some of many "four-way" relative work freefall formations.*

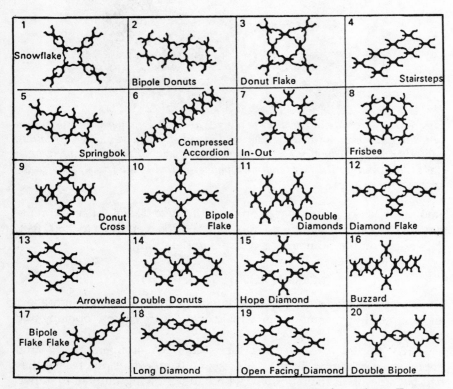

Fig. 6-8. *Several of numerous "eight-way" competition formations. Ten-way, 12-way, and 20-way formations are also made as part of "fun" relative work sky-dives, depending on aircraft availability.*

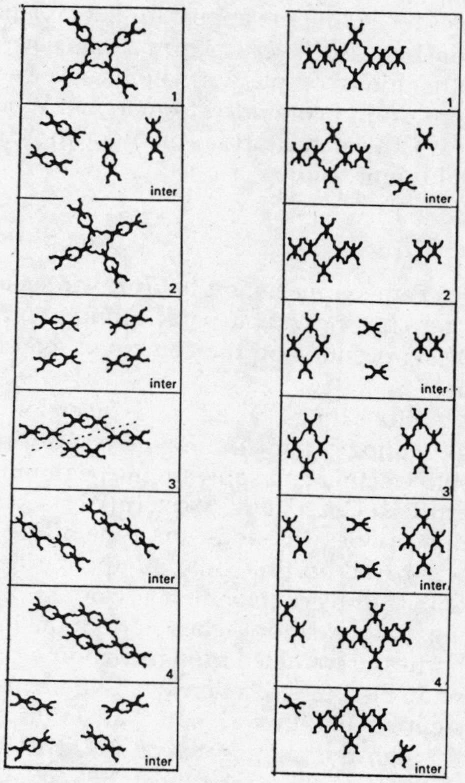

Fig. 6-9. Examples of "four-point", eight-way sequential relative work.

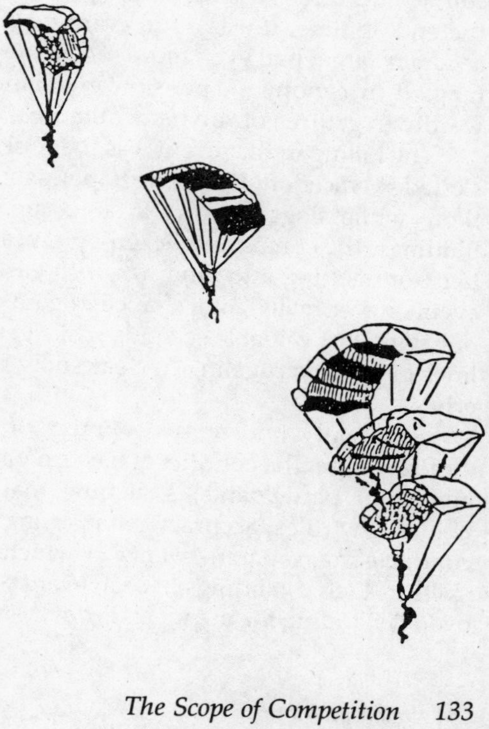

Fig. 6-10. Three jumpers have completed a canopy relative work "triplane" formation. The other two parachutists will, in turn, sink their canopies to lower altitudes, then each, in turn, will manuever into the formation from below to make a "five stack."

another, giving the appearance of biplane and triplane aircraft wing relationships. Such vertical formations have thus far exceeded 30 in number. Other more complex formations have been made in horizontal configurations and in combined formations. When performed by the best of the best CRW parachutists, many of the complex formations can be flown right until landing.

Para-Skiing

Para-ski meets are held in winter months, with scores given separately for individual parachuting accuracy and giant slalom alpine ski racing events, and the combined scores used to determine overall winners.

Para-skiing started as a diversion so jumpers could forestall any dwindling of parachuting interest during an "off season" brought on by cold weather and snow. In the beginning, there were two formats: "Eastern/East Coast" and "Western/West Coast." East Coast para-skiing was a nonserious, "hit-and-run" type of meet, in which a competitor's score was based on time only. Jumpers exited an aircraft, wearing ski boots, with the object of landing as close as possible to a target center. On landing, judges' stopwatches started; the jumper scrambled out of his or her harness; scrambled from the landing point to touch the dead center disc; scrambled to a location where personal skis were laid out, ready to be stepped into; then skied hastily to the slalom course starting line, darted through the many gates of a NASTAR-type giant slalom downhill race course and across the finish line where other judges' watches recorded the ending time. It was a fun event for contestants, but spectators at the accuracy target had even more fun as they watched hapless skydivers get tangled in canopy suspension lines as they tried hurriedly and awkwardly to get free of the parachute rig.

The failing in that event was that a skilled parachutist who was also a skilled ski racer often became hopelessly snarled in suspension lines and then, while slogging from a target area to the site for getting into ski bindings, the contestant picked up excessive snow that prevented him or her from getting into bindings with ease. Thus, a person skilled in two events never really got a chance to gain a good meet time solely because of having lost valuable seconds while getting untangled from suspension lines or while struggling to clear snow to make ski bindings work properly.

After only one or two winters of spectator-pleasing para-ski hit-and-run-type, the conduct of Eastern para-ski meets was changed for the benefit of participants, switching to the Western/West Coast format. Under new rules, accuracy parachuting and giant slalom ski racing were conducted as separate events in which competitors could truly display skills in each. Standings in each event were then combined to achieve an overall standing for the meet. From that point on, para-skiing burgeoned into a popular competitor activity for seasoned parachutists. However, participation was limited to contestants qualified to make exhibition-type jumps into DZs of limited size because activity took place on the slopes of downhill ski areas with potential hazards usually close by.

All these various parachuting competitive events take place at regional and national levels in countries around the globe, culminating in World Meets that usually bring a dozen or more countries together.

7

United States
Parachute Association
(USPA)

The United States Parachute Association (USPA) is a voluntary membership organization, with membership open to any individual, and consists primarily of persons interested in general aviation and the art and science of sport parachuting/skydiving. USPA's current active membership roster includes doctors, lawyers, government officials, airline pilots, construction workers, business owners, police officers, plumbers, mechanics, writers, military personnel, students, computer programmers, secretaries, insurance executives, psychologists, on and on and on.

USPA is incorporated as a nonprofit association; owners are the individual members, each owning an equal share. Ownership includes an equal voice and an equal responsibility.

USPA is a division of the National Aeronautic Association (NAA), the official skydiving representative of the Federation Aéronautiqué Internationalé (FAI) in the United States—and, very important, USPA is officially recognized by the FAA as the representative of skydivers in the United States. USPA also serves as a national representative body for parachute riggers and the parachute industry.

Here are highlight activities of today's United States Parachute Association:

- Promotes safety in parachuting and establishes safety standards and recommended procedures for safe jumping.
- Promotes and sanctions competitive sport parachuting and establishes standards for competition.
- Supervises and officially documents all record attempts in the field of parachuting.
- Encourages the study and knowledge of parachuting among the membership and the general public.
- Compiles, edits, and publishes monthly information regarding the sport and science of parachuting.
- In order to promote public safety, cooperates with all governmental agencies dealing with aeronautics.
- Selects and trains the United States Skydiving Team for international sport parachuting competition (See Chapter 6).
- Fosters and encourages development of parachuting as an intercollegiate sport through its affiliate, the National Collegiate Parachuting League (NCPL).
- Cooperates with other sporting and general aviation groups within the United States.

USPA benefits include:

- Public liability/property damage insurance.
- *Parachutist* magazine monthly. (See Chapter 8.)
- Representation at all levels of government.
- Eligibility for USPA- and NCPL-sanctioned competitions.
- Discount on NAA membership.
- Eligibility for membership in USPA-affiliated clubs.
- Eligibility for US/FAI parachuting licenses.
- USPA insignia and credentials.
- Guidance and assistance in all parachuting activities.

USPA has a long history, and its present name is the fourth in a series, each adopted to reflect the nature of the organization at various times. Its first name was National Parachute Jumpers Association (NPJA), when it was formed by Joe Crane and a small group of dedicated parachute jumping enthusiasts in 1932, with a headquarters of sorts in a suburb of New York City. Crane's goal was to gain recognition of parachuting as a professional aviation endeavor and to enhance the credibility of parachute jumpers in those times of widespread aviation barnstorming activities of every type. Crane wanted to band jumpers together so they could speak and act as a united group of professional-caliber parachutists and effectively deal with air show sponsors, other aviation organizations, and federal aeronautic agencies.

Crane had another purpose, too: to establish parachute jumping as an organized sport. He knew what the Russians had accomplished in their country and had similar hopes for America. Competition parachuting had been going on in the United States for several years, and the roster of competitors was growing at each of the hugely popular, successive national air shows (the Cleveland Air Races in 1929 lasted ten days).

As soon as Crane had formed the NPJA, a few nonjumping parachute riggers also joined; they liked the idea of "strength in numbers." So many persons started getting the then new federal parachute rigger's certificate and joined NPJA that the organization changed its name to reflect growing participation by parachute riggers, becoming the National Parachute Jumpers-Riggers Association (NPJRA) in 1947 and set up headquarters in Mineola, Long Island, another New York City suburb.

In the mid-1950s sport parachuting experienced a surge in popularity, and membership in the national parachuting organization grew steadily each year. With the great number of small groups of aficionados throughout the country, in 1957 the national organization changed its name to Parachute Club of America (PCA).

Headquarters was relocated again—this time to Mount Kisco, New York, a few miles north of New York City.

In 1968, with the growing national organization now with headquarters in Monterey, California, the final name change was made. Parachuting had become a mature sport, one with widespread activity and with an image-conscious membership. The membership opted for United States Parachute Association (USPA), a description that now seemed more fitting than one with a connotation of smallness, limited participation, and occasional activity. In 1976 USPA moved its headquarters east to a rented site in Washington, D.C., primarily to be close to the seat of federal government. The final move for the organization came in May of 1982, when USPA Headquarters was established in its own building in Alexandria, Virginia, only 10 minutes from the nation's capital.

Throughout name changes, the national organization's original objectives remained unchanged: to promote and organize parachute jumping as a sport and to have it be a safe, enjoyable, and satisfying form of recreation. As federal, state, and local governments persistently attempted to impose undue regulation, and in many cases to ban parachuting, the then PCA worked harder on behalf of its membership to resist regulation excesses and prohibitions. Also, PCA wanted to make it possible for members to acquire insurance at reasonable cost. To achieve that goal, it became necessary to establish standards for safe parachuting operations and methods for training beginners safely.

The first standards were termed "Basic Safety Regulations" (BSRs) (later *Regulations* became *Requirements*, as they are known today) and were complemented by training recommendations (doctrines) and by *license* and *rating* systems.

USPA is unique because the participants in the activity set their own standards and regulate themselves. *No other branch of civil aviation has that distinction.* At one time ultralight aircraft users controlled themselves, but they are now regulated by the FAA because of a demonstrated inability to effectively self-regulate. USPA steadily reminds its members that self-regulation is voluntary and depends on a collective desire for survival. In essence, it's a case of monitoring themselves so they "don't kill the goose that lays golden eggs."

Because skydiving is self-regulating, the USPA organization has been able to have rules flexible enough to keep pace with the sport's evolution—and those rules are established and modified by the USPA membership through its democratic participation in their national organization.

USPA operates under a constitution and bylaws, and it has a structure much like business corporations. There is an all-volunteer Board of Directors (BoD) that establishes USPA policies and procedures by means of a majority vote at BoD meetings held twice a year. The BoD comprises eight National Directors and 14 Conference Directors, the latter representing geographic regions, with all directors elected by the membership at large. A representative of the NAA is also an *ex officio* member of the board. The officers of the BoD are selected by board members and include a chairman (though the position is not restricted to males), president, vice president, secretary, and treasurer.

The officers, together with an elected member-at-large, constitute an Executive Committee that makes decisions and attends to important matters that arise between semiannual BoD meetings.

The BoD operates through a committee system; small committees of BoD members with special qualifications and interests offer advice and guidance concerning major activities of sport parachuting.

USPA's national headquarters site is in Alexandria, Virginia, just outside Washington, D.C. The headquarters houses an administrative staff that takes care of day-to-day business.

An Executive Director hired by the BoD manages the headquarters' operations and is given a variety of duties and responsibilities by the BoD. Besides clerical personnel, the administrative staff includes a Director of Publications and a Director of Training.

All in all, the job of headquarters' staff is to carry out instructions and policies of the Board of Directors, and the BoD has the purpose of following the members' wishes.

As would be expected of a mature organization, the USPA has reached a notable level of sophistication, and its efforts and achievements are well received by the membership and by other organizations in the various aviation communities.

8

Parachuting Literature

A substantial field of written material is available from which a beginning parachutist can readily learn more about the ultimate in free flight—skydiving. Over the nearly four decades since parachuting took hold as a sport in the U.S., a number of hopeful parachuting periodicals have been published. Some lasted briefly, others were produced for several years, others came and went, others appeared and continue today, and one has persisted since late-1957. Also, a goodly number of worthwhile books were produced to provide state-of-the-art information about quickly changing techniques and vastly improved products.

PERIODICALS

Despite high hopes, most of the periodicals, as good and useful as they were, for one reason or another, fell by the wayside. However, one stalwart effort has become a venerable publication; and a second shows promise of being around for quite a while.

Parachutist

Since its first eight-page, black-and-white, glossy paper, illustrated issue of September 1957, *Parachutist* has been the official publication of the United States Parachute Association (USPA). The magazine, published monthly, is 8½ × 11 inches in size, is printed on high-quality, glossy stock, contains many full-color photographs, and has at least 50 pages in each issue. Each edition contains new feature articles and regular "Departments" (Letters—Paragrams—At Presstime—Calendar—Wings and Things—Donors—Licenses/Ratings/Awards—Incident Reports—Group Members—Classified Ads). The yearly subscription cost of

$21.50 (United States, FPOs, and APOs) is included in annual USPA membership dues.

Skydiving

A tabloid-format monthly newspaper published in DeLand, Florida, *Skydiving* began publishing in 1979. It provides up-to-date news, editorials, feature articles, technical information, calendars, equipment, meet results, and regular information columns for sport parachutists. Publisher Michael Truffer is a veteran, highly skilled sport parachutist with a lot of jumps in his logbook and many parachuting accomplishments to his credit. *Skydiving* is packed with all kinds of good stuff for students who want to know more about the new, exciting sport in which they are now involved. The basic subscription rate is $16 for twelve issues and can be considered money well spent for both beginning sport parachutists and experienced skydivers.

BOOKS

Skies Call, Andy Keech[0] Skies Call, P.O. Box 57238, Washington, D.C. 20037 (Photographic essays published in three successive editions.).

Skies Call started as a one-time venture for Andy Keech, with a goal of providing skydivers with a lasting memento of the beauty, grace, color, and excitement of sport parachuting. Keech garnered a great number of color photographs about every aspect of skydiving, carefully pored over them, sifted and resifted, and ultimately grouped 150 high-quality photographs and brief descriptive passages into a 136-page, hardbound, oversize book that would be a permanent reminder.

His work received widespread acclaim, and, in time, there were calls for more such excellence. Keech responded with *Skies Call 2*, which was full of more wonderful photographic viewpoints of skydiving depicting new high-performance, colorful canopies and freefall formations of greater size and complexity.

With Skies 3, Keech produced his third photographic work with a greater number of illustrations than its predecessors, equally colorful, equally imaginative, equally worth having in one's skydiving library.

Parachuting Folklore—The Evolution of Freefall Michael Horan; Parachuting Resources, Richmond, Indiana, 1980 (167 pages, illustrated, $7^1/8'' \times 8^1/2''$, softcover).

The author of this information-packed work is now a doctoral student living in Florida and attending to studies for a doctorate in education. For the time being he has put full-scale parachuting activity on hold. However, as he can, he still gets to a nearby DZ for a soul-satisfying leap and to keep in touch with skydiver friends.

Horan began parachuting in 1963 while in the U.S. Marine Corps. Since that time he has logged over 2,500 jumps, become an FAA Master

Parachute Rigger, and held positions in the parachute industry testing and developing various systems. He is a longtime USPA member, holds a Class D (Expert) license, Jumpmaster and Instructor ratings, Diamond Wings (2,000 freefall jumps), and Gold Freefall Badge (twelve hours of accumulated freefall time). Also, he is USPA's Archivist and a former member of the USPA Board of Directors.

His book has stories about men and women who made parachute jumps for a variety of reasons—for the fun of it, to make money, in defense of their country, or to satisfy a competitive spirit.

Included in his book are many thoroughly interesting accounts:

- Balloonists who, for nearly 200 years, used smoke-filled bags to lift themselves high into the sky, then leaped from their aerial platform with all sorts of parachutes. Advertising their planned events brought flocks of curious spectators, and the fame of exhibition parachute jumpers spread quickly.
- A long look at the life of Joe Crane, perhaps the one person, who from the 1930s onward, did the most to elevate the risky endeavors of post-World War One barnstorming parachutists (often using the crudest equipment) from recklessness to the extraordinary sophistication of present-day sport parachute techniques and gear.
- Icarus, Charles A. Lindbergh, Leo Valentin, Käthe Paulus, Clem Sohn, Georgia "Tiny" Broadwick, Jacques-André Garnerin, Charlie Dame, Leslie Irvin, Roy "Red" Grant, Arthur Starnes, Jacques-André Istel, the Montgolfier brothers, Lew Sanborn, Muriel Simbro, Lt. Harold R. Harris, and Cheryl Stearns make only a handful of other parachuting achievers studied to varying degrees throughout *Parachuting Folklore*.
- Beyond folklore, Mike Horan presents a long, detailed, factual narrative about an Ohio city that was made well known by the Wright brothers: *Dayton: Cradle of U.S. Parachuting*. In 1918 McCook Field became the hub of activity for developing a parachute for use by crew members in aircraft emergencies. For the next 10 years McCook Field was a major parachute development and testing center. What was learned there was disseminated into the military and civilian parachuting communities. Thereafter, rapid strides were made in safety and techniques.

Index to Parachuting: 1900–1975/An Annotated Bibliography, Michael Horan; Parachuting Resources, Richmond, Indiana, 1979 (173 pages, illustrated, 5^1/$_2$" × 8^1/$_2$", softcover).

Mike Horan's first-published book can be considered the best single source for anyone seeking information about parachutes, parachuting, people involved in parachute history, technical information, techniques, a variety of analyses, so on and so forth. It is an especially valuable publication for researchers, writers, and historians.

What Horan has done is compile an index of more than 2,500 articles that have been published in periodical publications, articles related to just about every aspect of parachuting, including poetry and making your own canopy. After a brief history of parachuting, there is both a thorough listing of the addresses of periodicals indexed and an explanation of how to gain access to material cited in the index.

The index is divided into 59 categories, with several of them having subcategories. Some of the categories are: Accuracy, Aerodynamic Decelerators, Automatic Openers, Collegiate Parachuting, Competition, Equipment, Helmets, High Altitude Parachuting, Humor, Instructing, Jumpmastering, Night Parachuting, Para-Skiing, Psychology, Relative Work, Rigging, Safety, Water Parachuting, Women, World Championships.

Horan's bibliography matches the scope of the rest of his work; it lists 158 books published about many facets of parachuting.

One reviewer noted, ". . . immensely valuable . . . a public, school, or industry aeronautical library would be remiss in not having Horan's book in its science/technology reference section."

Parachuting: The Art of Freefall Relative Work, Pat Works; Aero-Graphics, DeLand, Florida, 1988 (230 pages, 5¹/₂″ × 8¹/₂″, softbound).

The first edition of this outstanding publication dealing exclusively with relative work (RW)—one of the most difficult, complex, and satisfying elements of sport parachuting—was published in 1975. At that time it was the result of 15 years of experience and 4 years of research and writing.

That 160-page book was copiously illustrated with fine diagrams, line art, and 17 black-and-white photographs. Its 15 chapters clearly explained how freefall relative work could best be learned quickly. Many skydivers studied and heeded the authoritative book (which quickly became known as "the relative worker's bible") and were the beneficiaries of the backgrounds and lucidity of the author.

A revised edition has since been published, crammed with information for both the beginning RW worker and skydivers using advanced techniques. This edition includes chapters about equipment, body positions, basic maneuvers, aircraft exits, "swooping," docking, flying a formation, four-person competition, large and *really* large formations, "how-to" techniques, and something new—"sky dancing," exquisite movements that epitomize the gracefulness that can be freefall skydiving. And there's much more in the latest edition that can take you to the heights.

Body Pilot, Carl Nelson, Jr.; Abstract Publishing, Chicago, Illinois, 1981 (Freakfanalia, J. Nelson, Rte. #34, Skyline Center, Sandwich, Illinois 60548) (112 pages, 8¹/₂″ × 11″, softbound).

The author/photographer has produced a graphic guidebook "to explain how to fly your body in freefall."

In 1958 two freefalling parachutists passed a wooden baton between them. Much previous experimentation by many jumpers had been done trying to solve the mysteries of aerial maneuvering after leaving an aircraft and before opening a canopy. Whenever more than one jumper exited a plane the attraction was enormous to "reach out and touch someone," but awkwardness and lack of knowledge adversely affected attempts to make intentional contact.

However, once the first baton pass was made and the "know how" was widely disseminated, others quickly got to doing the new parachuting activity—relative work (RW). Ultimately, RW achieved "official" recognition by being included as events in national and international championships.

The author has written an instructional work, with techniques given in a specific order, starting with level flight and flying as a "base" (holding a body position and a heading) until a "pin" jumper aggressively moves in to make contact and complete a formation; then being an "aggressor" skydiver, and so on, through team formations and team flying.

Studying and applying what the author details in words and illustrates with superior color photographs and excellent drawings will help speed learning the satisfying art of skydiving RW.

Canopy Relative Work, Terry Parsons; Skydiving Book Service, P.O. Box 1520, DeLand, Florida, 32721, 1981.

This book explains and illustrates the complexities of canopy relative work (CRW).

The Skydiver's Information Manual; United States Parachute Association, Alexandria, Virginia (145 pages, 8½" × 11", three-ring binder, $14).

The Skydiver's Informational Manual provides valuable, up-to-date information on every aspect of sport parachuting. Its three-ring binder format simplifies making revisions as USPA issues periodic revisions and special bulletins.

Specific information includes the following:

- The United States Parachute Association
- Constitution and By-Laws
- Group Membership Program
- Basic Safety Requirements and Waivers
- Basic Safety Requirements (BSRs)
- Waivers to the BSRs
- Classification of Skydivers
- USPA Licenses

- USPA Instructional Rating Requirements
- Beginning Skydiving—First-Jump Training
  - —Training Options
  - —Supervision and Schools
  - —Registration and Eligibility
  - —FAA Regulations
  - —Rules and Requirements
  - —Parachute Equipment
  - —Weather
  - —Aircraft
  - —Exit
  - —Parachute Opening
  - —Canopy Steering
  - —Landing
  - —Emergency Situations
  - —Recurrent Training
- Static Line Progression Method
- Accelerated Freefall Progression Method
- Graduate Student Progression
- Level 8—Continuing Education
- Prejump Safety Check and Briefing Recommendations
- Skydiving Equipment Recommendations
- Relative Work Recommendations
- Freefall Rate of Descent and Exit Altitude Tables
- Advanced Progression
- Night Jump Recommendations
- Water Landing Recommendations
- CRW Recommendations
- Demonstration Jump Recommendations
- High Altitude Jump and Oxygen Use Recommendations
- Awards
- Expert Wings and Freefall Badges
- Sequential RW Awards
- CRW Awards
- Membership Seniority Certificates
- Federal Aviation Regulations
- Glossary
- Applications and Forms

The Parachute Manual—A Technical Treatise on Aerodynamic Decelerators (3rd Edition), Dan Poynter; Parachuting Publications, Santa Barbara, CA, 1984 (499 pages, 2,000-plus illustrations, 8½" × 11", softcover, $44.95).

If you really want to learn more about parachutes, particularly technical aspects, there is a single source to which you can go that will assuredly give you far more information and specific detail than perhaps you would really want—unless you are an aeronautical engineer, or want to be one; but Dan Poynter's manual is today considered to be the standard in parachuting—and not just in sport parachuting. In fact, it is referred to as the "bible" by parachute riggers everywhere. All branches of the U.S. military services use it for reference, as does the U.S. Forest Service. Many foreign governments have also ordered it. *Aviation/Space* magazine has said of it: "The definitive work on the history, development, design, repair, and maintenance of parachute equipment."

The Parachute Manual took Dan Poynter more than eight years to compile. When he started skydiving in the early '60s, he decided he also wanted to be a parachute rigger as another step in being a "compleat" parachutist, but there was little documentation from which to learn. What had been published was hard to find. The little he could gather revealed there was a large information gap for rigger candidates—and for those who were already FAA-certificated parachute riggers.

He kept on with his research and in several years had garnered, sifted, sorted, and collated a huge amount of technical data. When information was lacking, he researched published history and lore, then wrote descriptions, captions, and narratives. Then he entered the publishing field, successfully producing the first edition of *The Parachute Manual* in 1972. A single information source was finally at hand for everyone involved in parachuting.

More printing runs were made to meet the demand. Meanwhile, evolution in parachuting was carrying on rapidly. Dan steadily compiled more information to keep pace with changes, and in 1975 published a second, revised edition of the manual. Parachuting evolution did not slow at all. Dan's research and information gathering continued. In several years it was time for another new, updated version. In 1984 the "Third Edition, Completely Revised" was published.

At $44.95, it might seem to be more than you would want to pay for something you know little, if anything, about—but the tome is an extraordinary store of information. *The Parachute Manual* is truly a huge treasury at a bargain price.

Chapter I: 1.0 Regulations (18 pages).

The FARs (Federal Aviation Regulations), NAS-804, TSO C-23, USPA Parts, etc., with a discussion of how they relate to one another and how they affect the parachute rigger.

Chapter II: 2.0 The Parachute Rigger Certificate (3 pages).

What it means and step-by-step instructions for obtaining one.

Chapter III: 3.0 The Parachute Loft (30 pages).

The basic layout, tools, sewing machines; their use, function, and repair; forms.

Chapter IV: 4.0 Parachute Materials (98 pages).

Cloth, cord, tape, thread, webbing, hardware, etc. A listing and description of those types common to parachute construction.

Chapter V: 5.0 Personnel Parachute Assemblies (86 pages).

A history of the personnel parachute. A description of all personnel parachutes manufactured in the U.S.

Chapter VI: 6.0 Parachute Component Parts (135 pages).

A listing and description of all personnel parachute component parts manufactured in the U.S.

Chapter VII: 7.0 Maintenance, Alteration, and Manufacturing Procedures (81 pages).

Specifications and methods; step-by-step instructions for making repairs and manufacturing new parachute items.

Chapter VIII: 8.0 Design and Construction (32 pages).

Parachute design criteria and construction details.

Chapter IX: 9.0 Parachute Inspecting and Packing (72 pages).

Inspection and identification of damage, assembly instructions, packing instructions.

Glossary/Index: (18 pages).

Almost 900 parachute-related terms explained succinctly.

Parachute Rigging Course, Dan Poynter; Parachuting Publications, Santa Barbara, California. (60 pages, 8½" × 11", softcover, $11.95).

Poynter did not stop at providing information for parachute riggers, equipment designers, and manufacturers. To help parachute rigger candidates wanting to obtain FAA certification, he also developed and published *Parachute Rigging Course*, a course of study for the Senior Parachute Rigger certificate. Riggers agree that this home-study course is a highly important adjunct in preparing for FAA written and practical examinations. It explains how to go about making application to the FAA; and it contains reading assignments, practical work, sample examination questions, and detailed answers. Using the course, about 90% of preparation can be done at one's convenience, resulting in less travel and expense to acquire a parachute rigger's certificate. (A comprehensive explanation of parachute rigger certification is given in Chapter 3.)

Dan Poynter was eminently qualified for publishing parachute rigging information, having had years of intensive, practical work at sport parachute DZs and for more than one manufacturer. He was also issued U.S. Patent No. 3,908,937 on September 30, 1975, for the "POP TOP Parachute Pack." The design was for a manually or automatically operated certificated chest-type parachute that accommodated 24-foot or 26-foot conventional canopies and other sizes and types of the same or less volume. A special and new feature of the container design was the *externally* mounted pilot chute. The new pack provided a thin profile when ready for use. There were other singular features of the design: The ripcord was operated from the back of the assembly. Thus, located between the container and the body of the user, the all-important locking pins were more safely protected than in other types of chest-mounted chutes in general use at the time. Maintaining straightness of ripcord pins is critical. Another new item was that ripcord pins, which keep the assembly closed, were held in place by fabric loops rather than by the then conventional metal cones.

Parachute Rigger Study Guide, Questions, Anwers, Explanations and References, Deborah Blackmon, Master Rigger; ParaPublishing, Santa Barbara, CA, 1989 (71 pages, 8¹/₂" × 11", softcover, $14.95).

Requirements for a parachute rigger certificate (Senior or Master), ratings for types of parachutes, and details of privileges, limitations, and general operating rules are given in Federal Aviation Regulation (FAR) Part 65. Anyone who meets the requirements and applies to the FAA is entitled to a parachute rigger certificate.

Blackmon's thorough guidebook provides accurate, authoritative information that greatly eases the task of understanding the complexities of parachute rigging.

In the first section, *Questions,* are the 291 actual questions the FAA uses to construct a series of written examinations, one of which a candidate must sit for as the initial formal step in certification.

The second section, *Answers and Explanations,* gives an answer to each FAA question, followed by a detailed explanation of whys and wherefores. For a rigger candidate's further follow-up, one or more specific references are given.

This work belongs in the reference library of any serious parachute rigger candidate. It's also a mine of information for any skydiver who wants to know more about parachute care and maintenance.

Parachute Rigger Question Book (FAA T-8080, AVN-130, 09/88), Aero-Graphic; P.O. Box 1520, DeLand, Florida (32 pages, 8¹/₂" × 11", softcover, $9.95).

This study guide is based on a publication of the U.S. Department of Transportation, FAA, Aviation Standards National Field Office. The guidebook contains the "pool" of actual questions used for the FAA Senior and Master Parachute Rigger written examinations. These written tests are difficult, and any candidate must seriously pursue required study to be successful. The book does not contain answers, but a written reference is given for each question. Examining those references will help you learn the right answer.

Parachuting I/E Course—A Program of Study to Prepare the Expert Parachutist for the U.S.P.A. Instructor/Examiner Written Examination, Dan Poynter; Parachuting Publications, Santa Barbara, California. (75 pages, 5¹/₂" × 8¹/₂", softbound, $10.95).

Dan Poynter's knowledge and experience are not limited to parachute rigging. He has made more than, 1,200 parachute jumps and was an early USPA Instructor/Examiner, after having helped formulate the stringent USPA Instructor/Examiner program. His home-study course is divided into sections, each concentrating on a specific area of parachuting. Each chapter has an introductory explanation of a lesson, reading assignments, sample typical questions and answers—with references for further study. Also, of particular value, hard-to-find articles are reprinted. A candidate then only needs to acquire readily obtainable required additional study items available through USPA.

The course has been published continuously for more than 15 years; thus, it is current and complete, making it most useful.

BASEics, by "BASE #3."

This is a brief but authoritative booklet, written for experienced parachutists who might have an interest in a controversial aspect of parachuting—BASE jumping. "BASE" is an acronym for **B**uilding, **A**ntenna, **S**pan (bridge) (also termed **S**tructure by some), and **E**arth (cliff). As said, BASE jumping is a hotly controversial activity and is not sanctioned by the USPA. Pro and con arguments are many. Proponents regularly point to local government recognition of such parachuting in the state of West Virginia by one day a year closing an approximately 900-foot-high bridge to vehicular traffic so parachutists can make leaps from the span into a narrow canyon to land on a tiny clearing on the edge of a narrow river. The booklet is must reading for contemplators of BASE-jumping, though it is limitedly informative and first-time BASE jumpers generally consult experienced BASE jumpers for specific and current aid in jumping from a particular site.

MISCELLANY

Para-Gear Equipment Company Catalog (Published annually, 160-plus pages, illustrated, $8^{1}/_{2}" \times 11"$, softcover).

This company has been in the sport parachute equipment sales business for more than a quarter of a century and has long been a reputable source for acquiring skydiving-related items. Para-Gear publishes a direct mail catalog—much of it in color—that is an excellent means for a beginning parachutist to become familiar with the wide range of parachute canopies, containers, harnesses, container/harness assemblies, accessories, replacement parts, tools, publications, emblems, judging equipment, trophies, so on and so forth. Para-Gear updates its catalog annually, and a typical edition has 160 or more pages, with more than 800 items illustrated clearly. A catalog can be obtained by mailing a $2 check that includes Third Class Postage. For customer order-placing convenience, there is a toll-free "800" telephone number for customers outside Illinois:

PARA-GEAR EQUIPMENT COMPANY
3839 West Oakton Street
Skokie, IL 60076 U.S.A.
(312) 679 – 5905
(800) 323 - 0437 (Outside Illinois Only)

A substantial number of parachute-related publications are listed in the bibliography at the end of this book. Anyone wanting to learn more about the history of parachutes and parachuting will welcome that resource.

9

Where to Jump

There are many places to make sport parachute jumps in the United States, Canada, South America, Europe, Asia—in fact, just about anywhere in the world.

UNITED STATES PARACHUTE ASSOCIATION
"GROUP MEMBERS"

The following sport parachuting centers, some commercially operated and some club-run, are Group Members of the United States Parachute Association. USPA says this of them: "They have pledged to follow USPA Basic Safety Requirements [BSRs] and Recommendations for students and advanced skydivers and to offer first-jump courses taught by USPA-rated Instructors."

USPA CONFERENCE REGIONS (alphabetically arranged):

Central Conference—Illinois, Iowa, Kansas, Missouri, Nebraska (25 drop zones, abbreviated DZs)

Eastern Conference—Maryland, New Jersey, New York, Pennsylvania—Canada (22 DZs).

Gulf Conference—Arkansas, Louisiana, Texas (13 DZs).

Mid-Atlantic Conference—North Carolina, South Carolina, Virginia (16 DZs).

Mideastern Conference—Indiana, Michigan, Ohio, West Virginia (16 DZs).

Mountain Conference—Colorado, Idaho, Utah (9 DZs).

North Central Conference—Minnesota, Wisconsin (16 DZs).

Northeastern Conference—Connecticut, Maine, Massachusetts, New Hampshire, Rhode Island, Vermont (6 DZs).
Northwest Conference—Alaska, Oregon, Washington (16 DZs).
Pacific Conference—California (5 DZs).
Southeast Conference—Florida, Georgia (17 DZs).
Southern Conference—Alabama, Florida, Kentucky, Tennessee (13 DZs).
Southwestern Conference—Texas, Oklahoma (11 DZs).
Western Conference—Arizona, California, Nevada (11 DZs).

NOTE: Three states, for varied reasons, are in more than one conference region. They are:

- **California**—Pacific Conference; Western Conference.
- **Florida**—Southeast Conference; Southern Conference.
- **Texas**—Gulf Conference, Southwestern Conference.

Central Conference—Illinois, Iowa, Kansas, Missouri, Nebraska (25 DZs)

Accelerated Freefall Iowa, Boone Municipal Airport, Boone, IA 50036, one mile north of Hwy 30, (515)432-6441.

Algona Skydivers, Algona Airport, Highway 18 West, Algona, IA 50511, (515)295-7572.

Archway Skydiving Centre, City Airport, Highway 4 North, Sparta, IL 62286, (618)443-2091, 441-2375.

Carmi Para Center, 3222 Copperline, Mt. Vernon, IN 47620, (812)783-1415.

Central Iowa Skydivers, Perry Municipal Airport, Perry, IA 50220, (515)278-4261.

Crete Skydiving Center, Inc., Crete Municipal Airport, Crete, NB 68333, (402) 488-7084.

Des Moines Skydivers, Inc., RR 4, Box 234A, Winterset, IA 50273, (515)244-1834.

Greater St. Louis PC, Greenville Airport, Greenville, IL 62246, (314)576-JUMP.

Horizon Skydiving School, 8608 East 32nd Street, Kansas City, MO 64129, (816)923-7006.

Illinois Valley Parachute Club, P.O. Box 284, Minier, IL 61759, (309)392-9111, 359-9068.

Kankakee Skydiving Center, Inc., P.O. Box 186, Braidwood, IL 60408, (815)458-2773.

Kansas Sky Ranch, 21 miles SSE of Wichita, Kansas on Hwy K-15, (316)782-3558, 682-3692.

Kansas State University Parachute Club, Wamego Airport, Wamego, KS, (913)456-8860, 776-4022.

Lincoln SPC, 929 Furnace Avenue, Lincoln, NB 68521, (402)477-7778, 267-6465.

Mid-American Sky Sports, Inc., Garnett Airport, Garnett, KS 66032, (913)489-2506, 448-2280.

Mid-American SPC, 119 South Cheney Street, Taylorville, IL 62568, (217)287-7347, 824-JUMP.

Missouri River Valley Skydivers, Lexington Airport, Rte 1, Box 455, Henrietta, MO 64036, (816)494-5315, 776-2372.

Northwood Skydiving Center, Hwy 105 East, Northwood Municipal Airport, Northwood, IA 50459, (515)324-2387.

Oz Sport Parachute Center, Rice County Airport, Rte. 3, Box 58A, Lyons, KS 67554, (316)257-5002.

Pegasus Skydiving, Jetmore Municipal Airport, P.O. Box 248, Jetmore, KS 67854, (316)357-6491.

Rivercity Skydivers, Inc., Martin's Airfield, South Sioux City, NB 68776, (402)494-6724.

Rock River Valley Skydivers, P.O. Box 1038, Sterling, IL 61081, (815)232-8431. 626-8772.

Skydive El Dorado, Inc., El Dorado Airport, 2 miles south of El Dorado, Kansas on Hwy 77, 1 mile east, (316)321-3060, 225-6356.

Skydive Sandwich, Inc., Route 34, Sandwich Airport, Sandwich, IL 60548, (815)786-8200.

Skydive St. Louis, Inc., P.O. Box 216, Jonesburg, MO 63351, (314)488-5969, 278-3388.

Eastern Conference—Maryland, New Jersey, New York, Pennsylvania (22 DZs)

AFF East/Skydive Chambersburg, 3506 Airport Road, Chambersburg, PA 17201, (717)264-1111, (800)526-3497.

Albany Skydiving Center, P.O. Box 281, Duanesburg, NY 12056, (518)895-8140.

AquaFoil, Inc., P.O. Box 3312, Crofton, MD 21114, (301)261-0188.

Erie Skydiving Center, Moorhead Airpark, 9125 Haskell Road, North East, PA 16428, (814)725-5314, (716)674-8543.

Extra Fine Skydives, Inc., Devener Airport, Route 194, Hanover, PA 17331, (717)843-3552.

Finger Lakes Skydivers, 9798 Congress Street Extension, Trumansburg, NY 14886, (607)869-5601, 387-5225.

Frontier Skydivers, Inc., Hollands International Airport, 3316 Bee Be Road, Newfane, NY 14108, (716)832-JUMP.

Gananoque Sport Parachuting Centre, Gananoque Municipal Airport, RR #1, Gananoque, Ontario, Canada K7G 2V3, (613)382-5114.

JAWCO, Inc. Parachute Center, 287 Little Conestoga, Road, Glenmore, PA 19343, (215)942-2286.

Long Island Sky Divers, Inc., Spadero's Airport, Montauk Highway, East Moriches, NY 11940, (516)589-2910.

Malone Parachute Club, Inc., Malone-Dufort Airport, Malone, NY 12953, (518)483-9892, (802)879-6193.

Maytown SPC, Donegal Airport, RD 1, Marietta, PA 17547, (717)653-9980.

Mifflin County Skydivers, Inc., Mifflin County Airport, Three Cent Lane, Reedsville, PA 17084, (814)237-1737, (717)667-6664.

Mon-Yough Skydivers, Inc., RD #1, Box 300D, Worthington, PA 16262, (412)297-3690.

Morgantown Skydivers Aeronautical Club, Willow Glen Rd. and Rte 23, Box 258A, RD #2, Morgantown, PA 19543, (215)285-6601.

NewCal Aviation, Inc., 14 Riser Rd. Little Ferry, NJ 07643, (201)440-1990.

North East Pennsylvania Ripcords, Cold Springs Farm, Sugarloaf, PA 18249, (717)788-2476.

Oneida County Skydivers, Curtis Airfield, Teuscher Rd., Verona, NY, (315)339-5017, 245-2362.

Skydive East, Skymanor Airport, Pittstown, NJ 08867, (201)996-6262.

Skydive Long Island Inc., Spadero's Airport, Montauk Highway, East Moriches, NY 11940, (516)878-1186.

The Ranch, P.O. Box 121, Gardiner, NY 12525, (914)255-4033, 255-9538.

United Parachute Club, Inc., New Hanover Airport, Route 663/Swamp Pike, Gilbertsville, PA 19525, (215)323-9667, 323-8565.

Gulf Conference—Arkansas, Louisiana, Texas (13 DZs)

Acadiana Skydivers, Rte. 1, Box 348, Jeanerette, LA 70544, (318)276-9296, 233-4115.

Aggies Over Texas, Inc., Coulter Field, 6120A, Highway 21 East, Bryan, TX 77803, (409)778-0245, 693-0415.

Airillusions Airshows, P.O. Box 27701-459, Houston, TX 77227, (713)481-0541.

Central Arkansas Para Center, Carlisle Municipal, Carlisle, AR 72024-0840, (501)552-3254, 835-0150.

Clear Sky SPC, Beaumont Municipal Airport, Beaumont, TX, (409)860-4699.

Jumpers Unlimited, Beaumont Municipal Airport, 455 Keith Rd., Beaumont, TX 77713, (409)866-0084, 860-3168.

Lake Area Skydivers, Southland Field, 7000 Southland Field Road, Sulphur, LA 70663, (318)583-9144.

Magic Valley Skydivers, San Benito Airport, San Benito, TX 78586, (512)399-9942.

Memphis Parachute Association, P.O. Box 381104, Memphis, TN 38183, (901)755-8710.

Sky's the Limit Parachute Center, Inc., P.O. Box 1539, Beeville, TX 78104, (512)358-9330.

Skydive San Antonio, Inc., Midlake Airport, $1/2$ mile N. of Elmendorf, Texas on Cassiano Road, (512)635-7013, 733-7453.

Skydive San Marcos, Inc., $1/2$ mile west of Fentress, Texas, on Hwy. 80, (512)488-2214.

Skydive Spaceland, Houston Gulf Airport, 2750 FM 1266, League City, TX 77573, (713)337-1713.

Mid-Atlantic Conference—
North Carolina, South Carolina, Virginia (16 DZs)

Astroid SPC, Rte 1, six miles east of Asheboro, NC off Hwy 42, (919)241-2270.

Cunningham Parachute Service, Laurinburg-Maxton Airport, Pinebluff, NC 28373, (919)281-3133.

Dismal Swamp Skydivers/Pepsi Parachute Team, Craft Field, Farmville, NC, (919)758-2428, 752-3169.

82nd Airborne Division SPC, P.O. Box 67, Reilly Road, Fort Bragg, NC 28307, (919)436-5858.

Flying Tigers SPC, Clemson-Occonee Airport, Clemson, SC 29631, (803)882-1928, 843-2151.

Franklin County SPC, Box 703, Louisburg, NC 27549, (919)496-2224, 496-5153.

Green Beret Parachute Club, P.O. Box 70241, Fort Bragg, NC 28307, (919)436-4056.

Hartwood ParaCenter, Inc., 194 Cropp Road, Hartwood, VA 22405, (703)752-4784.

Lugoff Para-Flite Club, Inc., Camden, SC. Grass strip off I-20, exit 92, Hwy 601, (803)432-0692, 438-3186.

Peninsula Skydivers, P.O. Box 904, West Point, VA 23181, (804)785-9990, 497-4655.

Raeford Parachute Center, P.O. Drawer R.A., Raeford, NC 28376, (919)875-3261.

Skydive Carolina!, Chester County Airport, Highway 909, Chester, SC 29706, (803)581-JUMP, (704)331-5131.

Skydive Orange, Inc., Orange Municipal Airport, 4 miles east of Orange, VA 22960, (703)672-5054.

Skydive Suffolk, Inc., Municipal Airport, Suffolk, VA 23434, (804)539-3929.

Skydive Walterboro, Walterboro Municipal Airport, Hwy 17A, Walterboro, SC 29488, (803)538-2547.

Vikings of Denmark, Barnwell Airport, Box 373, Denmark, SC 29042, (803)284-3178.

Mideastern Conference—
Indiana, Michigan, Ohio, West Virginia (16 DZs)

Aero Ventures, Inc., 211 East Clinton Street, Columbus, OH 43202, (614)263-3777, 363-JUMP.

Akron Skydivers, Inc., 2037 Sudomer Drive, Suffield, OH 44260, (216)630-DIVE.

Alliance Sport Parachute Club, 2 Hofmeister Rd., Petersburg, OH, (216)426-2565.

Canton Air Sports, Martin Airport, 5367 East Center Drive NE, Canton, OH 44721, (216)452-0560, 477-5533.

Cleveland SPC, Garretsville, OH; 35 miles southeast of Cleveland, (216)548-4511.

Green Beret Freefall Club, P.O. Box 130, Ceredo, WV 22507.

Illiana Skydivers, RR #1, Box 317A, Covington, IN 47932, (317)793-2816.

New Horizon Parachute Club, 1³/₄ miles east of Highway 3 on County Road 1200 North at 271 East, P.O. Box 361, Eaton, IN 47338, (317)396-3602, 396-9383.

Parachutes and Associates, Inc., Frankfort Municipal Airport, State Road 28, Frankfort, IN 46041, (317)654-6188.

Parahawks PC, Marine City Airport, Marine City, MI 48039, (313)765-3242.

Skydive Anderson, 7339 Sprague, Anderson, IN 46013, (317)642-7392, 642-1608.

Skydive Greene County Inc., 177 South Monroe Siding Road, Xenia, OH 45385, (513)372-0700.

Skydive Hastings, Inc., 2995 West Airport Road, Hastings, MI 49058, (616)948-2665.

Skydive Mentone, Inc., Highway 19 South, south of Mentone, then west 1 mile on CR600 South, Mentone, IN 46539, (219)353-7330.

Waynesville Sky Sports, Inc., 4925 North State Route #42, Waynesville, OH 45068, (513)897-3851.

West Virginia Skydivers, Jackson County Airport, 4 miles SW of Ravenswood, WV, (304)375-4855.

Mountain Conference—Colorado, Idaho, Utah (9 DZs)

Anderson Ranch, 3615 East Sunnyside Road, Idaho Falls, ID 83406, (208)529-5298.

Cedar Valley Freefall, 10 miles west of Lehi, Utah on SR73, (801)768-9054.

Colorado School of Skydiving, Inc., P.O. Box 637, Strasburg, CO 80136, (303)690-8583.

Front Range Skydivers, P.O. Box 25290, Colorado Springs, CO 80918. DZ 30 miles northeast of Colorado Springs at Calhan Airport, Calhan, Colorado, (719)591-1478, 347-9998.

Heber Valley DZ, Heber County Airport, Provo, UT 84601, (801)375-6168.

Ogden Sky Knights, 3911 Airport Road, Ogden, Utah 84401, (801)544-7638.

Skydive Colorado, Fort Collins-Loveland Airport, Loveland, CO 80537, (303)669-9966.

University of Southern Colorado SPC, Calhan Airport, Calhan, CO 80808, (719)347-9998.

Utah Sky Ranch, Airport #2, 7200 South 4450 West, West Jordan, UT 84084, (801)569-USPA, 322-JUMP.

North Central Conference—Minnesota, South Dakota, Wisconsin (16 DZs)

Baldwin SPC, Inc., P.O. Box 11879, St. Paul, MN 55111-0879, (715)684-3416, (612)436-5225.

Black Hills Skydivers, Black Hills Airport, Spearfish, SD 57783, (605)642-7839.

Buffalo Skydivers, Buffalo Municipal Airport/Maple Airport, Maple Plain, MN 55359, (612)479-2428, 472-9146.

Green Bay Skydivers, Carter Airport, Route 3, Pulaski, WI 54162, (414)822-5010, 434-0337.

Iron Range Skydivers, Inc., Eveleth-Virginia Municipal Airport, south of Eveleth off Hwy 53, Iron, MN, (218)744-3213.

Minnesota Skydivers, P.O. Box 250, Lakeville, MN, (507)645-8608, (612)451-1209.

Northeast Wisconsin Skydivers, Carter Airport, Route 3 and Hwy 32, Pulaski, WI 54162, (414)822-8418.

Para-Naut, Inc., 6 miles west of Oshkosh, WI, (414)685-5122.

Relatively North Skydiving Club of Michigan's Upper Peninsula, Houghton County Airport, Houghton, MI 49931, (906) 524-7976.

Seven Hills Skydivers, Inc., Mathaire Field, Marshall, WI, 16 miles northeast of Madison. (608)244-5088.

Sky Knights, East Troy Municipal Airport, East Troy, WI 53120, (414)542-9143.

South Dakota Skydivers, Inc., Box 63, Sioux Falls, SD 57101, (605)647-2381.

St. Croix Valley Skydivers, P.O. Box 92, Osceola, WI 54020, (715)294-2433.

Superior Skydivers, Belknap South Restaurant on Bong Airport, Superior, WI 54880, (715)392-8811, 392-6575.

Valley Skydivers, Inc., West Fargo Airport, West Fargo, ND 58078, (701)282-9394.

Wisconsin Skydivers, Inc., Aero Park, W204 N5022 Lannon Road, Menomonee Falls, WI 53051, (414)252-3434.

Northeastern Conference—Connecticut, Maine, Massachusetts, New Hampshire, Rhode Island, Vermont (6 DZs)

Connecticut Parachutists, Inc., Box 507, Ellington, CT 06029, (203)871-0021.

Pepperell Sport Parachute Center, Nashua Road, Route 111, East Pepperell, MA 01437, (508)433-9948, 465-1150.

Massachusetts Sport Parachute Club, P.O. Box 122, Turners Falls, MA 01376, (413)863-8362, 863-8783.

New England Skydivers, Northampton Airport, Old Ferry Rd., Northampton, MA 01060, (413)665-7577.

Skydive Lebanon, Upper Guinea Road, RFD #1, Box 1255, Lebanon, ME 04027, (207)339-1520.

Woodstock PC, Route 169, South Woodstock, CT 06267, (203)928-4652.

Northwest Conference—Alaska, Oregon, Washington (16 DZs)

Beagle Sky Ranch, 16000 Shiloh Road, White City, OR 97503, (503)826-2004.

Blue Skies of Alaska, 131 Concordia Drive, Fairbanks, AK 99709, (907)474-9433, 474-0566.

Fort Lewis Sport Parachute Club, P.O. Box 33987, Fort Lewis, WA 98433-0987, (206)967-3906.

Kapowsin Air Sports Ltd., 27611 146th Avenue, East, Kapowsin, WA 98344, (206)847-5766.

Microsoft Skydive Club, Snohomish Parachute Center, Harvey Airfield, Snohomish, WA 98290, (206)568-5960.

Montana Para-Sports/Silvertip Skydivers, Stevensville Airport, 8525 St. Vrain Way, Missoula, MT 59802, (406)721-1848, 777-9929.

Seattle Sky Divers, 9912 Airport Way, Snohomish, WA 98290, (206)568-9306.

Skydive Arlington, Arlington, WA, I-5, Exit 206, go east 2 miles, (206) 422-6911.

Skydive Lost Prairie, Inc., 3175 Lower Lost Prairie Rd., Marion, MT 59925, (406)858-2493.

Skydive Oregon, 12150 Hwy 211, Mollala, OR 97038, (503)829-DIVE.

Snohomish Parachute Center, Harvey Airfield, Snohomish, WA 98290, (206) 568-5960, (800) 338-JUMP.

Star Parachute Ranch, 4005 Can-Ada Rd., Star, ID 83669, (208)286-7059.

Southwind School of Skydiving, Vista Field, 309 S. Roosevelt St., Kennewick, WA 99336, (509)735-2814.

Spokane Parachute Club, N. 6227 Elm, Spokane, WA 99205, (509)328-3114.

Western SPC, Beaver Oaks Airport, 29388 SE Hieple Road, Eagle Creek, OR 97022, (503)630-JUMP, 654-0718.

Williamette Valley Parachute Training Club, 345 Scravel Hill Rd. SE, Albany, OR 97321, (503)926-5736, 928-4622.

Pacific Conference—California (5 DZs)

California PC, Box 1065, Livermore, CA 94550.

Madera Parachute Center, Madera Municipal Airport, Madera, CA 93637, (209)673-2688.

Skydance Skydiving, Rte. 2, Box 2410A, Yolo County Airport, Davis, CA 95616, (916)753-2651.

Skydive Hawaii, Dillingham Airfield, 68-760 Farrington Hwy, Honolulu, HI 96791, (808)521-4404.

Skydiving West Inc., Mendota Airport, Mendota, CA, (209)655-DIVE, 826-3933.

Southeast Conference—Florida, Georgia (17 DZs)

Air Adventures Florida, Air Glades Airport, Hwy 27, Clewiston, FL 33440, (813)983-6151, 983-2949.

Atlanta Airsports, Stockmar Airport, Villa Rica, GA, (404)948-3373, 333-0446.

Atlanta Skydiving Center, Inc., Rte. 1, County Line Road, Jenkinsburg, GA 30234, (404)775-9150.

Flagler Aviation, Flagler County Airport, SR100, Bunnell, FL 32110, (904)437-4547, 736-3202.

Freefall Ranch, Inc., Roosevelt Memorial Airport, Highway U.S. 27-A, P.O. Box 39, Warm Springs, GA 31830, (404)655-3373.

Keystone Air Sports, P.O. Box 566, Keystone Heights, FL 32656, (904)473-4491.

North Georgia Skydivers, Box 534, Ellijay, GA 30540, (404)635-4653, 276-4469, 276-9905.

Palatka Paracenter, Rte 1, Box 8350, Highway 100, Palatka, FL 32177, (904)325-4293.

Paragators, Inc., 19618 Eustis Airport Rd., Eustis, FL 32726, (904)357-7800, 669-3339.

Skydive DeLand, P.O. Box 3071, Deland, FL 32723, (904)736-1742.

Skydive Inc., 28700 S.W. 217th Avenue, Homestead, FL 33030, (305)SKY-DIVE.

Skydive Valdosta, Valdosta Regional Airport, Madison Highway, Valdosta, GA, (912)247-4229.

Silver Hawk Aviation, Inc., Richard B. Russell Airport, Rome, GA, (404)285-1009.

Skydive Tampa Bay, Inc., Exit 58 (I-75) north of Tampa, located 1^1/2 miles west on SR54 at Top of Tampa Airport, (813)973-3153, 726-1014.

Titusville PC, Dunn Airpark, Titusville, FL 32780, (407)267-0016, 269-3286.

U of Florida Falling Gators SPC, P.O. Box 12992, Gainseville, FL 32604-0992, (904)376-9471, 373-4247.

Williston Skydivers, Inc., Hwy 41 South, Williston, FL 32696, (904)336-7970.

Zephyrhills PC, east side of the Zephyrhills Municipal Airport, Zephyrhills, FL 33539, (813)788-5591, FAX (813)783-1339.

Southern Conference—Alabama, Florida, Kentucky, Tennessee (13 DZs)

Americair/Skyventures, Tuskegee Municipal Airport, 1727 Airport Road, Tuskegee, AL 36083, (205)727-7767.

Auburn University SPC, Elmore County Airport, Auburn, AL 36830, (205)821-6041.

Fort Campbell Sport Parachute Activity, P.O. Box 36, Fort Campbell, KY 42223, (502)798-4106.

Fort Rucker SPC, Hatch Stage Field, Fort Rucker, AL 36362, (205)598-8088.

Golden Eagle SPC, White County Airport, Sparta, TN 38505, (615)823-1561, 839-2550.

Greene County Sport Parachute Center/Kentucky, Airport Road, Bardstown, KY 40004, (502)348-6577, 348-9531.

Gulf Coast Air Sports, U.S. Hwy 90, St. Elmo, AL 36541, (205)865-4649, 957-6379.

MOA Parachute Rides, 7965 Beulah Rd., Pensacola, FL 32506, (904)944-3907.

Panhandle Parachute Center-Pensacola, Florida, Horak Airport, Elberta, AL 36530, (205)986-5618.

Skydive South, Inc., Sylacauga Municipal Airport, Airport Rd., Sylacauga, AL 35150, (205)870-0476, 245-3246.

Tennessee Skydiving Center, Inc., Tullahoma Municipal Airport, Northern Field, Tullahoma, TN 37388, (615)455-4574.

Thunderbird SPC, 121 Briarwood Drive, Berea-Richmond, KY, (606)873-4140, 986-8202.

20th Special Forces SPC, 2499 Johnson Rd., Huntsville, AL 35805, (205)883-7570, 883-4156.

Southwestern Conference—Texas, Oklahoma (11 DZs)

Aerodrome Freefall Society, Aerodrome Airpark, Highway 2933 at FM 997, McKinney, TX 75069, (214)542-7601.

Amarillo Skydivers, Gartell Airport, I-27 and FM2219, 2 miles west on FM2219 off I-27 on north side of road, Amarillo, TX 79109, (806)353-4019, 374-7049.

Dallas Skydiving Center, Seagoville Airport, Seagoville, TX 79359, (214)398-2360, 474-9002.

Fort Hood Sport Parachute Club, SHIPP DZ, Elijah Road and FM116, Fort Hood, TX 76544, (817)288-9422, 547-4051.

North Texas Parachute Center, P.O. Box 851, Gainesville Municipal Airport, Gainesville, TX 76240, (817)665-3211.

Oklahoma PC, Inc., Cushing Municipal Airport, Tulsa, OK 74110, (918)225-2222, 836-8888,

Skydive Eagles Nest, Rte. 5, Box 1725, Eagles Nest Airfield, Odessa-Midland, TX 79766, (915)697-JUMP.

Skydive New Mexico, Mountain Sun Aviation, 125 Exit 191 West, Belen, NM (505) 831-2177

Skydive Temple, Temple Municipal Airport, Temple, TX, (817)690-8286, 778-4200.

Slovak Air Skydiving Center, Ennis Municipal Airport, Ennis, TX 75119, (214)875-0445, 462-8791.

Westex Sky Sports, 1608 North Garfield, Midland, TX 79701, (915)367-JUMP, 683-JUMP.

Western Conference—Arizona, California, Nevada (11 DZs)

Bravo-Bravo Aviation, Skylark Airport, 17494 Cottrell Boulevard, Lake Elsinore, CA 92330, (714)678-5911.

Desert Sky Ranch, Buckeye Municipal Airport, Buckeye, AZ 85326, (602)377-1961, 271-0440.

Las Vegas Parachute Club, North Las Vegas Air Terminal, 5 minutes from downtown Las Vegas, New Mexico, (702)796-8888, 731-5858.

Marana Skydiving Center, Pinal Airpark, 35 miles northwest of Tucson, off I-10, Marana, AZ 85238, (602)682-4441, 791-2357.

Perris Valley Skydiving Center, 2091 Goetz Rd., Perris CA 92370, (714)657-9576, 657-3904.

Perris Valley Skydiving School, Perris Valley Airport, 2091 Goetz Rd., Perris, CA 92370, (714)657-1664, (800)832-8818.

San Diego Air Sports, Box 13531 Otay Lake Rd., Jamue CA 92035, (619)421-0968.

Santa Ynez Aviation, Santa Ynez Airport, P.O. Box 300, Santa Ynez, CA 93460, (805)688-8390, 688-7277.

Skydiving Adventures Parachute School, Hemet-Ryan Airport, Hemet, CA 92343, (714)925-8197.

Skydive Arizona, Coolidge Municipal Airport, Coolidge, AZ 85228, (602)723-3753, 723-3772.

Skydive Paso Robles, 4990 Wing Way, Paso Robles Municipal Airport, Paso Robles, CA 93446, (805)239-3483.

Southern California Skydiving Club, California City Airport, California City, CA 93505, (619)373-4826.

Overseas USPA Group Members (19 DZs)

1-6-5 Skydivers, Pondok Cibubor Blok F 111/4 Cisalak Pasar, Cimanggis, Jakarta, Indonesia, (082)122044.

A-1 Skydiving Centre, Ltd., Rectory Farm Abbotsley, Huntingdon, Cambs, England PE194UE, 076 77 7065.

Aero Fallschirm Sport, Inc., Flughafen, 3527 Calden, West Germany, 0011-49-5674-4119.

Allerod Faldskaerms Center, Allerod Flyveplads, Molleosevej 6, 3450 Allerod, Denmark, 0045-42-27-09-00.

A.S. Allmarche, localita Squartabue, Porto Recanti Macerata, Italy, (071)978932, (0731)202632.

Bad Tolz Sport Parachute Club, Box 394, APO, NY 09050, (080) 41-4659, 41-30-860.

British Skysports Paracenter, Bridlington Aerodrome, Bridlington, East Yorkshire, YO164YB, England, (0262)677367, 603435.

Centro de Paracaidismo Costa Brava, Apartado de Correos 194, Ampuriabrava, Gerona, Spain, 72-45-01-11.

Clark AB Sport Parachute Club, 3rd Combat Support Group/SSOP, Clark AB, Philippines, (63)4535-21287.

Fallschirmsport-Centrum Albatros GmbH, Flugplatz Hartenholm, 2359 Hasenmoor, West Germany, 04185-1355, 04195-1356.

Fallschirmsprungausbildung, Flugplatz Saarlouis-DUREN, D-6634 Wallerfangen-DUREN, Saarland, West Germany, (06837)74136, (06831)68127.

Japan RW Association, 5-F Oak Catherina 1-12-12 Shinjuku, Shinjuko-ku, Tokyo 160 (Japan) (03)350-5655, 350-5825.

Para Centro Sa Locarno, Aeroporto Cantonale, Lacarno, Switzerland, (093)67 26 51.

Paraclub Higuerote, Apartado de Correos 17.164, Parque Central, Caracas 1015-A, Venezuela, (02)573-1445, FAX (02)871-3808.

Paraclub Moorsele, Ledegemstraat 140, 8640 Moorsele, Belgium, (56)50-00-92.

Scuola Nazionale Di Paracadutismo, Via Tiziano 137, 41026 Pavullo, Italy, (0536)20320.

Skydive Kangaroo, Some DZs in southern Germany, Austria, and France, (089)612 5000, 611 1984.

Skydive Trinidad and Tobago, Waller Field, Trinidad, (809)662-1516, 632-1152.

Swakopmund Skydiving Club, Swakopmund Airfield, P.O. Box 821, Namibia, 0641 5862.

Unaffiliated Parachute Clubs, Associations, Centers, and Drop Zones

There are many other organizations with which to make sport parachute jumps. Though described as "unaffiliated"—referring to *affiliation* with the United States Parachute Association (USPA)—many of the officers and staff members of unaffiliated clubs, associations, and commercial centers are, however, individual USPA members; and though unaffiliated, these organizations ascribe to USPA Basic Safety Requirements and Recommendations because they have been developed from experience and they make sense.

To learn of parachuting activities in a local region the "yellow pages" of telephone directories can be looked at under headings of "Parachutes" and "Skydiving."

In foreign nations, the national aero club can be contacted for skydiving activity in that country.

10
Parachuting Rules and Regulations

United States Parachute Association (USPA)

Basic Safety Requirements (Part 100)

2–1.01 APPLICABILITY

A. These procedures apply to all jumps except those made under military orders and those made because of inflight emergencies. Voluntary compliance with these procedures will protect the best interests of both the participants and the general public.

B. A "skydive" is defined as the descent of a person to the surface from an aircraft in flight when he/she uses or intends to use a parachute during all or part of that descent.

C. All persons participating in skydiving should be familiar with:
   1. Section 2–1.
   2. Section 2–2.
   3. Section 3–1 USPA Licenses.
   4. USPA Recommendations.
   5. All federal, state, and local regulations and rules pertaining to skydiving.

2–1.11 COMPLIANCE WITH FEDERAL REGULATIONS

No skydive shall be made in violation of Federal Aviation Administration (FAA) regulations.

2—1.13 MEDICAL REQUIREMENTS

All persons engaging in skydiving should:

A. Carry a valid Class I, II, or III Federal Aviation Administration medical certificate; or
B. Carry a certificate of physical fitness for skydiving from a registered physician; or
C. Have completed the USPA-recommended medical statement.

2–1.15 AGE REQUIREMENTS

Civilian skydivers are to be at least:

A. The age of legal majority (to execute contracts); or
B. 16 years of age with notarized parental or guardian consent.

2–1.21 STUDENT SKYDIVERS

A. All student instruction is to be under the supervision of a currently and appropriately rated USPA Instructor.
B. All student skydives are to be made under the direct supervision of a currently and appropriately rated USPA Jumpmaster aboard the aircraft until the student has been cleared by a USPA Jumpmaster to jumpmaster himself/herself. Accelerated Freefall students on Levels I, II, or III require two currently rated USPA AFF Jumpmasters to accompany students in freefall. All jumps on Levels IV through VII require at least one USPA AFF Jumpmaster to accompany the student in freefall.
C. Student skydivers are to:
   1. Initially make five (5) static line and/or tandem jumps to include successfully pulling a practice ripcord on three (3) successive jumps while demonstrating the ability to maintain stability and control prior to being cleared for freefall; or
   2. Successfully complete all learning objectives of Accelerated Freefall Levels I through VII prior to being cleared to jump without direct supervision.
D. Maximum ground winds for all student skydivers are 10 m.p.h. for round main canopies and 14 m.p.h. for ram air main canopies. Maximum ground winds for licensed skydivers are unlimited.

2–1.23 MINIMUM OPENING ALTITUDES

Minimum container opening altitudes above the ground for skydivers are:

A. Tandem jumps—4,000 feet Above Ground Level (AGL).
B. All freefall students—3,000 feet AGL.
C. All static line jumps—2,800 feet AGL.
D. A and B license holders—2,500 feet AGL.
E. C and D license holders—2,000 feet AGL.

2−1.25 DROP ZONE REQUIREMENTS

A. Areas used for skydiving should be unobstructed, with the following minimum radial distance to the nearest hazard:

Classification	Using round canopy	Using ram air canopy
Students	300 meters	100 meters*
A license holders	200 meters	50 meters
B license holders	100 meters	50 meters
C license holders	100 meters	Unlimited

*With ground-to-air communication to assist the student in canopy control.

B. Hazards are defined as telephone and power line, towers, buildings, open bodies of water, highways, automobiles, and clusters of trees covering more than 3,000 square meters.
C. Manned ground-to-air communications (e.g., radios, panels, smoke, lights) are to be present on the DZ during skydiving operations.

2−1.27 PREJUMP REQUIREMENTS

The appropriate altitude and surface winds are to be determined prior to conducting any skydive.

2−1.29 EXTRAORDINARY SKYDIVES

A. Night, water, and demonstration jumps are to be performed only with the advice of the local USPA Safety and Training Advisor (S&TA) or Instructor/Examiner.
B. Preplanned breakaway jumps are to be made only by Class C or D license holders using FAA TSOed equipment.

2−1.31 PARACHUTE EQUIPMENT

Each skydiver is to be equipped with:
A. Flotation gear when the intended exit point, opening point, or landing point of a skydiver is within one mile of an open body of water. An open body of water is defined as one in which a skydiver could drown.
B. A light when performing night jumps.
C. For all students, except tandem students, a rigid helmet.
D. For Accelerated Freefall students, a piggyback harness/container that has a ripcord/activated, spring-loaded, pilot chute-deployed main and reserve parachutes and is equipped with an automatic activation device (AAD) on the reserve parachute.
E. For each individual Accelerated Freefall student and Jumpmaster, his/her own visually accessible altimeter.

2–1.41 SPECIAL ALTITUDE EQUIPMENT, SUPPLEMENTARY OXYGEN

Supplementary oxygen is mandatory on skydives made from over 15,000 feet Mean Sea Level (MSL).

Federal Aviation Regulations (FARS)

The Federal Aviation Administration (FAA) is part of the United States Government's Department of Transportation and is responsible for regulating every aspect of airspace use. It does so by means of Federal Aviation Regulations (FARS).

The FAA's primary responsibilities are safeguarding persons and property on the ground and providing adequate control with regard to how airspace is used. It does so by certificating pilots, mechanics, air traffic controllers, and parachute riggers, and, furthermore, requires approval data for aircraft and parachutes.

The FAA specifically regulates certain aspects of sport parachuting but relies principally on self-regulation by skydiving participants following guidelines and safety requirements published by the USPA; also relying on self-policing from within the skydiving community for most training and operational requirements.

The following publications pertain to sport parachuting/skydiving:
—Part 65—Certification:
Airmen other than Flight Crew Members.
   "Subpart F-Parachute Riggers" defines requirements for certification.
—FAR Part 91—General Operation and Flight Rules
—FAR Part 105—Parachute Jumping
—FAR Part 149—Parachute Lofts
—Advisory Circular 105-2—Sport Parachute Jumping
—Chapter 10/FAA Inspector's Manual 8440.5A (Chg 32)—Sport Parachuting

[NOTE: FARs are not necessarily numbered consecutively. Gaps in numerical sequence in the following information are as they occur in the regulations, except where noted that information not included is not pertinent to parachuting.]

The FAA has the authority to impose fines and suspend or revoke certificates it has issued, including pilots and parachute riggers. The FAA can also fine parachutists.

§65.11 Certificate required

(a) No person may pack, maintain, or alter any personnel-carrying parachute intended for emergency use in connection with civil aircraft of the United States (including the auxiliary parachute of a dual parachute pack to be used for intentional jumping), unless he holds an appropriate certificate and type rating issued under this subpart and compiles with §§65.127 through 65.133.

(b) No person may pack, maintain, or alter any main parachute of a dual parachute pack to be used for intentional jumping in connection with civil aircraft of the United States unless he has an appropriate current certificate issued under this subpart. However, a person who does not hold such a certificate may pack the main parachute of a dual parachute pack that is to be used by him for intentional jumping.

(c) Each person who holds a parachute rigger certificate shall present it for inspection upon the request of the Administrator or an authorized representative of the National Transportation Safety Board, or of any Federal, State, or local law enforcement officer.

(d) The following parachute rigger certificates are issued under this Part:

(1) Senior parachute rigger.

(2) Master parachute rigger.

(e) Sections 65.127 through 65.133 do not apply to parachutes packed, maintained, or altered for the use of the Armed Forces.

§65.113 Eligibility requirements: general.

(a) To be eligible for a parachute rigger certificate, a person must—

(1) Be at least 18 years of age;

(2) Be able to read, write, speak, and understand the English language, or in the case of a citizen of Puerto Rico, or a person who is employed outside the United States by a U.S. air carrier and who does not meet this requirement, be issued a certificate that is valid only in Puerto Rico or while he is employed by that air carrier, as the case may be; and

(3) Comply with the sections of this subpart that apply to the certificate and type rating he seeks.

(b) Except for a master parachute rigger certificate, a parachute rigger certificate that was issued before, and was valid on, October 31, 1962, is equal to a senior parachute rigger certificate and may be exchanged for such a corresponding certificate.

§65.115 Senior parachute rigger certificate: experience, knowledge, and skill requirements.

Except as provided in §65.117, an applicant for a senior parachute rigger certificate must—

(a) Present evidence satisfactory to the Administrator that he has packed at least 20 parachutes of each type for which he seeks a rating, in accordance with the manufacturer's instructions and under the supervision of a certificated parachute rigger holding a rating for that type or a person holding an appropriate military rating;

(b) Pass a written test, with respect to parachutes in common use, on—
   (1) Their construction, packing, and maintenance;
   (2) The manufacturer's instructions;
   (3) The regulations of this subpart; and
(c) Pass an oral and practical test showing his ability to pack and maintain at least one type parachute in common use, appropriate to the type rating he seeks.

§65.117 Military riggers or former military riggers: special certification rule.

In place of the procedure in §65.115, an applicant for a senior parachute rigger certificate is entitled to it if he passes a written test on the regulations of this subpart and presents satisfactory documentary evidence that he—

(a) Is a member or civilian employee of an Armed Force of the United States, is a civilian employee of a regular armed force of a foreign country, or has, within the 12 months before he applies, been honorably discharged or released from any status covered by this paragraph;
(b) Is serving, or has served within the 12 months before he applies, as parachute rigger for such an Armed Force; and
(c) Has the experience required by §65.115 (a).

§65.119 Master parachute rigger certificate: experience, knowledge, and skill requirements.

An applicant for a master parachute rigger certificate must meet the following requirements:

(a) Present evidence satisfactory to the Administrator that he has had at least three years of experience as a parachute rigger and has satisfactorily packed at least 100 parachutes of each of two types in common use, in accordance with the manufacturer's instructions—
   (1) While a certificated and appropriately rated senior parachute rigger; or
   (2) While under the supervision of a certificated and appropriately rated parachute rigger or a person holding appropriate military ratings.

An applicant may combine experience specified in subparagraphs (1) and (2) of this paragraph to meet the requirements of this paragraph.

(b) If the applicant is not the holder of a senior parachute rigger certificate, he must pass a written test, with respect to parachutes in common use, on —
   (1) Their construction, packing, and maintenance;

(2) The manufacturer's instructions; and

(3) The regulations of this subpart.

(c) Pass an oral and practical test showing his ability to pack and maintain two types of parachutes in common use, appropriate to the type ratings he seeks.

§65.121 Type ratings.

(a) The following type ratings are issued under this subpart:

(1) Seat.

(2) Back.

(3) Chest.

(4) Lap.

(b) The holder of a senior parachute rigger certificate who qualifies for a master parachute rigger certificate is entitled to have placed on his master parachute rigger certificate the ratings that were on his senior parachute rigger certificate.

§65.123 Additional type ratings: requirements.

A certificated parachute rigger who applies for an additional type rating must—

(a) Present evidence satisfactory to the Administrator that he has packed at least 20 parachutes of the type for which he seeks a rating, in accordance with the manufacturer's instructions and under the supervision of a certificated parachute rigger holding a rating for that type or a person holding an appropriate military rating; and

(b) Pass a practical test, to the satisfaction of the Administrator, showing his ability to pack and maintain the type of parachute for which he seeks a rating.

§65.125 Certificates: privileges.

(a) A certificated senior parachute rigger may—

(1) Pack or maintain (except for major repair) any type of parachute for which he is rated; and

(2) Supervise other persons in packing any type of parachute for which he is rated.

(b) A certificated master parachute rigger may—

(1) Pack, maintain, or alter any type of parachute for which he is rated; and

(2) Supervise other persons in packing, maintaining or altering any type of parachute for which he is rated.

(c) A certificated parachute rigger need not comply with §§65.127 through 65.133 (relating to facilities, equipment, performance standards, records, recent experience, and seal) in packing, maintaining, or altering (if authorized) the main parachute of a dual parachute pack to be used for intentional jumping.

§65.127 Facilities and equipment.

No certificated parachute rigger may exercise the privileges of his certificate unless he has at least the following facilities and equipment available to him:

(a) A smooth top table at least three feet wide by 40 feet long.
(b) A compartment for hanging parachutes vertically for drying and airing.
(c) Enough packing tools and other equipment to pack and maintain the types of parachutes that he services.
(d) Adequate housing facilities to perform his duties and to protect his tools and equipment.

§65.129 Performance standards.

No certificated parachute rigger may—

(a) Pack, maintain, or alter any parachute unless he is rated for that type;
(b) Pack a parachute that is not safe for emergency use;
(c) Pack a parachute that has not been thoroughly dried and aired;
(d) Alter a parachute in a manner that is not specifically authorized by the Administrator or the manufacturer;
(e) Pack, maintain, or alter a parachute in any manner that deviates from procedures approved by the Administrator or the manufacturer of the parachute; or
(f) Exercise the privileges of his certificate and type ratings unless he understands the current manufacturer's instructions for the operation involved and has—
    (1) Performed duties under his certificate for at least 90 days within the preceding 12 months; or
    (2) Shown the Administrator that he is able to perform those duties.

§65.131 Records.

(a) Each certificated parachute rigger shall keep a record of the packing, maintenance, and alteration of parachutes performed or supervised by him. He shall keep in that record, with respect to each parachute worked on, a statement of—
    (1) Its type and make;
    (2) Its serial number;
    (3) The name and address of its owner;
    (4) The kind and extent of the work performed;

(5) The date when and place where the work was performed; and

(6) The results of any drop tests made with it.

(b) Each person who makes a record under paragraph (a) of this section shall keep it for at least 2 years after the date it is made.

(c) Each certificated parachute rigger who packs a parachute shall write, on the parachute packing record attached to the parachute, the date and place of the packing and a notation of any defects he finds on inspection. He shall sign that record with his name and the number of his certificate.

§65.133 Seal.

Each certificated parachute rigger must have a seal with an identifying mark prescribed by the Administrator, and a seal press. After packing a parachute he shall seal the pack with his seal in accordance with the manufacturer's recommendation for that type of parachute.

PART 91—
GENERAL OPERATING AND FLIGHT RULES
SUBPART A—GENERAL

(§§91.1 through 91.14 not listed here, not being pertinent to parachuting.)

§91.15 Parachutes and parachuting

(a) No pilot of a civil aircraft may allow a parachute that is available for emergency use to be carried in that aircraft unless it is an approved type and—

(1) If a chair type (canopy in back), it has been packed by a certificated and appropriately rated parachute rigger within the preceding 120 days; or

(2) If any other type, it has been packed by a certificated and appropriately rated parachute rigger—

(i) Within the preceding 120 days, if its canopy, shrouds [suspension lines] and harness are composed exclusively of nylon, rayon, or other similar synthetic fiber or materials that are substantially resistant to damage from mold, mildew, or other fungi and other rotting agents propagated in a moist environment; or

(ii) Within the preceding 60 days, if any part of the parachute is composed of silk, pongee, or other natural fiber, or materials not specified in subdivision (1) of this paragraph.

(b) Except in an emergency, no pilot in command may allow, and no person may make, a parachute jump from an aircraft within the United States except in accordance with Part 105.

(c) Unless each occupant of the aircraft is wearing an approved parachute, no pilot of a civil aircraft carrying any person (other than a crew member), may execute any intentional maneuver that exceeds—
  (1) A bank of 60 degrees relative to the horizon; or
  (2) nose-up or nose-down attitude of 30 degrees to the horizon.
(d) Paragraph (c) does not apply to—
  (1) Flight tests for pilot certification or rating; or
  (2) Spins and other flight maneuvers required by the regulations for any certificate or rating when given by—
    (i) A certificated flight instructor; or
    (ii) An airline transport pilot instructing in accordance with §61.169 of this chapter.
(e) For purposes of this section, "approved parachute" means—
  (1) A parachute manufactured under a type certificate or a technical standard order (C-23 series); or
  (2) A personnel-carrying military parachute identified by an AF, AAF, or AN drawing number, or any other military designation or specification number.

PART 105-
PARACHUTE JUMPING
SUBPART A—GENERAL
§105.1 Applicability

(a) This Part prescribes rules governing parachute jumps made in the United States except parachute jumps necessary because of an in-flight emergency.
(b) For the purposes of this Part, a "parachute jump" means the descent of a person, to the surface from an aircraft in flight, when he intends to use, or uses, a parachute during all or part of his descent.

SUBPART B—OPERATING RULES

§105.11 Applicability

(a) Except as provided in paragraphs (b) and (c) of this section, this subpart prescribes operating rules governing parachute jumps to which this Part applies.
(b) This Part does not apply to a parachute jump necessary to meet an emergency on the surface, when it is made at the direction, or with the approval, of an agency of the United States, or of a State, Puerto Rico, the District of Columbia, or a possession of the United States, or of a political subdivision of any of them.
(c) Sections 105.13 through 105.17 and §§105.27 through 105.37 of this subpart do not apply to a parachute jump made by a member of an Armed Force—

(1) Over or within a restricted area when that area is under the control of an Armed Force; or

(2) In military operations in uncontrolled airspace.

(d) Section 105.23 does not apply to a parachute jump made by a member of an Armed Force within a restricted area that extends upward from the surface when that area is under control of an Armed Force.

§105.13 General.

No person may make a parachute jump, and no pilot in command of an aircraft may allow a parachute jump to be made from that aircraft, if that jump creates a hazard to air traffic or to persons or property on the surface.

§105.14 Radio equipment and use requirements.

(a) Except when otherwise authorized by ATC—

(1) No person may make a parachute jump, and no pilot in command of an aircraft may allow a parachute jump to be made from that aircraft, in or into controlled airspace unless, during that flight—

(i) The aircraft is equipped with a functioning two-way radio communications system appropriate to the ATC facilities to be used;

(ii) Radio communications have been established between the aircraft and the nearest FAA Air Traffic Control Facility or FAA Flight Service Station at least 5 minutes before the jumping activity is to begin, for the purposes of receiving information in the aircraft about known air traffic in the vicinity of the jumping activity; and

(iii) The information described in subdivision (ii) has been received by the pilot in command and the jumpers in that flight; and

(2) The pilot in command of an aircraft used for any jumping activity in or into controlled airspace shall, during each flight—

(i) Maintain or have maintained a continuous watch on the appropriate frequency of the aircraft's radio communications system from the time radio communications are first established between the aircraft and ATC, until he advises ATC that the jumping activity is ended from that flight; and

(ii) Advise ATC that the jumping activity is ended for that flight when the last parachute jumper from the aircraft reaches the ground.

(b) If, during any flight, the required radio communications system is or becomes inoperative, any jumping activity from the aircraft in or into controlled airspace shall be abandoned. However, if the communications system becomes inoperative in flight after receipt of a required ATC authorization, the jumping activity from that flight may be continued.

§105.15 Jumps over or into congested areas or open air assembly of persons.

(a) No person may make a parachute jump, and no pilot in command of an aircraft may allow a parachute jump to be made from that aircraft, over or into a congested area of a city, town, or settlement, or an open air assembly of persons unless a certificate of authorization for that jump has been issued under this section. However, a parachutist may drift over that congested area or open air assembly with a fully deployed and properly functioning parachute if he is at a sufficient altitude to avoid creating a hazard to persons and property on the ground.

(b) An application for a certificate of authorization issued under this section is made in a form and manner prescribed by the Administrator and must be submitted to the FAA Flight Standards Service Office having jurisdiction over the area in which the parachute jump is to be made, at least four days before the day of that jump.

(c) Each holder of a certificate of authorization issued under this section shall present that certificate for inspection upon the request of the Administrator, or any Federal, State, or local official.

§105.17 Jumps over or into airports.

Unless prior approval has been given by the airport management, no person may make a parachute jump, and no pilot in command of an aircraft may allow a parachute jump to be made from that aircraft—

(a) Over an airport that does not have a functioning control tower operated by the United States; or

(b) Onto any airport.

However, a parachutist may drift over that airport with a fully deployed and properly functioning parachute if he is at least 2,000 feet above that airport's traffic pattern, and avoids creating a hazard to person and property on the ground.

§105.19 Jumps in or onto control zones with functioning control towers operated by the United States.

(a) No person may make a parachute jump, and no pilot in command may allow a parachute jump to be made from that aircraft, in or into a control zone in which there is a functioning control tower operated by the United States without, or in violation of the terms of, an authorization issued under this section.

(b) Each request for an authorization under this section must be submitted to the control tower having jurisdiction over the control zone concerned and must include the information prescribed in §105.25.

§105.20 Jumps in or into airport radar service areas.

(a) No person may make a parachute jump and no pilot in command may allow a parachute jump to be made from that aircraft in or into an airport radar service area without, or in violation of, the terms of an ATC authorization issued under this section.

(b) Each request for an authorization under this section must be submitted to the control tower at the airport for which the airport radar service area is designated.

§105.21 Jumps in or into positive control areas.

(a) No person may make a parachute jump, and no pilot in command of an aircraft may allow a parachute jump to be made from that aircraft, in or into a positive control area without, or in violation of, an authorization issued under this section.

(b) Each request for an authorization issued under this section must be submitted to the nearest FAA Air Traffic Control Facility or FAA Flight Service Station and must include the information prescribed by §105.25 (a).

§105.23 Jumps in or into other airspace.

(a) No person may make a parachute jump, and no pilot in command of an aircraft may allow a parachute jump to be made from that aircraft, in or into airspace unless the nearest FAA Air Traffic Control Facility or FAA Flight Service Station was notified of that jump at least 1 hour before the jump is to be made, but not more than 24 hours before the jumping is to be completed, and the notice contained in the information prescribed in §105.25(a).

(b) Notwithstanding paragraph (a) of this section, ATC may accept from a parachute jumping organization a written notification of a scheduled series of jumps to be made over a stated period of time not longer than 12 calendar months. The notification must contain the information prescribed by §105.25(a), identify the responsible persons associated with that jumping activity, and be submitted at least 15 days, but not more than 30 days, before the jumping is to begin. ATC may revoke the acceptance of the notification for any failure of the jumping organization to comply with its terms.

(c) This section does not apply to parachute jumps in or into any airspace or place described in §§105.15, 105.19, or 105.21.

§105.25 Information required, and notice of cancellation or postponement of jumps.

(a) Each person requesting an authorization under §105.19 or §105.21, and each person submitting a notice under §105.23, must include the following information (on an individual or group basis) in that request or notice:

(1) The date and time jumping will begin.

(2) The size of the jump zone expressed in nautical mile radius around the target.

(3) The location of the center of the jump zone in relation to—

   (i) The nearest very high frequency omnidirectional range (VOR) facility in terms of the VOR radial on which it is located, and its distance in nautical miles from the VOR facility when that facility is 30 nautical miles or less from the drop zone target; or

   (ii) The nearest airport, town, or city depicted on the appropriate Coast and Geodetic Survey WAC or Sectional Aeronautical Chart, when the nearest VOR Aeronautical facility is more than 30 nautical miles from the drop zone target.

(4) The altitudes above the surface at which jumping will take place.

(5) The duration of the intended jump.

(6) The name, address, and telephone number of the person requesting the authorization or giving notice.

(7) The identification of the aircraft to be used.

(8) The radio frequencies, if any, available in the aircraft.

(b) Each person requesting an authorization under §105.19 or §105.21, and each person submitting a notice under §105.23, must promptly notify the FAA Air Traffic Control Facility or FAA Flight Service Station from which it requested authorization or which it notified, if the proposed or scheduled jumping activity is canceled or postponed.

§105.27 Jumps over or within restricted or prohibited areas.

No person may make a parachute jump, and no pilot in command may allow a parachute jump to be made from that aircraft, over or within a restricted area or prohibited area unless the controlling agency of the area concerned has authorized that jump.

§105.29 Flight visibility and clearance from clouds requirement.

No person may make a parachute jump, and no pilot in command of an aircraft may allow a parachute jump to be made from that aircraft—
- (a) Into or through a cloud; or
- (b) When the flight visibility is less, or at a distance from clouds that is less, than that prescribed in the following table:

Table 10-1. Flight Visibility and Clearance from Clouds Requirement.

	Altitude	Flight Visibility	Distance from Clouds
(1)	1,200 feet or less above the surface regardless of the MSL Altitude	3 statue miles	500 feet below 1,000 feet above 2,000 feet horizontal
(2)	More than 1,200 feet above the surface but less than 10,000 feet MSL	3 statute miles	500 feet below 1,000 feet above 2,000 feet horizontal
(3)	More than 1,200 feet above the surface and at or above 10,000 feet MSL	5 statute miles	1,000 feet below 1,000 feet above 1 mile horizontal

§105.31 [Deleted]

§105.33 Parachute jumps between sunset and sunrise.

- (a) No person may make a parachute jump, and no pilot in command of an aircraft may allow any person to make a parachute jump from that aircraft, between sunset and sunrise, unless that person is equipped with a means of producing a light visible for at least three statute miles.
- (b) Each person making a parachute jump between sunset and sunrise shall display the light required by paragraph (a) of this section from the time that person exits the aircraft until that person reaches the surface.

§105.35 Liquor and drugs.

No person may make a parachute jump while, and no pilot in command of an aircraft may allow a person to make a parachute jump from that aircraft if that person appears to be, —
- (a) Under the influence of intoxicating liquor; or
- (b) Using any drug that affects his faculties in any way contrary to safety.

§105.37 Inspections.

The Administrator may inspect (including inspections at the jump site) any parachute jump operation to which this Part applies, to determine compliance with the regulations of this Part.

SUBPART C—PARACHUTE EQUIPMENT

§105.41 Applicability

(a) Except as provided in paragraph (b) of this section, this subpart prescribes rules governing parachute equipment used in parachute jumps to which this Part applies.

(b) This subpart does not apply to a parachute jump made by a member of an Armed Force using parachute equipment of an Armed Force.

§105.43 Parachute equipment and packing requirements.

(a) No person may make a parachute jump and no pilot in command of an aircraft may allow any person to make a parachute jump from that aircraft, unless that person is wearing a single harness dual parachute pack, having at least one main parachute and one approved auxiliary parachute that are packed as follows:

(1) The main parachute must have been packed by a certificated parachute rigger, or by the person making that jump, within 120 days before the date of its use.

(2) The auxiliary must have been packed by a certificated and appropriately rated parachute rigger:

(i) Within 120 days before the date of use, if its canopy, shroud [suspension lines], and harness are composed of nylon, rayon, or other similar synthetic fiber or material that is substantially resistant to damage from mold, mildew, or other fungi and other rotting agents propagated in a moist environment; or

(ii) Within 60 days before the date of use, if it is composed in any amount of silk, pongee, or other natural fiber, or material not specified in paragraph (a) (2) of this section.

(b) No person may make a parachute jump using a static line attached to the aircraft and the main parachute unless an assist device, described and attached as follows, is used to aid the pilot chute in performing its function, or, if no pilot chute is used, to aid in the direct deployment of the main parachute canopy.

(1) The assist device must be long enough to allow the container to open before a load is placed on the device.

(2) The assist device must have a static load strength of—

(i) At least 28 pounds but not more than 160 pounds, if it is used to aid the pilot chute in performing its function; or

    (ii) At least 56 pounds but not more than 320 pounds, if it is used to aid in the direct deployment of the main parachute canopy.

  (3) The assist device must be attached—

    (i) At one end, to the static line above the static line pins, or, if static pins are not used, above the static line ties to the parachute cone; and

    (ii) At the other end, to the pilot chute apex, bridle cord or bridle loop, or, if no pilot chute is used, to the main parachute canopy.

(c) No person may attach an assist device required by paragraph (b) of this section to any main parachute unless he has a current parachute rigger certificate issued under Part 65 of this chapter or is the person who makes the jump with that parachute.

(d) For the purposes of this section, an "approved" parachute is—

  (1) A parachute manufactured under a type certificate or a technical standard order (C-23 series); or

  (2) A personnel-carrying military parachute (other than a high altitude, high speed, or ejection kind) identified by an NAF, AAF, or AN drawing number, an AAF order number, or any other military designation or specification number.

EXTRACT—FAA INSPECTOR'S MANUAL 8440.5A (CHG 32)

Chapter 10—Sport Parachuting

141. Purpose. This chapter provides necessary guidelines to ensure uniform application of FAR Part 105 which regulates all parachute jumping except that of an emergency nature. In addition to this chapter, AC 105-2A, Sport Parachute Jumping, provides added guidelines.

142. General. As directed by the FAA Act of 1958, Part 105 was written primarily to ensure protection of other users of the national airspace system and the general public from sport parachuting activities. Congress determined that parachute jumping is a sport and should be subject to Federal regulation only to the extent necessary to protect others.

143. Parachute Associations/Organizations. Parachutists who are not members of a recognized parachute organization and wish to participate in a demonstration/exhibition jump over or into a congested area, must present satisfactory evidence of the necessary experience, knowledge, and skill that is comparable to those required by the United States Parachute Association (USPA). If the applicant is unable to provide this information, inspectors may require a demonstration jump/s as a prerequisite for approving the request. The USPA, located at 1440 Duke Street, Alexandria, Virginia 22314, (703)836−3495, has adopted its own safety rules and licensing standards for parachutists, instructors, and jump-masters. The USPA has pledged to implement a policy of self-policing to assist the FAA in avoiding conflicts with other airspace users and to maintain a high level of safety. Toward this end, the USPA has supplied every GADO/FSDO with a brochure of its rules and safety programs, and [has] offered [its] assistance any time the FAA encounters problems with a particular club or has questions regarding parachuting.

144. Certificate of Authorization. Section 105.15 is applicable to jumps over or into congested areas or open-air assemblies of persons. A Certificate of Waiver or Authorization, FAA Form 7711−1, is required for any jump OVER or INTO a congested area. The drift-over provision of Section 105.15 permits a jumper to exit an aircraft over something other than a congested area, and with a fully deployed parachute, drift over a congested area or open-air assembly of persons, and land in an open area. Under these circumstances a **certificate of authorization is not required**. The key to determine if an authorization is required are the words "over or into." In other words, the drift-over provision does not permit any jump that results in landing into a congested area or open-air assembly of persons unless the parachutists have obtained a Certificate of Authorization.

145. Parachutists' Competency. The competence of the parachutists is extremely important when evaluating the suitability of a landing site. Holders of USPA Class C and D licenses have proven themselves to be highly skilled, and anyone holding such a license and actively participated in the sport within the last 12 months, should be competent to participate in any jump where the separation criteria meets or exceeds that established in a Level One Landing Area. Those persons holding a USPA Class D license with a current exhibition rating have demonstrated the additional skills that are necessary to permit exhibition demonstrations in accordance with the separation criteria established in a Level Two Landing Area.

NOTE: USPA demonstration (PRO) ratings are issued to members who have a USPA D license who have accomplished 10 successive jumps into a 10-meter (32 feet) diameter target area in accordance with the following criteria:

(a) All landings must be made standing up.
(b) The size of the canopy used during qualification will determine the canopy limitations allowed during actual demonstration jumps (i.e., smallest canopy demonstrated).
(c) Demonstration jumps must be witnessed by either an S&TA [Safety and Training Advisor] or by an I/E [Instructor/Examiner], and at least two other spectators.

(d) The completed application must be signed by the S&TA or I/E and by applicant's Conference Director and forwarded to USPA HQ along with a current, suitable photograph of the applicant.

(e) USPA HQ will issue the rating with an expiration date 12 months from the issue date. Members will be renewed on the basis of continued demonstration of the original rating requirements.

146. Landing Areas. Landing areas will be divided into two distinct categories, dependent on the demonstrated competency of the parachutists.

(a) *Level One*. Parachutists who hold a USPA Class C or D license must select a landing area that will permit the jumper to land not closer than 50 feet from any spectator and will not involve passing over persons on the surface at an altitude of less than 250 feet.

(b) *Level Two*. Parachutists who hold a USPA Class D license with an exhibition rating, who certify that they will use a steerable square main and reserve canopy, will be permitted to exit over or into a congested area. The selected landing area must permit the jumper to land not closer than 15 feet from any spectator and will not involve passing over persons on the surface at an altitude of less than 50 feet.

147. Alternate Landing Areas. Regardless of the experience of the parachutist, "runoffs" or "escape areas" must be considered. Small target areas may be acceptable when a suitable alternate landing area is available in the event of unexpected conditions.

148. Application. When an authorization is required, the applicant will submit FAA Form 7711-2, Application for Certificate of Waiver or Authorization, in triplicate, to the GADO/FSDO having jurisdiction over the area in which the jump is to be made. Before approval, the inspector must coordinate any request involving controlled airspace with the controlling air traffic facility. Approval or denial of the application will be documented on the front side of FAA Form 7711-2, with supporting information entered in the remarks section on the reverse side. If the request is approved, a copy of FAA Form 7711-2, and the original Certificate of Waiver or Authorization, FAA Form 7711-1, will be signed and dated by the authorizing inspector and returned to the applicant. The original FAA Form 7711-2 and a copy of FAA Form 7711-1 will be retained in the district office file.

149. Aircraft Used in Parachute Operations. Any aircraft engaged in sport parachuting operations must be operated in accordance with rules prescribed in FAR Part 91. In some cases, a large aircraft may be subject to the applicability of FAR Part 125. The operators of these aircraft must hold an operating certificate under Part 125 or a letter of deviation authority permitting operation under Part 91 for the purpose of intentional parachute jumping. Many aircraft involved in parachute jumping have been modified to accommodate the jumpers. These modifications may involve seatbelt attachments and arrangements, attachments to the structure, or emergency exits, and will require documentation of field approval by the FAA, or a Supplementary Type Certificate (STC). Changes in the configuration of the aircraft must be reflected in the weight and balance documents.

150. Military Exhibition Teams. (Information not included here because of limited value to a general reader of this guidebook.)

151. Assistance. It would be impossible for every aviation inspector to be knowledgeable about sport parachuting activities. While the majority of contacts with the parachutists are made by operations inspectors, technical questions concerning airworthiness or engineering should be referred to the appropriate office for resolution. In some cases, USPA may be able to provide assistance.

Appendix

EQUIPMENT/ACCESSORY
MANUFACTURERS AND DISTRIBUTORS

This partial list of companies in the U.S. shows the great number of manufacturers and distributors involved in the sport parachute field. Many of these firms also supply standard emergency-type parachute equipment and accessories. Many of the companies listed also have fax or telex numbers. You can call them for that information.

California

- Action Air Parachutes, Rte. 2, Box 2410A, Yolo County Airport, Davis, CA 95616-9734, (916)753-2650. (Stocks, sells, and services major brands of parachute and related equipment; member, Parachute Industry Association.)
- Butler Parachute Systems, 6399 Lindbergh Boulevard, California City, CA 93505. (Equipment designer, special products.)
- Flite Suit, P.O. Box 4, Pope Valley, CA 94567, (707)965-2503. (Designer/manufacturer of jump suits.)
- Rigging Innovations, 236-A East Third Street, Perris, CA 92370, (714)657-1769. (Piggyback container/harness system designer/manufacturer; member, Parachute Industry Association.)
- Square One Parachute Sales & Service, 2095 Goetz Road, Perris, CA 92370, (714)657-8260, Fax (714) 657-8179.
- Teva Sport Sandals, 25950 #2 Belle Port, Harbor City, CA 90710, 1-800-FOR-TEVA. (Designer/manufacturer of specialized footwear.)

Colorado

- Edge Enterprises, 3507 Morrison Street, Denver, CO 80219, (303)935-8830. (Sales, service, and manufacturing, ram air main and reserve canopies, piggyback harness/container systems, accessories.)

Connecticut

- New England Parachute Company, P.O. Box 126, Hampton, CT 06247, (203)779-0229. (Major ram air canopy designer/manufacturer; also custom piggyback container/harness assemblies; provides complete repair services.)

Florida

- Air Time Designs, Inc., P.O. Box 1145, Zephyrhills, FL 34283-1145, (813)788-4753. (Designer/manufacturer of jump suits.)
- Jump Shack, 1665 North Lexington Avenue #106, DeLand, FL 32724, (904)734-5867. (Major designer/ manufacturer of piggyback container/harness assemblies.)
- Performance Designs, 2761 78th Street, Hialeah, FL 33061, (305)558-6178. (Ram air canopy designer/manufacturer.)
- Relative Workshop, 1725 Lexington Avenue, DeLand, FL 32724, (904)736-7589. (Major designer/manufacturer of piggyback container/harness assemblies; also *one of only two U.S producers of tandem parachuting systems*.)
- Strong Enterprises, 11236 Satellite Boulevard, Orlando, FL 32821, (305)859-9317. (Major designer/manufacturer of ram air and other canopies and piggyback container/harness systems; also *one of only two U.S. producers of tandem parachuting systems*; offers various catalogs of diversified product line; provides complete repair services.)
- Sunshine Factory, 819 5th Avenue, Zephyrhills, FL 34248, (813) 788-9831.

Georgia

- F.T.S. Incorporated, 4125 McFarland Drive, Alpharetta, GA 30201, (404)475-7181. (Ram air canopy designer/manufacturer.)
- Aerosports, P.O. Box 39, Warm Springs, GA 31830, (404) 655-3373.
- Glide Path International, 2348 John Glenn Drive, Chamblee, GA 30341, (404)458-1516. (Major designer/manufacturer of ram air canopies.)

Illinois

- Para-Gear Equipment Co., 3839 West Oakton Street, Skokie, IL, (312)679-5905. (Major distributor with extraordinarily diversified line of equipment and accessories; annually produces an excellent comprehensive 160-plus-page catalog; provides complete repair services; member, Parachute Industry Association.)

Maryland

- Kroop's Goggles, Dept. P. 9865E North Washington Boulevard, Laurel, MD 20707, (301)498-5848. (Major manufacturer of lightweight goggles with assorted lens colors and custom, color-coordinated edging.)

New Hampshire

- The RW SHOP, Route 13, Box P, Brookline, NH 03033, (603)673-JUMP (5867). (Major supplier of equipment and accessories; also manufactures some products; provides complete repair services.)

New Jersey

- National Parachute Industries, Inc., P.O. Box 1000, 47 East Main Street, Flemington, NJ 08822, (201)782-1646. (Major designer/producer of ram air and other canopies and piggyback and other container/harness assemblies; 40-page catalog available; provides complete repair service.)
- North American Aerodynamics, Inc., Highway 202, Flemington, NJ 08822, (201)782-5758; also 110 Carver Drive, Roxboro, NC, (919)599-9266. (Major canopy designer/manufacturer of ram air canopies.)
- Parachute Associates, Inc., P.O. Box 428, Lumberton, NJ 08048, (609)859-3397. (Distributors of ram air and other canopies, piggyback container/harness assemblies, and accessories.)
- Para-Flite, Inc., 5800 Magnolia Avenue, Pennsauken, NJ 09109, (609)663-1275. (Major ram air canopy/accessory designer/manufacturer.)

New York

- Cummings Rigging Works, Inc., 15 Gaynor Ave. #2H, Manhassett, NY 11030, (516)627-1432. (Distributor of equipment and accessories; provides complete repair services.)

North Carolina

- North American Aerodynamics, Inc., 110 Carver Drive, Roxboro, NC, (919)599-9266; also Highway 202, Flemington, NJ 08822, (201)782-5758. (Major designer/manufacturer of ram air canopies.)

Ohio

- Stewart Systems (SSK Industries, Inc.), 4925 N. Street, Route 42, Waynesville, OH 45068, (513)897-6165. (Designer/manufacturer of piggyback container/harness assemblies.)

Oregon

- Western Parachute Sales, Inc., 29388 SE Heiple Road, Eagle Creek, OR 97022, (503)630-JUMP, 654-0718. (Distributor of ram air and other canopies, container/harness systems, and accessories.)

Pennsylvania

- Para Loft, Inc., (Dave De Wolf, FAA DPRE), 26 West Bainbridge, Elizabethtown, Pa 17022. (Operates a parachute rigger training school; as an FAA-Designated Parachute Rigger Examiner (DPRE), is authorized to administer parachute rigger oral and practical examinations and to issue temporary rigger certificates.)

Tennessee

- Precision Aerodynamics, Inc., Highway 127-N, P.O. Box 386, Dunlap, TN 37327, (615)949-4688. (Major ram air canopy designer/manufacturer.)
- Signal Parachutes, 401 Pine Street, Signal Mountain, TN 37377. (Buys and sells preowned parachute equipment.)
- Skydance Photography, 4518 Granny White Turnpike, Nashville, TN 37204, (615)297-9751. (Designer/manufacturer of stock and custom freefall photography systems, including still film and video camcorder.)
- Far West Parachute, 3139 Renaissance Dr., Dallas, TX 75287, (214)307-2091 (Master rigger repair services; distributor of parachute systems and accessories, member, Parachute Industry Association).

Texas

- The Adventure Loft, Inc., 1425 Century #100, Carrollton, TX 75006, (214)245-4256. (Designer/manufacturer, including piggyback container/harness system, round reserve canopy, reserve pilot chute.)

Utah

- The Hat Shoppe, 268 East Kathryn Circle, Sandy, UT 84070, (801)572-3883. (Designer/manufacturer of custom leather skydiving hats, a.k.a., "soft helmets.")

Washington

- Para-Phernalia, Inc., 1045 12th Avenue, N.W., #F-8, Issaquah, WA 98027, (206)392-9534. (Designs/manufactures piggyback container/harness systems; member, Parachute Industry Association.)

Glossary

Skydiving has a great number of special terms associated with it. Understanding the jargon of the sport and its associated elements will make it easier to know what is going on at a drop zone (DZ) and in parachuting.

AAD—*See* AUTOMATIC ACTIVATION DEVICE.

"A" Basic License—The first of a series (and lowest) of four sport parachutist skill-level licenses issued by the UNITED STATES PARACHUTE ASSOCIATION. Such licenses are indicators of various abilities that have been demonstrated by a candidate for a specific license. The "A" license is issued to a student with a minimum of 20 jumps and who is no longer on student status. (*See* Chapter 3 for qualification details.)

above ground level—Abbreviated AGL or agl. Not to be confused with ABOVE SEA LEVEL. Altimeters are adjusted to a "zero" setting based on the ground level of where a jump is to be made. This consideration could be important in the event of jumping onto a DROP ZONE (DZ) that might be much higher—or lower—in elevation than the location from which an aircraft departed, for instance making an exhibition jump in a high-ground region away from a low-land airport where a customary DROP ZONE (DZ) is situated.

above sea level—Abbreviated ASL or asl. A height indicator designating the altitude of a location in relation to sea level. Not to be confused with ABOVE GROUND LEVEL.

AC—*See* ADVISORY CIRCULAR.

A/C—*See* AIRCRAFT.

accelerated freefall—Abbreviated AFF. A parachuting instruction technique in which a student makes a freefall parachute jump accompanied by one or two appropriately rated ACCELERATED FREEFALL (AFF) instructors. (The number of instructors depends on a student's skill level.) In Canada the same teaching method is termed *Progressive Freefall*. ACCELERATED FREEFALL (AFF) is one of two state-of-the-art instruction methods. (*See* TANDEM PARACHUTING.)

adapter—An item of parachute hardware: manufactured in *adjustable* and *nonadjustable* configurations.

advisory circular—A publication of the FEDERAL AVIATION ADMINISTRATION (FAA) intended to clarify FEDERAL AVIATION REGULATIONS (FARs).

aircraft—A machine or device capable of atmospheric flight; used by skydivers to gain sufficient altitude for making a safe skydive (e.g., powered fixed-wing plane of every size, helicopter, dirigible, ultralight aircraft, hang glider, balloon). Though ram air parachute canopies make it possible to duplicate many features performed by an aircraft, such canopies are not considered "aircraft."

AFF—*See* ACCELERATED FREEFALL.

AGL—*See* ABOVE GROUND LEVEL.

alteration—Also MODIFICATION or CONVERSION. A change to a manufacturer's original configuration: e.g., removing canopy panels and gores to achieve steerability and additional thrust, installing harness D-RINGS for AUXILIARY (RESERVE) PARACHUTE attachment; adding a deployment retardation device (such as a sleeve, bag, or similar article) to intentionally slow deployment inflation of a canopy; and a host of other features.

altimeter—A "flight instrument" accessory carried by skydivers that shows height above the ground. Altimeters are manufactured in varied sizes and are extremely reliable. Some jumpers locate them on a harness chest strap, on a harness main lift web, or at other suitable, visually accessible places.

approved—A term signifying FEDERAL AVIATION ADMINISTRATION (FAA) certification of an item for use in aviation.

ASL—*See* ABOVE SEA LEVEL.

automatic activation device—Abbreviated AAD. A generic term for a self-contained device to remove ripcord pins from closure devices that keep a RESERVE PARACHUTE closed. The automatic opening feature can be based on preset altitude, time, percentage of terminal velocity, or a combination thereof. Development for sport parachuting use began in 1959, and the first such device was patented the following year. Over many years many lives were saved using AADS. (At one time an AAD was known as an automatic *opening* device. Sometimes that term was thought by students and novice skydivers to mean *canopy* opening instead of *container* opening. Manufacturers took to referring to their product as an automatic *activation* device, and adding stronger wording in instructions that an AAD was, under prescribed conditions, for activating the opening sequence of a container.)

auxiliary parachute—*See* RESERVE PARACHUTE. British parachutists use this term to refer to what Americans call a PILOT CHUTE.

"B" Intermediate License—The third highest of four United States Parachute Association-issued skill-level certificates that verify an individual's parachuting abilities. *See* Chapter 3 for qualification details.

back loop—A freefall aerial maneuver. Intentional back loops are a requirement for a UNITED STATES PARACHUTE ASSOCIATION (USPA) "A" Basic license. Back loops are also included in the set of prescribed turns and loops of LEFT SERIES, RIGHT SERIES, and CROSS SERIES of STYLE events in parachute competitions.

back slide—Horizontal movement in freefall in a rearward direction from that being faced by a skydiver. Caused primarily by arms (but also hands) being improperly positioned, even though a skydiver might otherwise be in a STABLE FALL position. Unintentional backsliding can be most frustrating to a student jumper learning RELATIVE WORK. However, it is a simple problem to overcome and jumping with an experienced skydiver who can observe what a student is doing is the best method for improving freefall skills.

bag—A DEPLOYMENT DEVICE into which a canopy is stowed when a parachute is ready for use, and which aids in the orderly deployment of the canopy during a jump.

bag lock—A predicament for a parachutist attributable to a packing error or to putting equipment on incorrectly and failing to have an equipment check before boarding an aircraft. A jumper's emergency procedure is to deploy the RESERVE PARACHUTE.

barrel roll—An aerial maneuver for a freefall parachutist. Doing a left and right barrel roll is a requirement for a UNITED STATES PARACHUTE ASSOCIATION (USPA) "D" ADVANCED LICENSE.

base—The first entity (individual, group) in a freefall RELATIVE WORK work formation toward which the rest of the participants move to complete a formation—to PIN a base (*See* PIN). In a "two-way" (two-person) formation the base would be one jumper, pinned by a second jumper; in a "hundred-way" from a Hercules C-130, the base could be a "ten-way" taken off the tailgate, with many following skydivers pinning the base. Also, the term applies to the first person/canopy in a CANOPY RELATIVE WORK formation.

BASE jumping—BASE is an acronym for **B**uilding, **A**ntenna, **S**pan, **E**arth; pertains to the controversial facet of parachuting whereby people leap from those sites rather than skydiving from an aircraft.

basic parachutist course—The complete course of instruction from a first-jump course through completion of all requirements for obtaining a United States Parachute Association "A" BASIC LICENSE. Completing such a course signifies a person is capable of safe, competent sport parachuting without JUMPMASTER supervision, but there is still quite a way to go in becoming an "honest-to-goodness," "gen-you-wine" SKYDIVER!

basic safety requirement(s)—United States Parachute Association-designated minimum standard(s) for safe SPORT PARACHUTING. BSRs have been developed over a long period of time and are the result of a vast amount of experience gained from about the country and about the world. They are common sense applications of safety pertaining to every aspect of skydiving.

baton pass—An accomplishment of RELATIVE WORK from the early days of sport parachuting; passing a baton from one jumper to another in freefall was proof of relative work skill. A baton was most often a wooden rod, some 12 inches long and an inch or so round—say a piece of broom handle. In time, batons often became ornately adorned, a tangible memento of parachuting achievement. One jumper serving as a BASE left an aircraft carrying a baton and a second jumper was to PIN the baton-carrier. As skills improved more complex baton passes were made, three-way, four-way, and so on. When a conventional baton was not available, *anything* was passed—ballpoint pens, mechanical pencils, short lengths of twig-size tree limbs, and so forth. In "fun" competitions passing a raw egg in its shell greatly tests individual skills.

batwings—Flexible, semiflexible, or rigid devices used by exhibition jumpers in the 1930s and early, 40s as aids in slowing rate of fall and increasing horizontal gliding movement during freefall. Leo Valentin (*see* bibliography) was a foremost proponent and practitioner of rigid batwings. On May 21, 1956, near Liverpool, England, he died while testing his latest concept. Batwings are prohibited by UNITED STATES PARACHUTE ASSOCIATION (USPA) BASIC SAFETY REQUIRE-MENTS (BSRs).

bomb-out exit—A diving exit from an aircraft; *see* DOOR EXIT and UNPOISED EXIT.

braking/brakes—By manipulating the control lines of steerable parachutes, a jumper beneath an open canopy can vary forward speed of the canopy. Such braking action will also alter rate-of-descent characteristics. Altering horizontal and vertical rates to slow and increase canopy movement is standard practice on every jump and parachutists, early on, learn braking techniques.

breakaway—*See* CUTAWAY. An emergency procedure for separating from a malfunctioned main canopy by jettisoning that canopy by means of CANOPY RELEASES, returning to freefall, followed by actuating a RESERVE PARACHUTE.

break off—A term used in both freefall RELATIVE WORK (RW) and CANOPY RELATIVE WORK (CRW). In RW, refers to the point in freefall jumpers in or near a formation separate from one another so as to have sufficient space to safely open parachutes. In CRW, it is the altitude at which no more incoming canopies are permitted to "dock" on the formation, and the altitude at which the formation begins to disengage and separate for landing.

buffeting—Up-and-down (head-high, head-low) movement during freefall brought about by asymmetrical body position.

burble—An area of "dead" air space (negative pressure) above a skydiver's body resulting from relative air flow about his or her body during freefall.

"C" Intermediate License—The second highest of four United States Parachute Association-issued skill-level certificates. *See* Chapter 3 for qualification details.

canopy—The fabric used to form that part of a parachute assembly that encloses air and provides the shape that serves as a fall-retarding/gliding device. As a usual matter, speaking nontechnically, canopy nearly always includes the canopy's SUSPENSION LINES, and sometimes includes RISERS. Most inflated "round" canopies have the appearance of an inverted bowl. However, generically speaking, there are other canopies referred to as round, though they are only nearly so—such as a conical canopy, usually found in RESERVE PARACHUTES, or a "Para-Commander" sport main canopy. A RAM AIR CANOPY usually has two rectangular surfaces (upper and lower) of varied measurements separated by a compartmented area (open across the front of the canopy's width (span) and closed along the rear width) that traps air and gives the canopy its unusual shape. A WHUFFO often likens the shape to a "flying mattress."

canopy relative work—Abbreviated **CRW**, pronounced "crew." Intentional flying of two or more ram air canopies to create simple or complex aerial formations during canopy descent from aircraft to landing. CRW became a competition event in U.S. National Parachuting Championships in 1982.

canopy release(s)—A mechanical device (almost always used in pairs, except for some older military rigs available as government surplus) enabling a parachutist to readily separate from a canopy in a variety of circumstances, e.g., in the air, separating from a malfunctioned canopy before actuating a RESERVE PARACHUTE; on the surface, landing in water, being suspended after a tree landing, being dragged in high winds, and so on. Such devices are conventionally integrated into right and left main lift webs at the front of a harness in the region of a wearer's shoulders. Risers of a canopy assembly are securely mated to release mechanisms during normal parachute service. If a situation calls for it, canopy releases are readily actuated and risers separate from the harness, freeing a parachutist.

canopy transfer—A technique for changing from a main canopy to an AUXILIARY PARACHUTE canopy in an emergency situation.

capewell—An item of specialized CANOPY RELEASE hardware, generally still found only on military and government surplus parachutes. The term *capewell* (lower case "c") has been in use in sport parachuting since the 1950's, when most skydiving equipment was modified military surplus gear. The word derived from the name Capewell Manufacturing Company, of Hartford, Connecticut, a major producer of military specification CANOPY RELEASE hardware. Simply through usuage by unknowledgeable people, Capewell incorrectly came to be a parachuting jargon generic description for a canopy release device. Canopy release devices of simpler design and operation (*see* THREE-RING RELEASE) are now used with sport-type parachuting equipment (including that used by select military personnel).

Caterpillar Club—An informal organization of people whose lives have been saved by making an emergency parachute jump from a disabled aircraft. (Does not include skydivers or military personnel who have used a RESERVE PARACHUTE while making an intentional parachute jump.) The organization was formed in 1922 by three men after Lt. H. R. Harris had made the first recorded emergency from a powered aircraft. The trio thought it would be a good idea if there were some way to recognize those whose lives had been saved by a parachute. The Irving Air Chute Company supported the idea and issued miniature lapel pins in the form of the caterpillar insect (symbolic of silk production) to such parachutists, at first only to those using an Irving chute, then later to any emergency parachutist. Switlik Parachute of Trenton, New Jersey also provided much support to the loosely organized Caterpillar Club, improving matters substantially by maintaining detailed records and presenting lapel pins and certificates. (*See* bibliography: *JUMP! Tales of the Caterpillar Club*, Don Glassman, 1930.)

cell—One of the COMPARTMENTS (or *divisions*) of a RAM AIR CANOPY that make up the shape of the canopy. RAM AIR CANOPIES usually are classified by number of cells, e.g., five-cell, seven-cell, nine-cell. Cells are often subdivided by a vertical "wall" added for additional canopy integrity. Most RAM AIR CANOPIES have a CROSSPORT in all interior vertical walls to aid and speed canopy inflation.

certificated—Refers to approved, commercially made equipment that the Federal Aviation Administration (FAA) deems airworthy. The FAA also uses the term to describe persons it has approved for various aviation functions, such as pilot, mechanic, parachute rigger, and so forth.

chord—The front-to-rear distance of a RAM AIR CANOPY, usually referring to a top surface measurement.

chord construction—A manufacturing technique for producing a ram air canopy in which the long axis of fabric for upper and lower surfaces is chordwise (front to rear).

clear and pull—*See* JUMP AND PULL.

compartment—Generally refers to a stowage area of a PIGGYBACK RIG sport parachute assembly used for holding a packed canopy assembly during service. *See* CONTAINER and PACK.

conference director—An elected "middle management" administrative position of the UNITED STATES PARACHUTE ASSOCIATION (USPA). The U.S. is divided into 14 geographic areas (*see* Chapter 9), each under the supervision of a Conference Director, who is responsible for representing the interests of skydivers in a Conference area.

connector link(s)—Metal hardware of various configurations used as connector between a group of canopy SUSPENSION LINES and a RISER attached to a HARNESS.

container—*See* PACK or COMPARTMENT. That part of parachute equipment used to stow a canopy in preparation for use. With present-day sport equipment the term *compartment* is often used because once-separate container and harness units are now built as integrated harness/dual main-reserve-container assemblies. There is occasional insistence that the term *container* be used in place of *pack*, to avoid terminology confusion, but, like it or not, both terms have been used interchangeably for more than 40 years, probably even longer.

control line(s)—*See* STEERING LINE(s). Those complementary lines attached to either certain SUSPENSION LINES or to portions of a canopy itself and used to alter the canopy form to achieve steerability, resulting in changing direction of flight or for modifying rate of descent.

"conventional" gear/rig—Refers to a dual sport parachute system comprising a back-type main parachute assembly and a front-mounted RESERVE PARACHUTE on a single harness.

crab/crabbing—A canopy-handling technique used during descent under a parachute as a means of compensating for being off a "WIND LINE" while approaching a target from an OPENING POINT.

crew—Pronunciation for CRW— abbreviation for CANOPY RELATIVE WORK.

cross connector—(a) An optional, complementary item of parachute equipment, mostly used on sport parachuting main canopies, intended to provide additional safety. Construction is simple enough, usually being a short length of strong tubular webbing with a small loop sewn in place at each end. One loop is placed onto a CONNECTOR LINK of a right-side RISER and the other loop is put onto the CONNECTOR LINK of a left-side RISER. Connectors generally are used in pairs for strength; between both front RISERS, and between both rear RISERS. If a CANOPY RELEASE should unexpectedly release, or if an intentional BREAKAWAY/CUTAWAY is started and one canopy release does not function readily, the canopy will not collapse. The benefit of having a cross connector is additional time gained to complete an emergency procedure. (b) For CANOPY RELATIVE WORK (CRW), cross connectors are arranged differently, from a front riser to a rear riser, and are used to keep a parachutist from sliding back up suspension lines once canopy engagement has been made. Such risers are required equipment when performing PLANE CRW formations.

crossport—An opening in a "cell divider" of a RAM AIR CANOPY that allows incoming airflow between adjacent interior cells as a means of speeding inflation of the canopy and to ensure even pressurization. Each major CELL of a RAM AIR CANOPY is divided in two, lengthwise along the canopy CHORD (front/rear dimension), for structural integrity, resulting in subcells. With RAM AIR CANOPY configurations growing in number of CELLS/subcells and size (square feet of area of the upper surface), crossports are an important consideration when designing canopies.

cross pull—Refers to reaching across one's chest, from right to left, in order to grip a ripcord handle. In early sport parachuting years this technique was standard for deploying a main parachute and was a holdover from military methods when a ripcord pocket was mounted on the left side of a harness. Main parachute ripcords were later moved to the right side of a harness making it easier to retain stability during a ripcord pull to end freefall.

cross series—A direction-specific set of turns and loops performed during freefall. *See* STYLE SERIES.

CRW—*See* CANOPY RELATIVE WORK.

cutaway—*See* BREAKAWAY. An emergency procedure for separating from a malfunctioned main canopy by jettisoning that canopy by means of canopy releases and returning to freefall, followed by actuating a RESERVE PARACHUTE. Cutaway derives from a time when parachutists of the last century and earlier, rising to altitude while suspended beneath a passenger basket of a hot air balloon, actually cut an attachment line so the parachute descent could be started. Later, parachutists using body harnesses and fortunately having an AUXILIARY PARACHUTE along on a jump, resorted to cutting the suspension lines of a damaged main canopy so the canopy could be gotten rid of and the RESERVE canopy deployed and manipulated. As will happen with words and phrases in our language, the term cutaway as an emergency procedure lingered in skydiving jargon and is probably used more often than the more correct *breakaway*.

D-bag—Abbreviation for *deployment bag*. *See* DEPLOYMENT DEVICE.

D-ring—Refers to a RIPCORD handle and its shape, though the *ring* portion of the term is not really apropos. Early configurations of ripcord handles were circular in form, but though the handle configuration soon after changed to various forms resembling the alphabet letter "D," the word *ring* remained attached and another parachuting jargon term came into being and endured.

"D" Master License—The fourth and highest in the series of United States Parachute Association-issued skill-level certificates. (*See* Chapter 3 for qualification details.)

delta position—A body position used by a freefall parachutist to achieve horizontal movement in addition to ever-present vertical fall. *See* TRACKING/TRACK.

demonstration jump—More often referred to as a "demo"; also termed EXHIBITION JUMP or, less often, DISPLAY JUMP.

deploy/deployment—A dictionary definition of DEPLOY includes "to open out," "to extend. . .; the act of deployment." In essence, the definition defines what happens when a skydiver pulls a ripcord to open a parachute container or uses a THROW-OUT PILOT CHUTE, in either case to actuate a sport main parachute. The PILOT CHUTE, DEPLOYMENT DEVICE (bag, sleeve), SUSPENSION LINES, and CANOPY "open out," are "extended" until there is an open canopy. (*See* Chapter 4.)

deployment device—Can refer to a number of items related to controlling orderly deployment of a parachute canopy, e.g., sleeve, bag, direct bag, free bag, diaper, POD, etc. (*See* Chapter 5.)

Designated Parachute Rigger Examiner—Abbreviated DPRE. An appointed position of the FEDERAL AVIATION ADMINISTRATION (FAA). A DPRE acts as a surrogate for the FAA in administering oral and practical examinations to qualified candidates who have previously passed an FAA written examination for the Senior PARACHUTE RIGGER certificate; also examines candidates for Master PARACHUTE RIGGER certification.

diaper—A retardation device intended to delay inflation of a parachute canopy until suspension lines have been completely deployed. A panel of fabric material is wrapped about the pleated, folded bottom portion ("skirt") of a RESERVE PARACHUTE canopy and is securely held in place until both the canopy and suspension lines have been fully elongated in an orderly deployment. Orderly deployment is the major contributing factor to proper operation of a parachute system. (*See* Chapters 4 and 5.)

display jump—Interchangeable with DEMONSTRATION ("demo") or EXHIBITION JUMP, though not a common usage in the U.S.

door exit—*See* UNPOISED EXIT and BOMB-OUT EXIT.

downplane—A term pertaining to CANOPY RELATIVE WORK (CRW) and describing a specific formation.

DPRE—Abbreviation for a FEDERAL AVIATION ADMINISTRATION (FAA) DESIGNATED PARACHUTE RIGGER EXAMINER.

DRCP—Abbreviation for DUMMY RIPCORD PULL.

drop zone—(Abbreviated DZ.) A location where parachute landings are made. Military usage provides the derivation of the term, pertaining to a site where jumpers landed after usually having boarded an aircraft at another location. (Also applies to a site where equipment is dropped.) In most sport parachuting activity, fortunate skydivers have a target area somewhere on the airport used for takeoff. Here and there, less fortunate jumpers have to board an aircraft at an airport, fly to a DZ location, make their jumps, and be shuttled back to the airport.

dummy ripcord pull—*See* PRACTICE RIPCORD PULL. A student uses a training aid that simulates an actual RIPCORD being pulled on a freefall jump, in preparation for the time a student ends static line training and is ready to make a freefall jump. Dummy pulls are also part of first-jump training for ACCELERATED FREEFALL students. (In a humorous vein, *dummy* refers to the simulation device—or practice movement in accelerated freefall training—not to the student, though there has sometimes been cause to wonder, in the opinion of some jumpmasters and instructors. Perhaps, in current times of raised consciousness, the negative connotation is why there is an inclination toward replacing *dummy* with *practice*.)

DZ—Abbreviation for DROP ZONE.

exhibition jump—*See* DEMONSTRATION JUMP.

exit altitude—The actual altitude above ground level at which a parachutist leaves an aircraft to begin a skydive.

exit point—The actual place above a ground reference point at which a parachutist leaves an aircraft to begin a skydive. Depending on wind conditions between the ground and the exit altitude, an exit point could be much different from an OPENING POINT. Early in learning, students are taught the difference between the two reference points.

FAA—Abbreviation for FEDERAL AVIATION ADMINISTRATION.

FAI—Abbreviation for FEDERATION AÉRONAUTIQUÉ INTERNATIONALÉ.

FAA Parachute Rigger—A federally certificated person who does any number of tasks related to parachute assembly, maintenance, overhaul, packing, repair, and so forth. Basic certification is as a Senior PARACHUTE RIGGER; the advanced certificate is for Master PARACHUTE RIGGER. Both certificates can be issued with single or multiple ratings (Back, Chest, Seat).

FAR—Abbreviation for **Federal Aviation Regulation**.

Fédération Aéronautiqué Internationalé—Abbreviated **FAI**. An international organization that governs aviation sports throughout the world. Among other responsibilities, it sanctions international parachuting competitions and approves parachuting records.

Federal Aviation Administration (FAA)—A federal governing agency, and part of the U.S. Department of Transportation, responsible for every aspect of United States aeronautical activity.

Federal Aviation Regulation—Abbreviated **FAR**. A regulation of the FEDERAL AVIATION ADMINISTRATION (FAA).

feet per second—Abbreviated **FPS** or **fps**. A figure used in calculating rates of descent, both in freefall and under a canopy.

fichet—A French term, and pronounced "fish-shay," the original meaning was the person who, when judging a parachuting accuracy competition, marked the first point of a parachutist's ground contact when striving for a target. The term later came to be used, now exclusively so, as the name of the marking device used by an accuracy judge.

fid—A parachute packing tool; usually a short length of smooth wood or metal; primarily used by a parachute packer for "dressing" (smoothing) the exterior of a parachute container as finishing step in packing.

Field Pack/ing—A quick method of gathering up a canopy and reducing its bulk to temporarily stow in bundled form to simplify transport over distance. (It's a handy technique to know for the time when a parachutist might land at some distance from a DZ because of exiting an aircraft at the wrong place; or being carried away from a DZ in unexpected winds; or landing on a reserve canopy instead of a main parachute.)

first-jump course—A course of parachute training leading to a person making his or her first sport parachute jump.

FJC—Abbreviation for **first-jump course**.

floater—The position of one or more specific participants in an exit sequence for a large freefall RELATIVE WORK (RW) formation attempt. As a way of speeding an exit (particularly in aircraft with a small door) and forming a BASE, as many RW participants as possible are positioned outside the aircraft, more or less "clinging" to door edges, to specially mounted handrails on the fuselage, and to other jumpers positioned in the door. At exit, those "hangers-on" have the assignment of extending to a fully open, spread-eagled body position so they can "float" while the BASE jumpers exit rapidly and start a formation so following skydivers can PIN the BASE. Depending on aircraft size, there can be several floaters on a given RW attempt.

forward loop—Same as FRONT LOOP, though the latter term is more often used.

FPS—Abbreviation for FEET PER SECOND.

freefall—A skydive on which a parachute is manually activated at a jumper's discretion; also refers to that portion of a jump between aircraft exit and parachute deployment.

frog position—A relaxed form of the basic full-spread freefall body position; easily learned by students and quickly adopted as the standard freefall position.

front loop—Also termed "forward loop," though the latter is less frequently used; a qualification requirement to acquire a United States Parachute Association (USPA) "D" (**Master**) license.

funnel—A term used in freefall RELATIVE WORK; describes appearance of a freefall formation that collapses inward and the participants seem to be falling into a funnel.

fun jump—A skydive made without the stress of competition; refers to most jumps.

glide—The horizontal, angular descent path of an open parachute canopy.

glide ratio—The relationship between the amount of horizontal movement and vertical descent of a canopy when it is open. A standard round canopy has a negligible glide ratio when it is manipulated by using risers/suspension lines to achieve "slipping" movement. A standard round canopy modified to a steerable configuration does then have a slight glide ratio, and that ratio goes up noticeably in the case of a Para-Commander or Papillon or similarly configured canopy. Ram air canopies routinely have a glide ratio of about 3:1, with certain models having a higher ratio.

glissade—An "ancient" sport parachuting term, rarely heard, seen, or used anymore. It is a French word describing an action in which a parachutist pulls down a canopy's front suspension lines and/or risers for more than a distance of a meter for the purpose of partially collapsing the canopy and increasing the rate of descent. (The canopy-handling technique was also referred to as a "front riser *slip*.") Such a maneuver was generally performed to avoid overshooting a target area. Early competition accuracy jumpers sometimes resorted to more than one glissade during a descent, some glissades lasting several seconds as an extreme measure to rapidly lose altitude. With the advent of the RAM AIR CANOPY for accuracy competition, glissade has disappeared into history.

Gold Wings—A notable United States Parachute Association (USPA) award presented to a qualified recipient for having made 1,000 freefall parachute jumps. Since the award signifies a milestone in a skydiver's career, presentation is done ceremoniously.

grommet—A circular metal fitting used in various items of parachuting equipment, e.g., containers, deployment bags, sliders.

GW—Abbreviation for UNITED STATES PARACHUTE ASSOCIATION (USPA) GOLD WINGS.

HAHO—An acronym for HIGH ALTITUDE, HIGH OPENING, a specialized type of military tactical parachute jump ("vertical insertion"). A parachutist exits an aircraft at as high as 40,000 feet in altitude, deploys a RAM AIR CANOPY after only a short delay, then soars a great distance, utilizing the high glide ratio of the canopy. Small teams, generally operating at night and unnoticed by ground forces because of being small, undetectable tracking targets, can thus fly several miles to a designated target area, to then carry on a mission.

HALO—An acronym for **High Altitude, Low Opening**, a specialized type of military tactical parachute jump. A jumper (or small team) exits an aircraft from an altitude of as high as 40,000 and remains in freefall for a long period—unnoticed by tracking equipment—deploying a RAM AIR CANOPY at about 1,500 feet, then utilizing the high-performance characteristics of the parachute to reach a target area. Operational missions are generally conducted at night, to avoid detection.

hardware—Various metal and plastic fittings used with parachute equipment.

harness—An arrangement of webbing and hardware that attaches to a parachutist's body and is used to support the jumper during descent under a canopy. (*See* Chapter 5.) There are varied configurations of each of many types of hardware used, giving a skydiver a wide range of choices to suit personal preference.

helmet—A useful, but not always required, skydiving accessory—though mandatory for static line and ACCELERATED FREEFALL (AFF) students.

hesitation—Abbreviated term referring to a PILOT CHUTE HESITATION.

hop 'n' pop—*See* JUMP AND PULL.

I—Abbreviation for INSTRUCTOR.

ICC—Abbreviation for INSTRUCTOR CERTIFICATION COURSE.

Instructor—A *rating* issued to a qualified UNITED STATES PARACHUTE ASSOCIATION (USPA) licenseholder, such rating indicating that an individual has completed specialized training related to teaching parachuting to others.

Instructor Certification Course—A protracted examination participated in to qualify for a United States Parachute Association (USPA) Instructor rating.

I/E—Abbreviation for INSTRUCTOR/EXAMINER.

Instructor/Examiner—A rating issued to a qualified UNITED STATES PARACHUTE ASSOCIATION (USPA) licenseholder, such rating going beyond skill levels and achievement requirements of the INSTRUCTOR rating.

inversion—A malfunction condition in which a canopy turns inside out—partially or completely. Generally, it is due to a disorderly deployment of a parachute system.

JCC—Abbreviation for **Jumpmaster Certification Course**.

Judge—A rating issued by the UNITED STATES PARACHUTE ASSOCIATION (USPA) attesting to an individual's skills in evaluating competitor performance; issued for various levels of expertise: Conference Judge, National Judge, FAI (*see* entry) International Judge.

jump and pull—*See* HOP 'N' POP. The technique of leaving an aircraft, maintaining stability, and promptly deploying a parachute. (Nervous student jumpers, poised facing forward on a "jump step," clutching a wing strut with both hands, suddenly lacking confidence, and given a firm "GO!" by a jumpmaster, have been known to make a "*pull* and jump," releasing only one hand from the wing strut and fiercely yanking a ripcord handle while still poised on the jump step, much to the consternation of the jumpmaster. Needless to say, the deploying parachute system quickly removes the student from the aircraft. Such an occurrence is always humorous after the student is safely clear of the plane.)

jump boots—Protective footwear used by parachutists. In days gone by, all parachutists wore heavy high-top boots offering firm ankle support and having thickly cushioned soles, both features meant to minimize landing shock; but the intent was not always successful. Such footwear is rarely seen at a skydiving DROP ZONE anymore. Instead, even student parachutists wear only jogger-type footgear. The slow rate-of-descent characteristics of modern ram air canopies have done away with the need for extreme measures in protecting feet and ankles. Jump boots, per se, are now primarily used in military parachutists engaged in military duties.

Jumpmaster—A rating issued by the UNITED STATES PARACHUTE ASSOCIATION (USPA) to qualified licenseholders, permitting direct supervision of student parachutists engaged in ground training and when making parachute jumps.

Jumpmaster Certification Course—A lengthy, detailed testing process participated in to qualify for a UNITED STATES PARACHUTE ASSOCIATION (USPA) Jumpmaster rating.

jump run—The direction in which an aircraft flies at a specified altitude preparatory to a skydiver exiting an aircraft; usually done by flying across a DROP ZONE target area toward a predetermined exit point.

jump ship—An aircraft used for SKYDIVING.

jump story—Fishers have "fish stories"; military and naval personnel have "war stories"; pilots have "There I was, . . ." stories—and student parachutists and skydivers alike have *jump stories*, limited only by imagination and the endurance of listeners.

L/D Ratio—Abbreviation for **lift-over-drag ratio.**

left series—A direction-specific set of turns and loops performed during freefall. (*See* STYLE SERIES.)

lift-over-drag ratio—An expression defining the distance a parachute canopy will glide horizontally in relation to the distance it will descend vertically, usually in the measurement of feet (e.g., 3:1 L/D—three feet of horizontal distance for each one foot of vertical descent).

lurk—"Hang around" RELATIVE WORK jumpers for a chance to get in on a RELATIVE WORK.

malfunction (minor/major)—A condition of a parachute system (or, for that matter, an individual) not functioning as it is supposed to.

major repair—A parachute rigging term; any repair that affects the "structural integrity" of a parachute system is classified as a major repair. Any other repair is a MINOR REPAIR.

military parachuting—Commonly refers to mass jumps made by parachute-equipped troops for tactical/strategic military purpose, usually by means of static line equipment and from altitudes ranging from 1,200 feet to as low as 500 feet. Qualified troops using special canopies also jump as low as 300 feet for specific purposes. However, much military parachuting also encompasses use of sport-type equipment by specially trained military personnel using techniques originally developed by civilian sport parachutists and enhanced by skydiving experience.

minor repair—A parachute rigging term; refers to any repair or alteration to a parachute assembly that does not affect the structural integrity of the system (*See* MAJOR REPAIR.)

modification—A change from the original configuration of any part of a parachute system.

NAA—Abbreviation for NATIONAL AERONAUTIC ASSOCIATION.

National Aeronautic Association—A voluntary membership national association encompassing many aspects of aviation activity in the U.S. The UNITED STATES PARACHUTE ASSOCIATION (USPA) is a member organization.

National Collegiate Parachuting League—Abbreviated **NCPL**. Formed in 1961; administers a sport parachuting program for college and university students;

sanctions and conducts various meets, including an annual national championship.

National Director—An elected "upper management" administrative position of the UNITED STATES PARACHUTE ASSOCIATION (USPA). Those elected biennially by the USPA membership serve a two-year term.

NCPL—Abbreviation for **National Collegiate Parachuting League**.

night jump—A parachute jump made from one hour after official sunset to one hour before official sunrise. This is the UNITED STATES PARACHUTE ASSOCIATION (USPA) standard for a night jump. The FEDERAL AVIATION ASSOCIATION (FAA) considers a night jump to be one made after sunset and before sunrise.

NOTAM—An acronym for the FEDERAL AVIATION ADMINISTRATION (FAA) *Notice to Airmen*. A NOTAM is an advisory notice filed by a user of airspace in an Air Traffic Control (ATC) unit's jurisdiction. DROP ZONES file a daily NOTAM with an ATC control tower so that facility can inform airspace users—particularly transients—of parachuting activity taking place in traveled air space.

novice—A beginning sport parachuting student. The designation usually lasts until a student has completed a BASIC PARACHUTIST COURSE and has acquired a UNITED STATES PARACHUTE ASSOCIATION (USPA) "A" BASIC LICENSE.

opening point—The point above the ground over which a skydiver should be in an open canopy so as to readily maneuver toward a target area. (Depending on wind conditions between an opening point and an EXIT POINT from an aircraft, there might be a substantial distance between the two locations.)

opening shock—Also termed *opening force*. The deceleration force exerted on a load as a parachute deploys and inflates. There are various influences on the degree of force experienced by a jumper when a canopy opens fully. By utilizing proper freefall techniques, opening force is generally insignificant.

oscillation—The swinging or pendulum-like motion of a suspended load beneath a canopy.

out—A term used with regard to RELATIVE WORK and accuracy. And it means what you think it would: Someone did not get into an RW formation; or, failure to land within a prescribed distance when making an accuracy parachute jump.

pack—This term, through usage, has become synonymous with CONTAINER, referring to that part of a parachute assembly in which a canopy and its related elements are stowed in preparation for use. (O.J. Mink, Manager, Parachute Division, Reliance Manufacturing Company, Chicago, in his 1944 book, *Meet the Parachute*, included this definition: "Pack—The. . .container into which the canopy, pilot chute and suspension lines are packed.")

packing paddle—A parachute packing tool of smooth wood or metal, similar to a FID except longer; used by parachute packers for "dressing" (smoothing) the exterior of a parachute container (pack) as a final step in packing.

paper—*See* WIND DRIFT INDICATOR. It comes about from the crepe *paper* used to make the most commonly used device for determining an EXIT POINT.

Parachute Club of America—Abbreviated **PCA**. Forerunner of today's UNITED STATES PARACHUTE ASSOCIATION (USPA). The new organization was the same as the previous one, but as sport parachuting matured, an image-conscious PCA membership approved a name change thought to have a better connotation than mere club-level activity.

Parachute Industry Association—Abbreviated PIA. A formal U.S.-based organization composed of manufacturers, material suppliers, and dealers selling parachutes, equipment, and accessories.

parachute landing fall—Abbreviated PLF. A prescribed technique for dissipating the force of landing under a parachute canopy. Performing a proper PLF is especially important for a student using a conventional round-type of canopy because of its higher rate of descent.

parachute rigger—Generally refers to a FEDERAL AVIATION ADMINISTRATION (FAA) parachute rigger, meaning a person who is federally certificated (licensed) to perform duties pertaining to packing, repair, care, and maintenance of parachutes. Also refers to non-FAA-certificated military and naval personnel assigned to parachute rigger duties.

parachutist—The accepted term for someone who parachutes.

para-skiing—A wintertime competitive skydiving activity that combines scores of accuracy parachuting with giant slalom ski-racing scores for a total meet result.

passenger—A term describing the person in the front location of a duo engaged in TANDEM PARACHUTING. Such person is most often a student parachutist, but an experienced jumper in training for a tandem jumpmaster (tandem pilot) rating also acts as a passenger to fulfill certification requirements.

PCA—*See* PARACHUTE CLUB OF AMERICA.

permeability—A measurement rate that defines the "mass rate of flow" (or the "volume rate of flow") for an area of cloth. In the U.S., permeability is measured by determining the amount of air passed through one square foot of fabric per minute using one half inch of water pressure. The term POROSITY is often incorrectly used in place of permeability.

PIA—*See* PARACHUTE INDUSTRY OF AMERICA.

piggyback rig—A combination main/reserve parachute assembly used for making sport parachute jumps. (Select military personnel also use piggyback rigs for special military parachuting operations.) Each main and reserve canopy is stowed in and deployed from a separate CONTAINER (COMPARTMENT, PACK) located on a skydiver's back. Both containers are positioned in line vertically (assuming a parachutist in an upright body position). A simile would be a tandem bicycle—with a reserve parachute in the forward location (*upper* container/compartment) and the main parachute in the rear position (*lower* CONTAINER).

pilot—Usually refers to the person flying an aircraft. However, with the advent of TANDEM PARACHUTING, the term has also come to refer to the INSTRUCTOR accompanying a student who is a PASSENGER while TANDEM PARACHUTING.

pilot chute—A miniature parachute with the function of aiding in orderly deployment of a parachute system when a freefall parachute jump is made. A pilot chute is almost always used when making sport-type static line training jumps—and a pilot chute is always used when making an instructor-assisted deployment student training jump. (A CONVENTIONAL RIG military main canopy used in mass training and operational jumps does not employ a pilot chute.) Pilot chutes are used in more than one manner. In an emergency freefall parachute, the pilot chute is connected to the peak (apex) of the canopy. In a sport parachute system, the pilot chute is attached to the DEPLOYMENT DEVICE such as a SLEEVE or a BAG into which a main canopy is stowed. When a pilot chute is deployed into an air stream, it serves to provide drag as a jumper continues to fall and the rest of the parachute system continues to deploy. The pilot chute continues to function until a canopy is inflated, at which point the pilot chute then deflates and rests on the canopy or trails behind the canopy. (*See* Chapters 4 and 5.)

pilot chute hesitation—Refers to the delay that might be experienced after a ripcord is pulled to open a "conventional" main parachute container so that a PILOT CHUTE can escape and serve to assist deployment of the main canopy. If a jumper's freefall stable body position is precisely correct, an unusual phenomenon can occur: fast-moving airflow about a jumper's body acts to press on the spring-loaded pilot chute, thus sometimes effectively counteracting the force of the spring, and thereby holding the pilot onto the now open container. (Occasional jumpers, students and experienced alike, have been seen to have a hesitation lasting several seconds.) However, most often swirling air will suddenly work the pilot into "clean" air above the jumper's back. In most cases student jumpers are not aware of experiencing a hesitation. If a jumper has an exceptionally long hesitation, simply turning his head enough to look clearly over a shoulder is usually sufficient to induce a slight body turn, thereby changing airflow pattern and letting the pilot chute to escape into clean air. Experienced skydivers, knowing what most often causes a hesitation, avoid having the delay by being slightly "head high" at the time of ripcord pull simply by raising arms a bit overhead, thereby tipping the body upward before reaching for the ripcord. The head-high, tipped-body position induces slight backsliding and the resultant airflow across the jumper's back will assure pilot chute deployment.

pilot chute in tow—A predicament for a skydiver encountered after putting out a hand-deployed pilot chute for an intended opening of a main container and deployment of a primary canopy. The problem is generally attributable to the jumper's error in packing. The hapless jumper's solution is deployment of the RESERVE PARACHUTE.

pin—The person in a RELATIVE WORK formation who is the "aggressor" in completing a freefall formation. Most commonly used when referring to a two-person formation where one jumper serves as a BASE while the second skydiver pins the first jumper. However, also refers to all other aggressor skydivers working toward completing a formation. On a 20-person Twin Otter flight many persons would pin a five-person (a.k.a., "five-way") BASE taken out of the aircraft door. Furthermore, the term applies to the second person/canopy in a CANOPY RELATIVE WORK formation.

plane—A CANOPY RELATIVE WORK (CRW) term denoting the configuration of two or more ram air parachute canopies flying in close formation, one canopy above the other with minimal clearance between canopies. To visualize a "biplane" CRW formation, picture a conventional aircraft biplane seen at airshows, such as a Stearman; for a "triplane," picture the aircraft of Snoopy's opponent, *The Red Baron*. As many as 32 canopies have been flown in a world record "megaplane" formation. A plane is a much "tighter" configuration of a STACK CRW formation.

PLF—Abbreviation for PARACHUTE LANDING FALL.

poised exit—A controlled exit from an aircraft to start a skydive; usually done from a position outside an aircraft on a wheel or a specially constructed "jump step"; can also be done from the door of a plane.

porosity—In a parachute canopy, refers to the ratio of space (or "void," or "interstitial area") to the total area of canopy fabric, expressed in percentage. An example would be a ROUND CANOPY modified for steerability by having portions removed to create combined drive/steering slots and thrust "windows" (openings). The percentage would refer to the material removed to create the openings desired. Porosity is often incorrectly used synonymously with PERMEABILITY.

practice ripcord pull—*See* DUMMY RIPCORD PULL. The latter term has been around in the sport so long that it is the more commonly used of the two choices.

PRCP—Abbreviation for PRACTICE RIPCORD PULL.

premature opening—Opening of a parachute container at a time other than when planned.

pull-up cord—A simple packing tool; a length of waste canopy suspension line used to assist closing a container as a final step in packing a parachute. At every DZ, skydivers can be seen with the pieces of line dangling from varied body locations.

ram air canopy—A high-performance, two-surface flexible gliding wing. (*See* Chapter 5.)

rapide link—A form of CONNECTOR LINK. Rapide is the manufacturer's name; the link is primarily used in sport-type parachute equipment for attaching canopy SUSPENSION LINES to risers that will be mated to harness fittings.

relative work—Abbreviated RW. Two or more persons working together in freefall to accomplish formations. A world record for large formation was set in the autumn of 1988, when 144 male and female skydivers completed a predetermined formation in the sky over Illinois. Efforts are continuing to exceed that superb, difficult accomplishment, with a goal of eventually forming a specific formation with 200 skydivers.

reserve parachute—*See* AUXILIARY PARACHUTE.

right series—A direction-specific set of turns and loops performed during freefall. (*See* STYLE SERIES.)

ripcord—A device for actuating deployment of main and reserve parachutes.

riser(s)—Connecting devices between a parachute harness and groups of canopy suspension lines.

running—Controlling a canopy so that its direction of flight is with the wind (compared with HOLDING or CRABBING). Running maximizes ground speed and horizontal distance covered during canopy descent.

RW—Abbreviation for RELATIVE WORK.

S&TA—Abbreviation for SAFETY & TRAINING ADVISOR.

saddle—A term describing the sling portion of a parachute HARNESS assembly; that part in which a parachutist is held (or "sits") while suspended beneath an open canopy. A HARNESS is an arrangement of webbing and hardware, and the saddle is an integral part of such construction. There are two saddle configurations—SOLID and SPLIT.

Safety & Training Advisor—An appointed UNITED STATES PARACHUTE ASSOCIATION (USPA) administrative position.

SCR—Abbreviation for STAR CREST RECIPIENT.

SCS—Abbreviation for STAR CREST SOLO.

shroud lines—Former term for canopy suspension lines.

single operation system—Description of the system used for automatically actuating a RESERVE PARACHUTE because of a main parachute malfunction calling for emergency procedure.

skydiver—Commonly used synonymously with SPORT PARACHUTIST.

skydive/skydiving—*See* SPORT PARACHUTING. Specifically, however, it refers to the freefall experienced after leaping from an aircraft.

skygod—Not a complimentary term; used to identify skydivers who have a lofty opinion of themselves and their parachuting abilities. Abilities might well be fact, but skygods hastily tend to forget they once knew nothing about skydiving and had usually "LURKED" experienced jumpers to garner tips, knowledge, help, and anything else in order to become good at skydiving as quickly as possible. Skygods tend to remain aloof from students, to keep apart from experienced jumpers who the skygods feel are not as talented as themselves; and skygods tend to form cliques. Skygods are an unfortunate "fact of life" at many DROP ZONES—but luckily they are few in number and can usually be quickly identified and avoided.

slider—A necessary item of parachute equipment when using a ram air canopy for sport parachuting. (*See* Chapter 5.) It is a device for retarding the inflation sequence of a "SQUARE" CANOPY so that opening of the canopy will not have an injurious effect on a skydiver. A slider usually has one of two forms: (a) a *solid* or separable square or rectangle of cloth fabric with a large metal grommet at each corner; or (b) two lengths of wide, soft webbing sewn in the form of an "X" and with a large metal grommet installed at each extremity. In all configurations prescribed groups of SUSPENSION LINES will pass through the grommets and the slider will be free to slide the length of the suspension lines. When packing, the slider is pulled upward to where suspension lines are attached to the canopy and generally held in place there by a rubber band as temporary stowage. (Some skydivers who prefer not to use the stowage band simply lay the collapsed, folder slider on the canopy.) In the deployment/ inflation sequence, the slider is at the top of the suspension line groups and serves as a retardant to high-speed inflation of canopy cells. As the cells inflate, the slider is forced down the suspension lines, the sliding continuing until all cells are inflated.

slider stop/bumper—A short length of soft plastic tubing placed completely over each CONNECTOR LINK used to connect SUSPENSION LINES to RISERS. Many times a slider will be forced down suspension lines quickly during an opening sequence. Before slider stops, deformation of a grommet sometimes occurred due to abrupt contact with exposed connector links. Such damage, though not significant in itself each time, occasionally lead to cumulative grommet damage, sometimes to a point where a damaged grommet then also damaged one or more suspension line, and on and on. Eventually, a lesson was learned when a slider "hang-up" occurred sufficiently high on the suspension lines to prevent proper inflation of the canopy, leading to a BREAKAWAY as an emergency procedure. Persistently damaging suspension lines also lead to line(s) replacement, with needless expense and "down-time." An "ounce of prevention" solution was adding an inexpensive stop/bumper at each connector link. (*See* Chapters 4 and 5.)

smokejumper—In the U.S., someone in the employ of the federal government who makes parachute jumps for the purpose of quickly reaching sites of forest fires, usually in remote places, and then, as a trained firefighter, works at extinguishing the fires. Smokejumpers have been used in America for more than 50 years. Until recent years, Canada had also made widespread use of smokejumpers, until helicopters became a more suitable means of transportation. Russia has also used smokejumpers for a long time.

sleeve—An inflation retardation device used to slow the opening sequence of parachute canopies and reduce OPENING SHOCK.

snap—An item of parachute hardware; manufactured in adjustable and nonadjustable configurations.

snivel—A term for describing excessively slow inflation of a canopy ("ROUND" or "SQUARE") after it has deployed from a container and is out of its deployment device. A snivel can be attributed to single or multiple causes, e.g., basic canopy design; an aging canopy resulting in increased canopy fabric porousness (increased PERMEABILITY); uneven suspension line lengths resulting in poor canopy TRIM; improper setting of BRAKE lines routinely stowed until the canopy opening sequence has been completed; a worn, weak-acting pilot chute; improper packing technique; or other faults. Continued canopy sniveling during opening sequence is certainly worth investigation, usually best done by a parachute rigger familiar with sport-type parachute equipment.

solid saddle—A form of parachute harness sling (SADDLE) configuration. In a solid saddle, individual harness leg straps are sewn to other parts of harness webbing to form a one-piece sling—wide, thick, stiff, uncomfortable. In early military surplus harnesses, "comfort pads" were designed and installed as an accessory to improve comfort for a parachutist suspended beneath a canopy for two or more minutes on an average jump.

SOP—Abbreviation for STANDARD OPERATING PROCEDURE (the way things are done).

SOS—(Also seen **S.O.S.**) Abbreviation for SINGLE OPERATION SYSTEM.

span—The side-to-side-distance of a RAM AIR CANOPY, usually referring to a top surface measurement.

span construction—A manufacturing technique for producing a RAM AIR CANOPY in which the long axis of fabric for upper and lower surfaces is spanwise (side to side).

split saddle—The basic SADDLE term refers to the sling of a parachute HARNESS. A split saddle is formed of independent lengths of webbing that encircle a parachutist's legs and are usually fitted with adjustable snap fittings for securing the leg straps to the main lift web portion of a HARNESS. There is also a STEP-IN HARNESS preferred by some skydivers. SADDLE is a holdover description from earlier parachuting (but now firmly in place in skydiving jargon) when harness leg straps were sewn to other parts of harness webbing to form a SOLID SADDLE—wide, thick, stiff, uncomfortable, and it restricted leg movements so useful in RELATIVE WORK. As early-on skydivers improved at freefall RELATIVE WORK, modifying the SOLID SADDLE of a HARNESS was one of the early measures taken to refine equipment to improve freefall performance.

sport parachuting—*See* SKYDIVING. Generally refers to all activity associated with recreational parachuting.

sport parachutist—*See* SKYDIVER. A person who participates in the recreational/sport aspects of parachute jumping, as opposed to those who make parachute jumps as a job or duty, e.g., military parachutist (paratrooper, pararescue), smokejumper.

spot—The EXIT POINT.

spotting—The technique of guiding a pilot to a position directly over a predetermined ground reference point known as the SPOT for exiting an aircraft on a skydive (*See* EXIT POINT).

square canopy—Square is a misnomer for describing the appearance of a RAM AIR CANOPY, but it is a term now firmly entrenched in sport parachuting jargon. When the RAM AIR CANOPY was introduced it had the look of being nearly square in shape when observed from below or above. It was not square, but it was close enough to quickly be so nicknamed. Though ram air canopies soon got larger and clearly were rectangular in form, the square sobriquet stuck. (Similes include scotch tape coming into language usage as a generic term for *pressure-sensitive transparent tape*, but "Scotch" is a brand name; and CAPEWELL incorrectly encompassing canopy release devices.)

square reserve—A ram air canopy for use as an AUXILIARY (RESERVE) parachute.

squid/squidding—*See* SNIVEL.

stable fall—Describes a face-to-earth freefall body position.

stack—A CANOPY RELATIVE WORK (CRW) term describing the configuration of two or more ram air parachutes flying in proximity, one canopy above the other, with canopy-leg contact between a lower and upper participant in the CRW formation. An approaching parachutist flies a canopy from a position below another parachutist, adjusting flight so the canopy will move to a point where the canopy can contact the feet of the upper parachutist. The upper parachutist also adjusts flight to assist in the docking, thus making CRW a cooperative effort. Completed formations are referred to by number, e.g., two-stack, three-stack, six-stack, eight-stack, and so forth. A stack is a more open form of a PLANE CRW formation.

Star Crest Recipient—A UNITED STATES PARACHUTE ASSOCIATION (USPA) award earned by a sport parachutist for having participated in a RELATIVE WORK formation of at least eight freefalling skydivers. (*See* STAR CREST SOLO for a related award.)

Star Crest Solo—A UNITED STATES PARACHUTE ASSOCIATION (USPA) award earned by a sport parachutist for having participated in a RELATIVE WORK formation of at least eight freefalling skydivers, with a further skill qualification that the candidate had to have entered the formation as the *eighth or later* participant. (*See* STAR CREST RECIPIENT for a related award.)

steering line(s)—*See* CONTROL LINE(S). Specific lines used for causing a parachute canopy to change direction of flight or to vary rate of descent.

step-in harness—A HARNESS with adjustable leg straps formed into loops that encircle a parachutist's upper thighs. Instead of using an adjustable SNAP that mates to a HARNESS fixed V-ring to form the leg loop, the loop is formed by using an adjustable ADAPTER in which the running (free) end of the webbing cannot be unthreaded from the adapter. Thus, a user has to *step into* or *step out of* leg straps when donning or removing the parachute assembly. A STEP-IN HARNESS could be a drawback if a parachutist should need to quickly and easily get out of a HARNESS (e.g., tree or water landing).

Stevens Cutaway System—A BREAKAWAY method to simplify the emergency procedure for a parachutist when experiencing a malfunction of a main canopy. It is particularly useful for a student parachutist. With a conventional parachute system of separate back parachute and front-mounted (chest-mounted) RESERVE PARACHUTE, a student needs only to fully actuate CANOPY RELEASES on a HARNESS. A lanyard is connected between a RISER of the main canopy and the reserve parachute ripcord handle, and as the student drops away from a jettisoned main canopy, the lanyard attached to the departing *riser* pulls the reserve ripcord handle from its pocket, thereby extracting ripcord pins from locking devices, allowing the pilot chute of the reserve parachute to deploy and extract the canopy.

streamer—An often-used word in sport parachuting, with more than one meaning. One of the meanings is WIND DRIFT INDICATOR. A second meaning represents a serious malfunction of a parachute canopy. Its usage comes about from its appearance at a distance. Instead of a parachute opening normally, it remains closed for one reason or another and the closed canopy "streams" along above a still freefalling parachutist. A streamer is an extraordinarily rare occurrence and can result in emergency procedures being required.

student parachutist—A trainee who has not qualified for a UNITED STATES PARACHUTE ASSOCIATION (USPA) "A" BASIC LICENSE.

style—Refers to specific aerial maneuvers calling for completion of controlled movements that demonstrate an individual has control of his or her body in all axes while in freefall. A STYLE SERIES is a requirement for a UNITED STATES PARACHUTE ASSOCIATION (USPA) "C" INTERMEDIATE LICENSE. Style is also an event in parachuting competitions at every level, from local through international.

style series—A series of 360-degree turns and loops done in a prescribed sequence. Competitions prescribe any or all of three customary sets of maneuvers to be done by contestants in the least amount of time and precisely as possible to avoid penalties of time or points. Style Events are part of conference, national, and international championships.

suspension lines—The fabric lines that make up that part of a parachute canopy assembly that bears a suspended load. (*See* Chapter 4.)

tandem parachuting—A parachute jump made by two people at once using a single parachute system. One of the state-of-the-art parachute instruction techniques used throughout the world in the 1980s. Tandem parachuting also has military tactical applications. (*See* Chapter 3.)

target—Generally, a DROP ZONE (DZ) prepared landing area. Most often—and certainly in serious competitive accuracy events—a target area ranges in size, usually a diameter of from five to ten meters of softened landing surface (it is often referred to as "the pit." Softening can be as basic as turning soil over, "rototilling" and raking it, and thereafter keeping it in that condition by periodic maintenance. At a higher level of sophistication, a wide, deep-in-the-center mound of approximately pea-sized gravel is used as a target area (and many times called "the peas"). It might seem that landing on "a pile of rocks" doesn't make much sense, but a well constructed, well maintained *pea-gravel pit* is the favorite of "accuracy jumpers." A target, specifically, is a disc measuring as small as five centimeters (two inches), the standard at national and international accuracy parachuting competitions. "Accuracy-conscious" DROP ZONES often go to the considerable expense of purchasing electronic scoring pad equipment so parachutists can fine-tune accuracy skills.

Technical Standard Order—U.S. Government regulations that apply to specifications (standards) for aviation materials and products. *TSO-C23c* applies to specifications of parachute design and minimum parachute performance standards.

temporary pins—Usually found in a parachute rigger's kitbag or toolbox, such short lengths of metal (very often former ripcord pins salvaged from scrap ripcord assemblies) are used to temporarily hold a container closed while other work is done before ultimately installing a ripcord in place. Experienced parachute riggers usually tie separate pins at a distance along a substantial length of scrap suspension line as a means of accounting for all temporary pins used in packing.

Terminal/Terminal Velocity—This descriptor is often referred to in skydiving, most of the time only using "terminal;" also often adding a prefix to use "*sub*-terminal" when appropriate. Terminal refers to that approximate speed at which a skydiver (for that matter, any falling object) will fall at a maximum rate for a given set of conditions. As used in sport parachuting, it is calculated on a combination of an individual's total weight (mass) and size (area of resistance). In freefall, when a jumper's mass, being pulled earthward by gravity, is slowed to a constant rate due to the area of resistance of the jumpers body (usually enlarged by a jumpsuit), the steady rate is described as terminal velocity. After exiting an aircraft it takes approximately nine to twelve seconds to reach terminal, the time difference depending on mass/area factors. As an example, a five-foot-nine, 170-pound jumper using a 28-pound main/reserve parachute assembly, wearing a hard helmet, medium-weight footwear, and an average-size jumpsuit, and falling in a full spread-eagle body position, will take about 10 to 11 seconds to reach terminal. A larger, looser jumpsuit could mean a slower terminal speed; or tucking in arms and legs would mean reaching terminal sooner; getting into a head-down diving position with feet together and arms close at one's side would mean the size (area of resistance) would be greatly reduced and that terminal could be as high as 185-200 miles an hour. In short, there are many factors affecting terminal velocity.

TFTM—Abbreviation for *too far to measure*. A concise logbook entry used when landing nowhere near a DROP ZONE'S target area. There are multiple variations on the basic term—TDFTM (*too damn far to measure*; TGDFTM (*too goddam far to measure*); a couple for even landing completely off a drop zone, each a more profane descriptor for a successively greater, more humiliating distance—TFFTM, TFGDFTM. These two will remain as abbreviations here; but just use imagination to figure the colorful meanings. Other variations are limited only by a logbook owner's creativity.

three-ring release—(Usually appears as **3-ring release**.) A successor to the various configurations of a complex military specification canopy release device, many of which were manufactured by the Capewell Manufacturing Company; also successor to other canopy release models developed as replacement devices used to alter military surplus parachute harnesses. The 3-ring release allows a CANOPY, SUSPENSION LINES, and RISERS to be easily and effectively separated from a parachute HARNESS. Such a release is readily incorporated into the SINGLE OPERATION SYSTEM of sport-type equipment for performing an emergency BREAKAWAY.

throw-out pilot chute—A type of PILOT CHUTE used to deploy the main parachute of a piggyback system. (*See* Chapter 5.)

toggle(s)—Toggles initially were small lengths of wood, plastic, or light metal secured to the ends of CONTROL LINES and were gripped in a jumper's hands as a means of firmly handling CONTROL LINES while guiding a canopy throughout descent from canopy opening to landing. Large fabric loops made of light, narrow webbing are now generally in use with ram air/square canopies because more positive control is achieveable. "Toggle(s)" is another term entrenched in skydiving jargon and applies to whatever device is attached to CONTROL LINES and used for manipulation.

tracking—Horizontal body movement of a freefalling skydiver, achieved by using a DELTA POSITION. The horizontal movement is in addition to ever-present vertical fall. Tracking is a most desirable skill to learn early on in improving freefall RELATIVE WORK abilities. (It is such an important skill that a tracking demonstration is a requirement of the UNITED STATES PARACHUTE ASSOCIATION "A" BASIC LICENSE for sport parachutists.) There is more than one valuable benefit to quickly learning to track proficiently. Tracking provides a variable closing rate when a distance between freefalling RELATIVE WORK skydivers needs to be decreased; and tracking will help a jumper to achieve sufficient distance from other skydivers when it is time to deploy a main parachute, contributing vastly to a safe opening. However, there is a "cost" attached to gaining the horizontal movement; being in the head-down, arms-back DELTA POSITION also increases vertical fall rate—in other words, a skydiver goes down faster, diminishing available altitude at a faster rate—a factor to be always kept in mind.

tree landing— Rarely greatly hazardous; nonetheless a circumstance that could occur due to various reasons—e.g., poor SPOTTING technique, being on a RESERVE CANOPY. Special techniques should be learned by every parachutist in anticipation of being faced with the situation.

trim—Pilots of powered and engineless aircraft trim their craft so that it flies and can be controlled with the least amount of effort. Trimming is done by fine-tuning control surfaces and control systems to accomplish easy craft operation. Skydivers using a RAM AIR CANOPY also control a sophisticated, high-performance item of parachuting equipment requiring attention to ensure best performance. Parachutists can do much of the adjustment needed to achieve the best canopy trim, but sometimes the specific skills of a knowledgeable parachute rigger are needed in more difficult cases.

TSO—Abbreviation for TECHNICAL STANDARD ORDER.

turbulence—Rough air that can affect a canopy's handling characteristics and performance. The discomforting effects of turbulence can be greatly reduced (and often eliminated, depending on degree of turbulence) by using the canopy's *braking* system to reduce forward speed (see BRAKING/BRAKES entry).

unpoised exit—*See* DOOR EXIT and BOMB-OUT EXIT.

USPA—Abbreviation for UNITED STATES PARACHUTE ASSOCIATION.

United States Parachute Association—Abbreviated **USPA**. A voluntary membership national organization that provides self-regulation of sport parachuting in the U.S. (*See* Chapter 7.)

waiver—Permission to deviate from UNITED STATES PARACHUTE ASSOCIATION (USPA) BASIC SAFETY REQUIREMENT(S). Waivers can be granted only by specific USPA personnel.

water jump—There are two types: One a parachutist wants to make as a FUN JUMP, or an unintentional landing in an open body of water in which a parachutist could drown and brought about by any number of unplanned events. The latter can be a hazardous situation, particularly for an untrained person.

Use of ram air canopies, both as a main and a RESERVE CANOPY has greatly minimized the chance of an inadvertent water landing, but the problem has not been eliminated. Candidates for a (USPA) "A" BASIC LICENSE must possess documentation of training by a USPA INSTRUCTOR for an unintentional WATER LANDING. Candidates for a USPA "B" INTERMEDIATE LICENSE must possess documentation of WATER LANDING training with full equipment. (*See* Chapter 3, for information about WATER LANDING training.) Though an actual WATER JUMP is no longer required by the USPA for any license, many jumpers make one or more a year, simply for the fun of it and to better understand the hazards of an unintentional WATER LANDING.

water landing—An intentional or unintentional landing in a body of water in which a parachutist could drown.

WDI—Abbreviation for WIND DRIFT INDICATOR; also termed STREAMER and PAPER.

Whuffo—Sport parachutists's term for nonjumpers ("whuff" rhyming with "muff"). Spectators often ask skydivers why they jump. It's said that "whuffo" was derived from "Wha' fo' y'all jump out of an airplane?"—"wha' fo'" meaning "what for" instead of "why." It wasn't long before "whuffo" was part of American skydiving jargon. (Uppity pilots—many of them insisting "I can fly the crate my plane came in"—ask: "Why jump out of a perfectly good airplane?" Skydivers had a quick response: "There ain't no such thing as a perfectly good airplane!")

wind drift indicator—Abbreviated WDI; also termed STREAMER. An approximation device for predetermining an EXIT POINT to be used in skydiving. The most generally used device is a weighted, 10-inch wide, 20-foot-length of yellow crepe paper (rolled into a cylinder about one inch in diameter for ease of storing and handling). The WDI is dropped from a jump plane at customary altitude of 2,200 feet and directly above a target area. The WDI unrolls quickly and descends at a rate approximating a parachutist beneath an open canopy. The WDI is then observed from the circling aircraft until the WDI lands. The exit point selected by a jumpmaster or qualified parachutist will be a reference point on the ground that is 180 degrees and equidistant from where the WDI landed. A second method (less used because components are not readily and economically available) is by using a helium balloon and a theodolite. An inflated balloon is released from the ground and tracked for a specific time (usually two minutes) using the theodolite. Angle and direction degree readings are then used to calculate and mark an exit point on a map or photograph as a reference for DROP ZONE management and parachutists.

wind line—The invisible path that represents the ideal course a parachutist would follow from canopy opening to a target area. Being off the wind line means that a jumper would have to maneuver a canopy to crab crosswind (maneuver angularly through airflow) to a point of being directly in line with wind in order to most easily reach a target. Learning to remain on a wind line, or maneuver onto a wind line, is something that comes with experience under a parachute canopy.

wind sock—A device used to determine wind direction and approximate speed. A conventional configuration is to have a tapered cloth tube mounted on a pole in such a manner that the device can shift with wind changes through 360-degrees. Placed at a reasonable distance from a target, so as to not interfere with an approaching jumper's descent path (approach), the wind sock is used as a continuing reference by parachutists. As a substitute when a sock is not available, a crepe paper WIND DRIFT INDICATOR is suspended from a tall pole to serve as a wind indicator. Such wind speed/direction indicators located near a target area are particularly valuable to accuracy jumpers training for competition. Wind indicators in a target area—perpendicular to the WIND LINE—are a requirement of formal parachuting accuracy competitive events.

zap/zapped—Also: zap!, ZAP!, zapped!, ZAPPED!—as varied emphasis is needed to describe some occurrence in the course of telling a JUMP STORY.

Bibliography

Anderson, Alonzo. *Bag of Smoke*. New York: Alfred A. Knopf, 1968.

Army Air Forces Aid Society. *Official Guide to the Army Air Forces*. New York: Bonanza Books/Crown Publishers, (first published 1944) 1988.

Becker, Beril. *Dreams and Realities of the Conquest of the Skies*. New York: Atheneum, 1967.

Boase, Wendy. *The Sky's the Limit/Women Pioneers in Aviation*. New York: Macmillan Publishing Co., Inc. 1979.

Blackmon, Deborah. *Parachute Rigger Study Guide*. Santa Barbara: Para Publishing, 1989.

Caidin, Martin. *The Silken Angels/A History of Parachuting*. J.B. Lippincott, 1964.

Cooley, Earl. *Trimotor and Trail*. Missoula: Mountain Press Publishing Co., 1984.

Coombs, Charles. *Survival in the Sky*. William Morrow and Co., 1956.

Darby, Ray. *The Space Age Sport: Skydiving*. New York: Julius Messner, 1964.

Department of the Air Force. *Your Body in Flight*. (AFP 160-10-3). Washington, D.C.: U.S. Government Printing Office, 1960.

Dixon, Charles. *Parachuting*. London: Sampson Low, Marston & Co., 1930.

Dwiggins, Don. *The Barnstormers*. New York: Grosset & Dunlap, 1968.

_____. *Bailout/The Story of Parachuting and Skydiving*. Toronto: Collier-Macmillan Ltd., 1969.

Edwards, Roger. *German Airborne Troops 1936-45*. Garden City: Doubleday & Co., 1974.

Emrich, Linn. *The Complete Book of Sky Sports*. New York: Macmillan Co., 1970.

Fechet/Crane/Smith. *Parachutes*. New York: National Aeronautics Council, Inc., 1942.

Glassman, Don. *Jump!/Tales of the Caterpillar Club*. New York: Simon and Schuster, 1930.

Goldstrom, John. *A Narrative History of Aviation*. New York: Macmillan Company, 1942.

Greenwood, Jim. *Parachuting for Sport*. New York: Sports Car Press, 1962.

Gregory, Howard. *The Falcon's Disciples*. New York: Pageant Press Inc., 1967.

_____. *Parachuting's Unforgettable Jumps*. La Mirada: Howard Gregory Associates, 1974.

Gunby, R.A. *Sport Parachuting*. Denver: Jeppesen/Sanderson, 1972, 1974.

Haining, Peter. *The Compleat Birdman*. New York: St. Martin's Press, 1976.

Hickey, Michael. *Out of the Sky/A History of Airborne Warfare*. New York: Charles Scribner's Sons, 1979.

Horan, Michael. *Parachuting Folklore/The Evolution of Freefall*. Richmond: Parachuting Resources, 1980.

_____. *Index to Parachuting/An Annotated Bibliography*. Richmond: Parachuting Resources, 1979.

Hurst, Randle M. *The Smokejumpers*. Caldwell: The Caxton Printers, 1966.

Huston, James A. *Out of the Blue*. Lafayette: Purdue Research Foundation, 1972.

Langewiesche, Wolfgang. *I'll Take the High Road*. New York: Harcourt, Brace and Co., 1939.

Low, A.M. *Parachutes in Peace and War*. London: The Scientific Book Club, 1942.

Lucas, John. *The Big Umbrella*. New York: Drake Publishers, Inc., 1973.

Mink, O.J. *Meet the Parachute/Use and Maintenance*. Chicago: Reliance Manufacturing Co., 1944.

Mischke, Maj. F.O. *Paratroops*. New York: Random House, 1943.

Morris, Alan. *The Balloonatics*. London: Jarrolds Publishers, Ltd., 1970.

Nelson, Jr., Carl. *Body Pilot*. Chicago: Abstract Publishing, 1981.

Padden, Ian. *The Fighting Elite/U.S. Airborne.* New York: Bantam Books, 1986.

Poynter, Dan. *Parachuting/The Skydivers' Handbook.* Santa Barbara: Parachuting Publications, 1978, 1983, 1989.

——————. *The Parachute Manual/A Technical Treatise on the Parachute.* Santa Barbara: Parachuting Publications, 1977.

Rossetti, Steve. *Relative Work for Skydivers.* (No publishing data), ca. 1975.

Ryan, Charles W. *Sport Parachuting.* Chicago: Henry Regnery Co., 1975.

Sellick, Bud. *Skydiving/The Art and Science of Sport Parachuting.* Englewood Cliffs: Prentice-Hall, 1961.

——————. *Parachutes and Parachuting.* Englewood Cliffs: Prentice-Hall, 1971.

Shea-Simonds, Charles. *Sport Parachuting.* London: Adam & Charles Black, 1979.

Smith, J. Floyd. *Parachutes/Development-Use-Maintenance.* Manchester: Pioneer Parachute Co., 1942.

Starnes, Arthur H. *Aerial Maniac.* Hammond: Delaney Printing Co., 1938.

Thompson, Leroy. *United States Airborne Forces/1940-1986.* New York: Blandford Press, 1986.

Townsend, Peter. *Duel of Eagles.* New York: Simon and Schuster, 1971.

Tugwell, Maurice. *Airborne to Battle/A History of Airborne Warfare 1918-1971.* London: William Kimber, 1971.

U.S. Marine Corps. *Parachute Instruction Manual/Marine Parachute Troops-1943.* Sharpsburg: Republished by Antietam National Museum (date unknown).

U.S. Navy. *Parachutes.* Washington: U.S. Government Printing Office, 1944.

——————. *Parachute Sense.* Bureau of Aeronautics, 1943.

Valentin, Leo. *Bird Man.* London: Hutchinson, 1955.

Weeks, John. *Airborne Equipment/A History of its Development.* New York: Hippocrene Books, Inc. 1976.

——————. *The Airborne Soldier.* New York: Blandford Press, 1982 (reprinted 1983, 1985, 1986).

Weller, George. *The Story of the Paratroops.* New York: Random House, 1958.

Whiting, Charles. *Hunters from the Sky/The German Parachute Corps 1940-1945.* New York: Stein and Day, 1974.

Works, Pat. *Parachuting: The Art of Freefall Relative Work.* DeLand: Aero-Graphics, 1988 (2nd ed.)

Zim, Herbert S. *Parachutes.* New York: Harcourt, Brace and Co., 1942.
Zweng, Charles A. *Parachute Technician.* North Hollywood: Pan American Navigation Service, 1944.

Other print resources include: *Parachutist* magazine (United States Parachute Association, publisher); *Sky Diver* magazine (L. Cameron, publisher); *Spotter* newsletter/magazine (Northeast Sport Parachute Council, publisher/D. Poynter, Editor); *DZ-U.S.A.* magazine (C.E. Hunnell, publisher); *Truth News Trends* newspaper (Parachutes, Inc., publisher); *Skydiving* newspaper (M. Truffer, publisher); *National Geographic* magazine (National Geographic Society, publisher); *Time* magazine (Time, Inc., publisher); *Popular Mechanics* magazine; *Modern Mechanics and Inventions* magazine; *Reader's Digest* magazine.

Additional resources include a variety of other material—film and videos, commercial and military training and technical manuals and other documents; plus conversations—many of them vividly detailing first-hand experiences—with countless people in the aviation and parachuting communities.

Index

Caterpillar Club, 47-48
Cavendish, Henry, 36
Cayley, George, 37
center of gravity, 55
certification, riggers, 82, 168-171
Charles, J.A.C., 36
Chinese development, 24-27
Christenson, Carol, 16
cloud ceiling requirements, 179
clubs, 11
Cocking, Robert, 34, 37-41
Coleman, Ken Jr., 60
Commission Internationale de
    Parchutisme (CIP), 123
competitions, 10-14, 119-135
    canopy relative work (CRW),
        131-134
    chronology of, 119-124
    individual accuracy, 124-126
    para-skiing, 134-135
    relative work, 130-131
    scope of, 124-135
    starting in, 124
    style, 127-130
    team accuracy, 126-127
congested area, 176
containers, 110, 114-115
control lines, 110
control zones, jumps into or
    over, 176
Crane, Joe, 6, 10, 11, 119, 120,
    138, 139
crowds, jumping into or over,
    176

D

da Vinci, Leonardo, 22, 23, 24,
    28
Daedalus legend, 2-4
de la Loubere, Simon, 26
demonstration jumps, 167
deployment bags, 114
deployment devices, 110, 113-
    114
deployment sleeves (see
    sleeves)
deployment/inflation
    sequences, 90-99
Derry, Frank, 100
diapers (see sleeves)

Doolittle, Jimmy, 48, 85
drop zones, 13, 58, 153-163
    alternate, 183
    notification of use, 178
    safety requirements, 167

E

emergencies, 60, 173
English development, 37-41, 29
equipment, 109-118
    development of modern, 12
    Federal Aviation Association
        (FAA) requirements for, 180-
        181
    manufacturers of, 185-189
    safety requirements, 109, 167-
        168

F

Fair, Bob, 11
Federal Aviation Administration
    (FAA)
    FARs for parachuting, 168-184
    regulations, 165
Federation Aeronautique Inter-
    nationale (FAI), 137
Fenton, Valerie, 18
flaring, 99
flight service station (FSS),
    jumps into or over airspace,
    177
flying speed, 98
folktales, lore, and history, 21-
    50
footwear, 116
Fortenberry, Dick, 13, 121, 123
four-way relative work (see
    relative work)
Franklin, Benjamin, 48, 49
freefall parachuting, 8
    development of, 9
    night jumps, 9
    perfection of technique, 11
    sequential, 14
French development, 27-35
full spread body position, 54

G

Garnerin, A.J., 31-35
glissade, 99

National Judge Certification Program (NJCP), 81
National Parachute Jumpers Association (NPJA), 6, 138, 139
National Parachute Jumpers-Riggers Association (NPJRA), 10, 11, 139
Nelson, Carl Jr., 144
night jumps, 167, 179

O

off-hand turns, 99
opening altitude, minimum, 166
opening shock, sleeve to reduce, 11
Orange Sport Parachute Center (OSPC), 14
Osoaviakhim (Russian parachutist organization), 5
Ottley, William H., 18
Ovid, 2, 3, 4
oxygen, supplementary, 168

P

paper doll training model, 55-56
papillon canopies, 101
Para-Commander parachutes, 90, 91, 123
  steering, 101-103
Para-Gear Equipment Company Catalog, 150
para-opener device (POD), 93, 97
para-skiing competition, 134-135
Parachute Club of America (PCA), 121, 139
parachute landing fall (PLF), 59
Parachute Manual, The, 19, 146, 147, 148
Parachute Rigger Question Book, 83, 149
Parachute Rigger Study Guide, 149
Parachute Rigging Course, 148-149
parachutes, 85-108, 110, 115
  automatic opening devices, 15
  deployment/inflation sequences, 90-99, 111

emergency type, basic parts of, 86
harness of, 87, 88
historical development of, 21-27
line stowage, 92, 93
main, 109
opening/deployment time, 112
papillon canopies, 101
Para-Commander (P-C), 90, 91, 101
para-opener device (POD), 93, 97
ram air canopies, 14, 93-98, 103-108
reserve, 109
round canopies, deployment sequence, 96
round canopies, operation of, 91-93
sleeved parachute deployment, 94
slots in, 100
sport rig system, 89
square canopies, 99
steerability, 99-103
tandem parachuting, 72
Parachutes Incorporated, 13
Parachuting Folklore-The Evolution of Freefall, 142
Parachuting I/E Course, 149
parachuting, military, 44-45, 48-50, 52, 53
  development of, 6-7
  exhibition teams, 184
  HALO, HAHO, and LALO techniques, 15
  World War I and II, uses of, 7
parachuting, recreational
  club formation, 11
  competitions, 10-14, 119-135
  emergence of, 5-7
  equipment development, 12
  equipment improvements for, 14
  first recorded (Russia), 5
  first U.S., 5
  free fall, early attempts at, 8, 9

Other Bestsellers of Related Interest

UNCONVENTIONAL AIRCRAFT—2nd Edition—
Peter M. Bowers

From one of America's foremost aviation photographers and historians comes what is probably the largest collection of information on unconventional aircraft ever assembled. Far-out flying machines that have appeared in the last 80 years receive their due honor, humor, and respect in this salute to them and their creators. For this revised and expanded edition, Bowers has added 77 additional aircraft, including the Rutan Voyager, Beechcraft Starship, the Bell/Boeing V-22 Osprey tilt-rotor VTOL, and the Zeppelin-Staaken R-IV bomber. 336 pages, 437 illustrations. Book No. 2450, $19.95 paperback, $28.95 hardcover

THE JOY OF FLYING—2nd Edition—Robert Mark

Here are the answers to just about every question a nonflyer could have about flying. From practical information to humorous sidelights, Mark covers what it's like to be behind the controls of an aircraft, the ins and outs of pilot training, techniques for communicating with air traffic control, reasons and requirements for advanced pilot ratings, even the ten greatest lies to tell a nonflying spouse. It's a fascinating and fun-filled look at the pleasures, challenges, and requirements of learning to pilot an airplane. 176 pages, 67 illustrations. Book No. 2444, $14.95 paperback only

BEECHCRAFT STAGGERWING—Peter Barry

Featuring never-before-published facts and photographs from the archives of the Beechcraft Staggerwing Museum Foundation, this book is a complete illustrated record of the colorful history of one of the classic aircraft of the 1930s. Beginning with the early experiences of the Staggerwing's designer, aviation pioneer Walter F. Beech, Berry describes the Staggerwing's development and production, its foreign and domestic uses, and its record-breaking races. This is truly a necessary addition to the library of any clasic aircraft buff. 160 pages, 104 illustrations. Book No. 3410, $14.95 paperback only

AIRMAIL: How It All Began—Carrol V. Glines

"Colonel Glines has prepared a splendid, well-illustrated book." **Newport News Press**

Early airmail service was one of the most innovative business endeavors of the early 1900s. *Airmail* traces this fascinating segment of aviation history, with colorful anecdotes of the pony express, the days when pigeons flew mail in the service of man and country, early attempts to "buck the weather," navigation by road maps, and more. 176 pages, Illustrated. Book No. 22378, $14.95 paperback only

STEALTH TECHNOLOGY: The Art of Black Magic—J. Jones, Edited by Matt Thurber

Revealed in this book are the findings of careful research conducted by J. Jones, an expert in the area of military aviation stealth applications. The profound effect modern stealth technology is having throughout the United States and the world is discussed. Facts about the B-2 Stealth Bomber and the F117A Fighter are included. 160 pages, 87 illustrations. Book No. 22381, $14.95 paperback only

MAYDAY, MAYDAY, MAYDAY! Spin Instructions Please!—Bob Stevens

Pilots, aviation buffs, and anyone with a sense of humor will enjoy this all-new collection of cartoons created by the undisputed Dean of American Aviation Cartooning, Bob Stevens. Poking fun at every aspect of general aviation, from soloing to flying the airways (and battling the bureaucracy) to the inevitable hangar flying, *Mayday* doesn't dissapoint. 224 pages, Illustrated. Book No. 28964, $12.95 paperback only

THE LUFTWAFFE: A Photographic Record 1919-1945—Karl Ries

Written by German's premier Luftwaffe historian!

This book is a behind-the-scenes look at the Luftwaffe from a noted author who has studied and written about the subject for more than 20 years. Author Karl Ries provides an actual account of the German Air Force. Hundreds of previously unpublished photographs and accompanying text chronologically tell the Luftwaffe's origins, rise, combat, and ultimate decline. 240 pages, 450 illustrations. Book No. 22384, $14.95 hardcover only

THE ILLUSTRATED GUIDE TO AERODYNAMICS—Hubert "Skip" Smith

If you've always considered aerodynamic science a highly technical area best left to professional engineers and aircraft designers . . . this outstanding new sourcebook will change your mind! Smith introduces the principles of aerodynamics to everyone who wants to know how and why aircraft fly . . . but who doesn't want to delve into exotic theories or complicated mathematical relationships. 240 pages, 232 illustrations. Book No. 2390, $16.95 paperback only

THE BLOND KNIGHT OF GERMANY—Raymond F. Toliver and Trevor J. Constable

The fascinating biography of the most successful fighter ace in the history of aerial warfare—Erich Hartmann whose 352 victories amounted to more than six times those of the top U.S. ace! You'll relive Hartmann's extraordinary aerial achievements, the ordeals suffered during 10 years of post-war imprisonment by the Soviet Union, and his role in the new West German Air Force. 352 pages, 166 illustrations. Book No. 24189, $16.95 paperback only

THE CESSNA 172—Bill Clarke

If you need a quick reference to Cessna . . . you'll find all the information you need conveniently gathered together and clearly presented in this buyer's guide. It supplies all the background knowledge on these airplanes that you need to make a wise purchase (new or used) and to improve the performance and comfort of your Cessna. This guide will enable you to make sure your Cessna meets all the FAA requirements and is running safely and smoothly for years. 320 pages, 113 illustrations. Book No. 2412, $14.95 paperback only

Aero Series, Vol. 37, BOEING 737—David H. Minton

This book offers an accurate and complete historical record of the Boeing 737, including commercial uses, prototypes, variations, and military applications. More than 100 line drawings and photographs illustrate the 737 from every possible angle, showing details on wings, tails, engined, pylons, cockpit interiors, galleys, instruments, cabin layouts, and liveries in close-up detail. Includes a detailed scale modeler's section and eight pages of full-color photographs. 80 pages, 8-page full-color insert. Book No. 20618, $10.95 paperback only

---

Prices Subject to Change Without Notice.

Look for These and Other TAB Books at Your Local Bookstore

To Order Call Toll Free 1-800-822-8158
(in PA, AK, and Canada call 717-794-2191)

or write to TAB BOOKS, Blue Ridge Summit, PA 17294-0840.